The American Revolution

The
AMERICAN
REVOLUTION

Edward Countryman

I. B. TAURIS & CO LTD
Publishers
London

Designed by Claudia Carlson.

British Library Cataloging in Publication Data
Countryman, Edward
  The American Revolution.
  1. United States—History—Revolution, 1775–1783
  I. Title
  973.3   E208

ISBN 1–85043–029–2

Printed and Bound in Great Britain by
Redwood Burn Limited, Trowbridge, Wiltshire

For Alfred Young
with admiration and thanks

Acknowledgments

I could not have written this book by myself. My greatest debt is to the community of historians who have explored the Revolution during the past two decades. I have borrowed from almost all of them, and I hope I have not done violence to their work. Writing under the aegis of Arthur Wang and Eric Foner has been a pleasure. I am grateful to them for inviting me to do the book and for endless good advice, from first plans to final draft. I tried out my earliest sketch on friends scattered across America and Europe, and I appreciate the time and the effort they took in their replies. Among them are Hugh Bell, William Dusinberre, Richard Gildrie, Robert Gross, George Kirsch, Bruce Laurie, Callum Mac-Donald, Mary Beth Norton, and Mary Ryan. The book bears the marks of a summer of research at the American Antiquarian Society, and I want to acknowledge the award of a Samuel Foster Haven Fellowship which made the trip possible. The University of Warwick gave me a term off to write. A pamphlet-length version of my argument appeared in 1983 under the title *The People's American Revolution* in the series published by the British Association for American Studies. Donald Ratcliffe, who edited the pamphlet, may recognize his influence here as well.

Eyvonne von Heussen has been marvelously supportive throughout the project. So have her sparkling daughters, Karon and Kirstein. In a way, Sam Countryman got the book started, by asking his father to tell him about the Revolution while we were hiking in New Hampshire. Since the beginning, all four have reminded me that books are not the same as life.

E.C.

Contents

Prologue   3

1 · Living on the Edge of Empire   9

2 · British Challenge, Elite Response   41

3 · From Rioters to Radicals   74

4 · Independence and Revolution   105

5 · Fourteen States   138

6 · One Republic   175

7 · "Should I Not Have Liberty"   214

Bibliographical Essay   246

Index   275

The American Revolution

Prologue
October 1774

The Continental Congress had been in session for a month and a half. Its members had been sent to Philadelphia to discuss their common problems and now they knew they had done most of what they could. For the most part, they had been strangers as they made their way to Philadelphia in August. Not much more had united them than their agreement that Britain had gone too far. The punishments that the ministry in London had imposed on Massachusetts after Boston's Tea Party were severe: Boston's port was closed; the structure of the Massachusetts government was altered and the governorship of the province given to a general; that general, Thomas Gage, commander in chief of all British troops in America, had far greater powers to billet his troops on the people than any of his predecessors enjoyed; if officials under him did wrong, they had the comfort of knowing they could be tried not in a hostile Massachusetts court but far away, in another province or in Britain. The ministers had been sure as they finished their work that this time the colonials would retreat, that Boston would pay for the tea and Britain's authority over the provinces would, at last, be unquestionable.

But the colonials decided differently. That was why the congressmen were in Philadelphia, and by October they were no longer strangers. They knew who among them was hot, who was tepid, who was cool. The cool ones, such as Joseph Galloway of Pennsylvania, were already losing their influence. The hot ones—Galloway's colleague Thomas Mifflin, Virginia's Richard Henry Lee, earnest, anxious John Adams of Massachusetts—had worked out a position and a policy. Now, as the congressmen packed for home, they agreed to offer both to the whole continent.

Their position was that Boston's problems were everyone's. Their policy, adopted as the Continental Association, was to close off the American economy. Trade with Britain would end completely. Trade with the rest of the world would drop sharply. Americans, in their pursuit of liberty, would buy no more slaves or Madeira wines. They would stop racing their horses, fighting their gamecocks, spending their money on plays and finery. They would slaughter no more sheep, for soon there would be greater need for wool than for mutton. Selfish men who sought to profit from the association would make themselves liable to community contempt. In every "county, city and town" the people would gather and elect a committee. Its job would be to see that the association took hold.

To boycott British commerce was nothing new by 1774. Cutting off trade had been one of the means that the colonials had chosen to respond to the Stamp Act in 1765 and to the Townshend Acts in 1767, and both times they got most of what they wanted. Nor was there anything novel in a call to put an end to luxury and extravagance. Preachers, essayists, and the authors of high-sounding resolutions had been condemning both for as long as there had been Britons in America. But this time something was different. The Stamp Act boycotts and the non-importation that people used against the Townshend Acts had been organized and eventually ended by informal meetings of merchants in the major ports. No one could have argued that it was illegal for merchants to debate among themselves about whether or not they would buy and sell British goods. But no one could claim that there was any place in the imperial constitution for a Continental Congress, representing colonies whose only legal connection lay in their common Britishness. Nor could anyone argue that British law provided the slightest hint of legality for the election of committees "in every county, city and town," or for the powers that the association called on those committees to exercise.

There were precedents, to be sure. The Stamp Act Congress of 1765 had been no more legal than the Continental Congress was, and it had established a set of principles that most of America had accepted. Committees of correspondence had been busy for years, exchanging information on behalf of colonial assemblies, town meetings, chambers of commerce, and Sons of Liberty. Yet, when the congress adopted the association, it took what may have been the most important single step in the transformation of the American movement from one of resistance to one of revolution.

The thirteen colonies that made that Revolution were spread along fifteen hundred miles of the Atlantic seaboard. Beneath a veneer of Britishness, they were vastly different: in their economic lives, in their politics, in their cultures. They had a long history of squabbling with one another, and their people had a long history of conflict among themselves. Thinking of the vagaries of eighteenth-century timekeeping, John Adams once used the metaphor of thirteen clocks to describe them and asked how those clocks came to strike as one. Or, to put it another way, how did those congressmen go to Philadelphia, decide on a stance of defiance, and win enough support to make that stance effective?

This book will explore that problem, but not just from the congressmen's point of view. Revolutionary America produced an extraordinary group of leaders, in politics, ideas, finance, and war. But by themselves leaders have never made a revolution. The congressmen gathered in Philadelphia because their fellow colonials were outraged enough at British policies to send them there. The Continental Association

took hold because those same ordinary colonials were determined enough and organized enough to make it take hold.
The processes by which those people channeled the anger,
built the determination and put together the organization
that enabled them to confront Britain's might make up one
of the most dramatic episodes in American history. At its
center is the story of the popular committees, of how they
were formed, of who comprised them, of how they took and
wielded power, of what became of them after independence.

The story also reflects a larger transformation. The committees emerged from upheaval, for in late colonial America
it seemed that nothing was certain. Crowd action disrupted
the patterns of public life and often the lives of private
people. Political rhetoric escalated from the pettiest of disputes to the heights of principle. Even religion became an
arena of strife as men and women turned encounters with
their God into confrontations with one another. The committees gave way, however, to something different. The 1780s
and 1790s saw violence and heated words, but they also saw
people organizing themselves to take control of their governments and their lives in ways they never had before. The
uncertainties and the doubts that went with being colonial
subjects had been succeeded by purposeful self-seeking and
organized self-awareness. These went with being citizens of
the new republic.

When George Washington assumed the presidency, America was a very different place from what it had been when
George III assumed the throne. The transformations of the
revolutionary era touched every aspect of how people thought
about themselves and of how they dealt with one another.
By no means were these transformations what men and
women intended as they embarked on the road that led to
them. Nor were they unequivocally good: the way was
opened for slavery to spread across the South; the Indians'
ability to preserve their own way of life was lost forever. Yet
the difference between the strife-ridden colonies and the self-

confident republic is overwhelming. It stems precisely from the fact that the road from the one to the other, far from being smooth and easy, led through a massive, disruptive, immensely confusing but popular Revolution.

The popular dimensions of the Revolution have been the subject of intense investigation during the past twenty years. Historians have looked at crowds, at street radicals, and at committees. They have explored the experience, the consciousness, and the purposes of artisans, farmers, militiamen, blacks, and women. They have found in the Revolution a record of struggle, achievement, and liberation. They have also found a story of defeat, as old ways died and as attempts to create new ones failed. They have found a story of irony, as people who set out to do one thing found themselves accomplishing quite another. The result has been to give the specialist and the advanced student a coherent picture of the Revolution that is far removed from the one that traditional accounts present.

The American Revolution draws together these many reconstructions of the Revolution's different facets. By no means does it reduce the Revolution to one formula. The Revolution was no more a simple matter of poor versus rich, or of radicals versus conservatives, or of city versus country, or of good versus bad, than it was a simple matter of Americans versus British. The revolutionary movement was never a united front facing one enemy. It was a series of coalitions that formed, dissolved, and re-formed, as people considered what they needed, what they believed, and what their situations were. But underlying all the diversities was a set of questions and problems that confronted a whole generation, not just its leaders. The members of that generation differed enormously among themselves as they worked out answers to those problems. They created fresh problems that they and their children would eventually have to face. But all of them had a hand, one way or another, in the Revolution's two great achievements, the destruction of the British Empire in

America and the creation of the American republic. Some, at least, made themselves at the same time that they made their Revolution. This book's goal is to bring together the complexities and tangles, the unique peculiarities and the large questions that everyone faced. Only by understanding that all of them had a part in it can we understand what the American Revolution was.

· 1 ·

Living on the
Edge of Empire

1

To our eyes, if we could see it, the land as it was then would look empty. The rivers and harbors and mountains and plains would be recognizable enough, but where, we would ask, are the people? In 1763, fewer than three million people inhabited the whole thirteen provinces from Georgia to New Hampshire. They lived in places whose names we still use. Boston was a town of 15,000 perched on a peninsula whose only link to the mainland was a narrow spit. The 22,000 people of New York City were crammed into the area that the financial district now occupies, with the rest of Manhattan, and all of Queens, Kings, Staten Island, and northern New Jersey lying almost empty around them. Philadelphia was somewhat bigger, despite its being the newest of the major towns, but only by a few thousand people. Charleston's population was of the same order, and places like Salem, Hartford, Baltimore, and Savannah were little more than villages. North America had nothing to compare with the great cities of the Old World. Nor could it boast any town that even faintly resembled Lima or Mexico City in population, sophistication, wealth, or poverty.

It was more than coincidence that the major towns were of roughly the same size, for they occupied roughly the same position in the world of their time. Each was a capital, where

men who wielded power made decisions that affected everyone else. Some of these men were colonials: the great landowners, prosperous merchants, and sophisticated lawyers who
loom so large in most accounts of the era. Others were high
British officials: peers, knights, and gentlemen serving for a
time. Still others were placemen, come to the colonies to
make their fortunes by inching their way up the ladder of
preferment. The very makeup of this series of ruling elites,
with its mixture of officials serving Britain and representatives serving their communities, all of them simultaneously
serving themselves, exemplifies the situation in which the
colonials lived.

But there was more than politics to make the towns similar.
Each was the hub of a local economy as well as a link in a
larger imperial and Atlantic network. In each, a sizable group
of artisans, such as the Boston silversmith Paul Revere or
the New York instrument maker John Lamb, made goods to
meet the needs of their communities and of people nearby.
In each, there were traders like New York's Isaac Sears, men
whose small sloops and schooners plied up and down the
seaboard and into the West Indies, carrying Grand Banks
cod to Jamaica, Pennsylvania wheat to Charleston, Barbados
molasses to New York. But in each there were merchants on
a grand scale as well, men like John Hancock and Andrew
Oliver of Boston, and Henry Laurens of Charleston, who
sent their brigs and ships across the Atlantic. Such men were
far more locked into the imperial system of credit, personal
relations, law, and power than their lesser trading colleagues
and the artisans. They were far more likely to be serious
players at the game of Anglo-American politics as well, seeking
both local office and imperial patronage.

The towns these people lived in existed to channel American goods in ways that would serve Britain's empire. Over
the hundred years that had passed since Oliver Cromwell's
time, successive British governments had erected a ramshackle but quite real structure of laws designed to bind the

colonies into a peripheral relationship with the British metropolis. According to the Navigation Acts, there were some things the colonists had to do, such as send their most important goods only to British ports and ship all their goods only in British vessels. There were other things they were expressly forbidden to do, such as turn their sizable output of crude iron into finished goods, or sell beaver hats to one another, or buy molasses from the non-British Caribbean islands.

Admittedly, the system was leaky. Most of the Navigation Acts used stiff taxes to compel what they required. There were not many officials to collect those taxes, and often what few there were could be easily bribed. Admittedly, as well, the system conferred real benefits. It provided guaranteed markets, naval protection, and a network of credit. Since American-built ships were legally British, it stimulated the colonists to develop one of the Atlantic world's foremost shipbuilding industries. Not only ship carpenters but rope- and sailmakers, blacksmiths and the chandlers who dealt in ship goods, also profited. Admittedly, in all the ports there were tendencies at work that pointed to autonomy and internal development rather than to colonial dependency. Yet the fact remained: at best, the colonials were only partially masters of their own house. The political power wielded by British officials, the economic power given shape in the Navigation Acts, and, for many, the day-to-day patterns of colonial lives bore witness to the fact that they existed to serve needs other than their own.

One sign of their colonial situation was the power of the institution of slavery. Blacks, almost all of them in bondage, formed a huge proportion of the people of the Southern colonies, where they did most of the productive labor. They also made up a good-sized minority of Northerners, including a fifth of the people of New York City. Some were simply ornamental, human evidence of a great person's wealth. But in the North and the South alike, blacks did socially necessary work. Slavery was a benefit to the masters, of course. Thomas Jefferson, who gained more from it than most, tried to include a passage in the Declaration of Independence that blamed slavery on the king. He failed. In the midst of prose that otherwise rings true, Jefferson found himself reduced to using typographical tricks and artificial emotion to make his point, and his fellow congressmen had the good sense to take them out. Yet whites in Virginia and South Carolina extorted work from blacks for the same reason that Spaniards in Mexico and Peru were extorting it from Indians, and nobles in Russia and Poland were extorting it from serfs. Slavery, like the Peruvian *mita* or Russian serfdom, produced primary goods for which the European metropolis was hungry. All three developed in the same matrix of natural wealth that was virtually free for the taking, unwilling labor that was driven to the task, and governments that were willing to aid in the driving. Nowhere in the Western European core was such a pattern to be found. Its presence in North America provides powerful evidence of the colonials' place in their world.

Slaves and masters were not the only Americans who lived in social relationships that reflected that colonial situation. Nineteen of every twenty whites dwelt in the countryside, not the towns. For almost all of them the great goal in life was the freehold ownership of enough land to support their families and to guarantee the future of their children. Yet, by the third quarter of the eighteenth century, that goal was becoming an impossible dream for many. In New England, especially, towns that had been sparsely populated at the start of the eighteenth century were running out of farmland by mid-century. Moreover, throughout the colonies, country people lived with the growing reality of a society based on landlordism and tenantry rather than freehold farms.

That tendency was stronger in some places than in others. In New England, it existed mostly as a fear. The Puritan settlers had distributed the land in a way that worked against any individual gaining large holdings. But as overcrowding forced their descendants off the land, they began to use the word "slave" as a synonym for "tenant." The usage reflected both their memories of the England their forebears had left behind and an awareness of how things were done in large parts of nearby New York. From there to North Carolina, tenantry was widely prevalent among farmers.

In some places, tenantry even bore faint overtones of European feudalism. There were bearers of genuine titles in the colonies: the baronet Sir William Johnson in New York's Mohawk Valley, Lord Fairfax in Virginia's Northern Neck. There were others who held their land on terms that mixed economic right and political privilege. That mixture lay at the heart of feudal social relations, whether or not a landlord had a formal title. For some, the mixture was empty: the Livingstons, the Van Cortlandts, and the Van Rensselaers of New York never exercised the right to hold "one court leet and one court baron" that their status as manorial landlords conferred. For others, it was very real: what was the whole of Pennsylvania but an enormous fief, with the governorship descending from Penn to Penn just as an earldom or a duchy might descend in Europe? For still others, the link was there, even if it was absent in law. Sir William Johnson tried and failed to have his estate of Kingsborough made into a manor, but he still controlled elections, courts, and officeholding on New York's western frontier. Even the courthouse and the jail were his personal property.

But, more importantly, men whose grandfathers and grandmothers had amassed immense tracts of empty land in the seventeenth century were finding the landlord-tenant relationship a profitable way to exploit it in the eighteenth. By and large, tenantry meant the growing of wheat and the improvement of the land. By and large, landlordism meant the milling and the marketing of the wheat and the reaping of capital gains and rents. For some landlords, this blended with a vision of a stratified but nonetheless organic community. Mistress Anne Grant, a well-born young woman whose father projected an estate in the region that would become Vermont, mused on the "amiable and innocent tenants we were to have." Frederick Philipse of the Hudson Valley governed his tenants' lives but cared for their welfare as well. So did Sir William Johnson. But others ran their estates quite simply as moneymaking enterprises, with no pretense that they were in it for anything other than their own gain. Tenant labor was not serfdom, let alone slavery. But, like the growth of slavery, its rapid increase in the mid-eighteenth century reflected the fact that the colonies were subordinate parts of a far-flung empire.

There were, of course, large numbers of rural people who were simply freeholders. Some, in the deep New England interior, or on the west bank of the Hudson, or beyond the Alleghenies in Pennsylvania, or in the uplands of the Southern provinces, lived almost cut off from the imperial network of power and commerce. Others, such as the prosperous farmers who dwelt near New York City and in the lower Delaware and Susquehanna valleys, were deeply enmeshed in that network. Whether they grew their crops for commerce, for subsistence, or for a mixture of the two, freehold farmers were doubtless a majority in the countryside. But they, too, lived in an empire that was run in good part from afar. When that empire's masters began to institute reforms after the Seven Years' War, colonials of all sorts would find themselves reminded forcibly of their place in the world.

II

In 1763, Britain stood supreme in North America after its final victory over France. People of many different sorts inhabited its American provinces. The woodland Indians were still a powerful force; their major links to Britain were trade, warfare, and protection. The most successful of them, such as the Six Nations of the Iroquois Confederacy, had long since mastered the art of balancing one group of whites off against another, whether the balance was French against English or English against colonials. Though settlers had forcibly pushed them back and were willing enough to enslave them if they could, North American natives had not been turned into a subordinate caste, as natives of Mexico and the Andes had been. Rather, they lived beyond the edge. Britain gave that edge a formal definition in 1763, when it established a "Proclamation Line" intended to separate the two races. The line began at Chaleur Bay, on the Gulf of St. Lawrence, and ran down the crest of the eastern mountains to the border between Georgia and Florida. With the French gone, it formed the Indians' main safeguard. While British might existed to enforce this boundary, there was at least a chance that the Indians could stave off white men's hunger for their land. From New York to Georgia, men who felt that hunger were organizing land companies to deal in land they nonetheless planned to acquire.

But though the names of their tribes struck fear throughout the interior, and though the "Conspiracy of Pontiac" of 1763 marked a valiant attempt to push the settlers back to where Britain said they should be, the Native Americans were already few in number. The great dying off that followed their first contact with European diseases had guaranteed that their fate was to be pushed back and finally to be herded into reservations. They would be colonized in their own way, not in the manner of Africans or South Asians. In 1776 they could still maintain the fiction that theirs were great nations, as capable of demanding respect as any nation of Europe. In the Revolutionary War they would find their last chance to play different groups of whites off against one another. But, in the end, no matter which side they chose, they would lose.

Africans in America could never maintain any such fiction. By 1776 there were already hundreds of thousands of them, and almost all were slaves. But within that common plight there was enormous variety. To be a house servant in Boston was one thing; to work on a Dutchman's farm in the Hudson Valley was another. To tend tobacco in Virginia was a third, and to grow rice in the fever-infested Carolina lowlands was a fourth. Legally, all slaves were property, living extensions of their master's will. Legally, they had no rights to the fruits of their labor, to the members of their families, or to their own bodies. Legally, they could not carry arms, or learn to read, or buy and sell, or marry. But so diverse were their experiences and their situations that no single term is broad enough to describe them. In the Revolution, they would diverge still further. A sizable minority would win freedom, but for the great majority, slavery would persist. Free blacks and slaves alike, however, found in these years their chance to take the first steps toward making themselves a people.

Diversity among whites was much greater. More than either Indians or blacks, whites lived in a world riven by gender, a world that women and men experienced in different ways. But their world was also riven by class, by religion, by language, and by region. The interplay among their many differences will be central to this book's account of their Revolution. If the word "slave" obscures the differences between a black in Boston and one near Charleston, the word "colonist" obscures those between a Puritan blacksmith in Worcester, a Dutch trader in Albany, a Scotch-Irish farmer in Carlisle, and an Anglican planter near Williamsburg. What did these people have in common?

For all that they were descended from most of the nations of Western Europe, the answer is Britishness. They may have acquired it by birth, as did the Puritans of New England and the Anglican gentry of the Tidewater, or by being conquered, as did the Dutch of New York, or by migration, as did Huguenot French, Palatine Germans, and Sephardic Jews. But all of them were heirs to a political and cultural tradition that set them off sharply from the Creoles of Spain's American dominions or from the newly conquered Catholic

French of the St. Lawrence Valley. To a Chinese or a Persian, of course, all Western Europeans must have seemed much the same. But, in an age when absolutism ruled in much of mainland Europe, residents of Britain and its colonies could take pride in the fact that they lived in freedom.

What their freedom meant, however, is quite another matter. Were they asked to define it, some colonials, like some Britons, would have answered that it lay in the security of person and property that the common law guaranteed. Others might have said that it lay in specific privileges and liberties given to them by their colonial charters. Still others would have pointed to the Whig settlement under which England had ruled itself since the Glorious Revolution of 1688. They would have noted that the king could neither legislate nor tax without the consent of the people, who were represented in Parliament. They would have maintained that their own assemblies stood to them as the House of Commons stood to the people of England, Scotland, and Wales. If anything, they were even more free, in this sense, than Britons. In the metropolis, only a relative handful of people actually had the vote. Many years might elapse between chances to exercise it. In America, at least half and probably more of all white adult males could cast their ballot for assemblymen. In some of the provinces, the law gave them a chance to do so every year.

British freedom was thus no simple, easily grasped quality. It blended the right to be left alone under the law's protection and the right to take part in political affairs. By no means was it equivalent to a notion of abstract, universal human rights. People of different sorts had freedoms of different sorts. They enjoyed their particular freedoms as members of particular communities, inheriting them through tradition, custom, usage, and prescription. Any change in this fabric was likely to presage freedom's end and it had to be fought.

Yet the fact remains that colonists confronted political life in terms of a language that stressed rights rather than obligations. Through pamphlets, in newspapers, broadsides, poems, plays, songs, and sermons, that language permeated public discourse. It insisted that men became most fully human in public life. It insisted that different communities enjoyed different corporate rights. And it insisted that the British parliamentary tradition offered the best means men had yet found to safeguard freedom. If people outside the British tradition enjoyed little freedom or none at all, or if women enjoyed less than men, or if the propertyless enjoyed less than the well off, that made no difference. Freedom was specific and peculiar, not universal. It was to be inherited and pre-served, not sought and extended. One of the changes wrought during the Revolution would come as people who had long enjoyed less freedom began asserting a claim to equal rights with people who had long enjoyed more.

III

What whites shared, then, was their Britishness and their colonial status. One gave them a view of the world and a political language centered on the belief that being free, however one defined it, was a good state of affairs. It gave them a set of customs and institutions that enabled some of them to have some say in how their world was ruled. The other placed them in a predicament that colonial peoples have always faced. They were subordinate, living in societies that existed to serve purposes not necessarily their own.

What separated them, however, was just as powerful. The thirteen mainland provinces had thirteen separate histories, histories that had sometimes pitted them against one another. One colony might throw itself into war with the French; another would hold back. Two colonies might claim the same land, for the boundaries between them were often vague. Such a conflict might simply pit one group of specu-lators against another, as in the struggle that Pennsylvania and Virginia waged in the 1770s for control of the upper

Ohio Valley. But it might also pit two ways of life against each other. When the holders of New York land grants in the Green Mountains began to settle them, they envisaged a future of landlords and tenants. But as settlers with conflicting New Hampshire titles moved into the same region at the same time, they projected one of communal villages and small freehold farms.

Moreover, the thirteen separate provinces were not necessarily cohesive. Lowland white South Carolinians valued their social harmony. They had reason to, for the huge majority of slaves among them presented the constant threat of retribution for the Middle Passage, or for the fierce exploitation of the early days of rice planting, or for the enduring reality of the lash. Yet, in the 1760s and 1770s, whites in both Carolinas would break into armed conflict. During the Revolutionary War they would slaughter one another. Virginians were genuinely cohesive, at least in political terms, but they disputed fiercely over religion, and their differences rested on social perspective as well as on theological differences. Marylanders, so much like Virginians in their economic and racial life, broke into angry dispute after independence, large numbers of them carrying arms for the king. In Pennsylvania the backcountry marched on Philadelphia in 1763, and the state constitution adopted in 1776 became a focus for dispute, not a basis for agreement. Land rioters in central New Jersey, the Hudson Valley, and the Green Mountains struggled against the dominion of real or would-be landlords between 1745 and 1775. Militant loyalists kept the struggle going during the war years. People in Massachusetts tore down the institutions that had governed them in 1774 and kept their courts closed until 1786, only submitting when armed force finally crushed them. Later chapters will deal with these tangles and conflicts. For the moment, the simple listing of them shows that revolutionary America was a turbulent, divided place.

More immediately, let us examine some specific people in

specific communities. How did they live? Who was important in their lives? How far did their horizons extend? What problems did they face? Historians of the colonial period and the Revolution have uncovered the lives that people led at levels far removed from the one inhabited by a John Adams or a Thomas Jefferson. They have shown both what such people did before and during the Revolution and what the Revolution did to them. Though each lived a unique life, each led that life within a framework of social relations that shaped the lives of many other people. Each found in the Revolution a chance to change that framework. Each emerged from it a different person, living in a different world.

Our portrait gallery is small. It contains likenesses of George Robert Twelves Hewes, Rebecca Owen Alford, Abraham Yates, Jr., James Beekman, Richard Henry Lee, and a man simply called Sam. Hewes, a cobbler, lived in Boston. Yates had begun in the same trade, but by the crisis years he was practicing law and dabbling in politics. He spent his life in Albany, New York. Alford had married into an old but not notable Connecticut family. Beekman was a New York City merchant, and Lee a Virginia planter, perhaps too outspoken for his own good. Sam was a South Carolina slave. What were the worlds of these people like?

We can begin with Hewes. His Boston was a stagnating town. Once the foremost center in North America, it had seen its population stop growing around 1750, at about 15,000 people. Unlike Philadelphia or New York, Boston had gained little from the fevered economy generated by the Seven Years' War. Some of its merchants—the patriot-to-be John Hancock, the loyalist-to-be Andrew Oliver—were prosperous enough. It did provide a market for luxuries like the silverware of Paul Revere or the paintings of John Singleton Copley. Yet well-off Bostonians embarking to cross the Charles River for a Harvard graduation might find their carriages or slaves or boats pelted with stones thrown by a hostile crowd. Could an apprentice like Hewes, who knew that Harvard was not for him, have been among the pelters? Did Hewes join the crowds that gathered each year on November 5 to celebrate the discovery of Guy Fawkes's plot to blow up the House of Commons? If he did, did he realize that such pageantry helped keep alive the most radical traditions of the English revolution? Had his parents passed on to him memories of the regicides who found refuge in New England after the Stuarts returned to the English throne in 1660? Hewes was religious; he may well have attended the inflammatory political sermons that the Reverend Jonathan Mayhew preached. He was also literate, and he probably read the endless stream of inflammatory essays that the printers Edes and Gill published in their *Boston Gazette*.

Hewes was five years old in 1747, when an attempt by a British man-of-war to impress seamen into its crew provoked riots that turned the town upside down for three days. He probably remembered that, and he may have remembered the importance in it of merchant seamen, who had to face the horrors of naval life directly. He may have remembered a crowd shouting, "Let it burn," when the house of the prominent Bostonian Thomas Hutchinson caught fire a few years later. He certainly had experienced tumultuous town meetings. He was eighteen when the would-be great men who made up the "New and Grand Corcus" mooted plans in 1760 to put an end to town meetings and replace them with a mayor-and-council form of government. He may have had a hand in choosing the committee of artisans that gathered to oppose the change.

In all probability, Hewes had no idea how striking was the eighteenth-century increase in the sum the town had to spend to support the very poor. It rose from £18 per thousand people per year in the second decade of the century to £158 per thousand per year after 1770. Nor was it likely that he knew of the fall in the percentage of Boston property held by the middle four-fifths of its people, the ones who were in neither the top nor the bottom 10 percent. They held more than half the town's wealth in 1687, but only 36 percent of it in 1771. But Hewes did know that he was an underling in his world. He showed as much by his nervous, trembling deference when he called on John Hancock after that great merchant invited him to pay a visit on New Year's Day, 1763. The portrait that Alfred Young has given us of Hewes shows us a short, common man we might not expect to become a revolutionary, but become one he did.

Like Hewes, Rebecca Owen Alford was an ordinary New Englander, but that was the end of their similarities. Born in Windsor, Connecticut, in 1736, in 1761 she married the widower Benedict Alford, twenty years her senior. Twenty-five years was a somewhat late age for a Yankee woman to marry, and she was not among the 50 percent of eighteenth-century New England brides who were pregnant at their wedding, though her husband's first wife had been. Such women, and the young men whom they were marrying, may have been seeking a measure of autonomy against the restraints of life in a Puritan village. They may have been rebelling against the power their parents held. But by 1761 Benedict Alford was his own man. In any case, by the time Rebecca married him, she had lived through stirring events.

She grew up in years of seemingly endless warfare. Windsor, in the valley of the Connecticut River, was far from the area of combat, but she would have learned about danger from sermons, and perhaps from her reading the many published accounts of women captured by the French and the Indians. Invariably, these women told of how they were ripped from secure environments and of how when they finally returned they no longer saw the world in the same way. Rebecca Owen would have seen young men volunteering to fight on the frontier, and she would have heard her parents' generation grumbling about the taxes the Connecticut government imposed to pay for the costs of war. These farming people had little coin or currency in which to pay. But other events struck closer to her own life.

The foremost, without question, was the Great Awakening. By the time of Rebecca Owen's childhood, New Englanders had been living for more than a century with a remarkable social, religious, and political synthesis. The family into which she married settled in Windsor before 1640, and remained there. In such a town, families were patriarchal; an aging father would hold on to his land until death and he would use his property to control his sons' lives well into their adulthood. Town meetings were consensual; the same representatives and the same local officers were likely to be elected year after year, and the people valued unanimity, not dispute. Churches were disciplined; to join one meant to accept that the minister, the deacons, and the congregation would become a primary force in one's life. People in these towns lived by agriculture, supplying themselves with most of what they needed. But by the time of Rebecca's birth, the synthesis was growing weaker: fathers, running out of land to distribute to their children, were losing power over them. The land itself was becoming tired. Epidemics were more common, and life expectancy was falling. Town meetings were being transformed: where people once tried to agree, now they were willing enough to contend. Matters came to a head in the 1740s and the 1750s over religion.

The Great Awakening began with the intense, emotional sermons of the touring Englishman George Whitefield and of American ministers like Jonathan Edwards and Gilbert Tennent. They abandoned the dry, logical, academic style that ministers had used ever since New England's founding and offered a simple message: Cast yourself on the Lord's mercy and be saved. In fact, their preaching presented a powerful challenge to the highly structured and institutionalized lives that New Englanders had led. People who heard it found the energy to cut through the ancient network of churchly control and face their God on their own. When they found that the organized clergy and their political leaders were trying to put an end to the revival, they refused to knuckle under, splitting congregations and voting out of office men who had grown used to ruling. Suddenly Connecticut and Massachusetts had become places of contention. Rebecca Owen was only a child when all this happened; even if she had been a grown woman, her sex would have kept her from the angry elections and church meetings to which the Awakening led. But the revival was a force that surged through the life of every New Englander.

All these elements probably contributed to the decision that she and her husband made in 1767 to break away from Windsor and move to the Green Mountains. England's victory in the Seven Years' War meant that the danger from the French and the Indians was gone, but the move was still burdened with uncertainty. Connecticut people called the Green Mountains the New Hampshire Grants. They acquired their land titles from that province's governor, Benning Wentworth. The governor was not particularly worried about the fact that New York and Massachusetts claimed the region as well; all he wanted was the share of each grant that he claimed as his fee. People like the Alfords acquired New Hampshire Grants at least partly in the hope of recreating the stable village life their families had known for three and four generations. Other people with an interest in the region had other ideas.

New Yorkers in particular were interested in the area, and they knew that in 1764 the Privy Council had given their province title to it. Though their government was forbidden to make grants there, it did so anyway. Some New Yorkers who invested were simply speculators; in their province, unlike New England, speculation on a grand or a petty scale had always been the rule. Others had a larger vision. Seeing the rewards that the lordship of great estates had given to families like the Hudson Valley's Philipses, Livingstons, and Van Rensselaers, they envisaged a similarly happy future for themselves, with tenants to make them wealthy and to bow to them as they passed. But people like Benedict and Rebecca were not the sort who bowed. The movement by which they and their neighbors thwarted the New Yorkers ended in the creation of Vermont. It was the most successful but by no means the only insurrection that rural people mounted in eighteenth-century America.

Yet Rebecca Owen Alford's significance does not end there. Like all women of her time, she was born into a pattern of beliefs, customs, and laws that dictated much of the course of her life. She could expect to learn less than her husband about the world of affairs. She would have no legal right to her property once she married; effectively, it would be his. She could expect to bear child after child. Though more likely than her husband to become a member of the church, she would have no real voice in making policy or calling a minister. She would, in short, spend her life as a dutiful daughter and then as a good wife. Rebecca gave her husband five more children to add to the nine he fathered by his first wife. Her son Ashley would sire fifteen. Yet this woman did break away from the community in which she was so deeply rooted. During the revolutionary years she and other American women would strike out on their own in many ways. The Revolution made a difference in their lives.

Our third portrait is of Abraham Yates, Jr., of Albany, New York. Albany was a Dutch enclave, legally a city despite its size, and very much an isolated community. It had built its first prosperity on the fur trade, in which its merchants sometimes competed with the French at Montreal and sometimes cooperated with them. Now its rich hinterland had become developed farm country, and it shipped grain, forest products, and ashes to distant markets. Albany was surrounded by the enormous manorial estate called Rensselaerwyck, which stretched for forty miles up and down the Hudson Valley and for twenty-five on either side of the river. The Van Rensselaers were not the only great family in Abraham Yates's world; the Livingstons with their own manor below Rensselaerwyck; the Schuylers, Ten Broecks, and Van Schaicks, who intermarried with the Van Rensselaers; and Sir William Johnson's family in the Mohawk Valley all moved on the same social level. A tax list from the 1760s shows the enormous gap between the best and the rest in Rensselaerwyck. The taxes were assessed on the values of lease-hold farms and, for the Van Rensselaers themselves, on the small part of the estate they ran on their own. Assessments did not reflect the value of either the lordship or the land lying waste. Of the 560 taxpayers, 495 held property rated at less than £10. The property of 158 of these was rated at only £1. Only ten held property assessed at £40 or more. But among those ten were Stephen Van Rensselaer, rated at £270, Rensselaer Nicol at £88, Johannes Van Rensselaer at £125, and their kinsman Abraham Ten Broeck at £100. Abraham Yates grew up and lived, in other words, in a grossly unequal society.

Yates himself came from a Yorkshire family that settled in Albany not long after the English seized New York from the Dutch. His people and the Dutch quickly intermarried, and in his long public career Yates never faced any problems of ethnic hostility. In other ways, however, Yates encountered a great many powerful people who did not like him simply because of what he was.

Unlike his fellow cobbler George Robert Twelves Hewes, Yates had no intention of spending his life making and repairing boots. He slowly learned that there was no point in licking them, either. He taught himself as much law as he needed to go into practice, and by mid-century he was beginning to rise in politics. He progressed from a seat on the Albany Common Council to become sheriff of Albany County, a position he held for five years. The patronage of the great landlord Robert Livingston, Jr., was what made his rise possible. In 1761, when the governor called one of the infrequent general elections for New York's tiny provincial assembly, Livingston invited Yates to run for a seat, promising his backing. But Sir William Johnson, who cut a mightier figure, demurred, and Yates suddenly found that he had gone as far as he could go.

Yates had already begun to learn what inequality meant in New York. During his time as sheriff, he had had to deal with angry tenants on both Rensselaerwyck and Livingston Manor. Some were New England migrants, some long-term residents, but they all knew how uncertain were the legal titles on which some of the great estates rested. The Livingstons, for instance, had expanded a grant of a few thousand acres into a holding of 160,000 acres by simple fraud when they laid out its boundaries. Moreover, the boundary between New York and Massachusetts, which marked Livingston Manor's eastern limits, was uncertain. As late as 1774, the Livingstons were still claiming land that now lies in Massaschusetts, and in the Connecticut border town of Salisbury. Life on the manor could be onerous, for the Livingstons were interested in gain far more than they were interested in creating a stable society. By the time Robert Livingston made Abraham Yates sheriff, tenants were using both the vagueness of the border and the manor's dubious origins in order to claim freehold titles to their farms. One of Yates's tasks was to deal with them. He learned how determined they were when he went to arrest them and instead found himself carted off to jail in Massachusetts.

After Yates's humiliation by Johnson and abandonment by Livingston, he stopped thinking that great men's preferment was the way to a better life. He began to question what great men were doing in his society. He could see that Albany and its county were thriving; between the first colonial census in 1695 and the last in 1771, the county's annual growth rate was 4.8 percent, well above the rate for the province as a whole. He could also see the visible signs of increasing prosperity, most especially the elegant mansions that landlords were beginning to regard as necessities. Sir William Johnson moved from the rigor of Fort Johnson to the charm of Johnson Hall; Philip Schuyler erected The Pastures just south of

Albany City; various Livingstons were dotting their family's manor with imposing dwellings. Yates began to write a history of how New York's class-ridden society came to be, using Rensselaerwyck as his example. It was the first of many writings, some to be published, in which he mused on the evil ways of the sort he would come to call "high flyers." He also continued to think about the arrogance of the British officers whose troops had marched and countermarched through his city during the Seven Years' War; often enough, he had had to deal as sheriff with disputes between troops and citizens. Yates began to talk to friends, relatives, and neighbors about the dual plight in which the people of the upper Hudson Valley found themselves, as subjects in an empire and as members of an unequal society. In 1775 he found the chance to wipe out the earlier false start in his public career, when his fellow Albanians made him chairman of their revolutionary committee. But though he would go from that to considerably higher posts, Yates would never lose contact with the people from whom he had sprung. He would never think himself born to command, in the way his fellow Albanian Philip Schuyler did.

James Beekman's New York City was unlike either Hewes's Boston or Yates's Albany. Whereas Boston was stagnating, New York was growing. Whereas Albany was isolated and insular, New York was already cosmopolitan. The Seven Years' War in particular had done wonders for the city. It became a major command and staging point, and military spending swelled the pockets of artisans and great merchants alike.

Beekman was one who gained handsomely. He did not grow immensely wealthy, in the manner of Oliver De Lancey, whose fortune stood at the war's end at well over £100,000 sterling. Nor did he have the connections of De Lancey, whose sister married a knighted admiral and whose brother was close to the Archbishop of Canterbury. But during the war years Beekman was importing more than £5,000 worth of goods annually and living on a scale that was appropriate. This Dutch Calvinist was doing well as a subject of the British Empire. He and his fellow merchants began to realize that they had interests distinct from those of the rest of the community. So they established a chamber of commerce, and a sympathetic provincial government gave them a charter of incorporation.

But they did not live in a world of free trade. In addition to the restrictions that living in the empire imposed, American merchants had to live with a long-standing tradition that the community had some voice in what they did with their goods. In time of shortage and depression, especially, their right to seek a profit became less important than their neighbors' right to the goods they needed, at prices they could afford. Some historians have called this way of doing business "corporatism," because it rested on the belief that the whole community formed one body. Some have called it a "moral economy." In varying ways, it governed eighteenth-century market relations in Britain, in much of mainland Europe, and in both the British and the Spanish American colonies. Governments restricted sales of foodstuffs and other necessary goods to controlled markets; they regulated prices; they published an "assize of bread," which established the quality, the weight, and the price of the ordinary loaf. Some of the controls New York's government imposed were for the sake of maintaining the province's good name in the markets of the world. But others were for the sake of maintaining social peace.

Early American townspeople knew that if government control failed during a crisis, popular action was likely. On one occasion early in the eighteenth century, Bostonians had forcibly kept a grain-laden ship from sailing because they needed the grain. In 1753, New York street demonstrations protested against the city's merchants' refusal to accept halfpenny coins at the old rate. Generally, such popular action was not needed in early American towns. On the whole, supplies were available, and when they were not, the government stepped in. But the traditions that made protest legitimate remained alive in popular culture, and most people knew that in England and Europe such action broke out much more often. A merchant like James Beekman knew that most of the time he could run his business as he saw fit, but he also knew that there were likely to be occasions and situations in which he would not have the only voice in the disposal of his property.

As the Seven Years' War ended, Beekman learned that the days of prosperity were over. After 1764, the average annual imports of his trading house dropped off to only £2,045, for without the demands of the army and navy the economy slumped. For Beekman, depression meant reduced profits, but most of the luxuries in his life remained. There were still the summer concerts in the Ranelagh Gardens to attend. The officers of the British garrison that remained would still give dances for the town's elite. Well-to-do men continued to import carriages and fine clothing. A theater would shortly be opening in town. But for New Yorkers who were less well off, the depression was another matter. It might mean the poorhouse or a debtor's prison. It might mean competing for scarce employment with off-duty soldiers and with sailors from the Royal Navy ships that wintered in the harbor. When Beekman and other New Yorkers faced the Stamp Act in 1765, they also faced a depressed economy.

Everything in Richard Henry Lee's life told him that he had been born to rule. By the eve of the Revolution, his Virginia was the jewel of Britain's mainland American colonies. Though its population was far larger than that of any other province, it had no major cities or towns. Instead, its people were spread through a landscape characterized, as Rhys Isaac puts it, by "water and trees, trees and water." Some of those Virginians, Richard Henry Lee's people among them, could tell themselves that theirs was the perfect way for human beings to live. They were close to nature, yet they could keep up with Europe's intellectual and cultural currents. Their estates were almost self-contained, yet they lived with comfort and grace. They were proudly individualistic, yet they cared about their community and their lives were open and convivial. In their world the best men ruled, and a careful system of vetting guaranteed that no one would join the circle of power who had not earned his place there. Lesser men stood back. They accepted the hospitality that the planters lavishly provided, followed the planters' lead at the annual open-air, open-voice elections for the House of Burgesses, and joined them to worship in Virginia's version of the Anglican religion. In church, as in so much of the rest of their lives, almost everything the Virginians did had the effect of making the planters' way seem the right way.

It had not always been so. As the historian Jan Lewis notes, "Virginia was founded in 1607 but it was not settled until nearly a century later." The years between were an ordeal, not an idyll. In the early decades, when the price of tobacco was high and the prices of land and of human life were low, disease, starvation, and human malevolence wiped out English servants brought to work in the fields. Public officials shamelessly used their positions to line their pockets. Planters appropriated land on a vast scale and then passed punitive laws to keep lesser men under their control. Such an agony was not unique to Virginia; it was repeated so often in the history of the South and the Caribbean that it seems a necessary stage in the establishment of a New World plantation society. Virginia was different only because its earliest laborers were white, not black. Small wonder that in 1676 Nathaniel Bacon, an adventurer newly arrived in the colony, was able to launch a major rebellion. Small wonder that, after they put the rebellion down, Virginia's leaders started to change their ways.

They achieved something remarkable, creating a social synthesis that transformed white Virginia from a warring, violent class society into an organic community. The replace-

ment of white servants by black slaves in the fields was central to how they did it. But the way of life that the planters
developed in their great houses, their county courts and
House of Burgesses, their churches, and even their taverns
was also important. No one ever pretended that all white
Virginians were equal. Yet the plantation was a social institution as well as the home of a private family. Life in a great
house was open, with people coming and going. It was also
highly structured, with people knowing their places and what
was expected of them. An elaborate set of social codes, partly
home-grown and partly copied from the gentry of England,
governed people's behavior. A planter might bemoan the
cost of the endless entertaining that was expected of him,
but he knew that he could expect similar hospitality wherever he traveled. He also knew that he could expect everyone
on his plantation—slave, guest, family member, employee—
to do as he bade.

If the great planter ruled as an individual on his own
estate, he and his peers ruled as a group in the courthouse
and the church. Like plantation life, the politics and the
religion of Virginians were theatrical, ritualized. County
courts were where Virginians gathered to do the business of
their local communities. They were not assemblies of equals,
the way a New England town meeting may have looked.
Nor were they simply the expressions of one man's will, in
the way that the court of Tryon County, New York, expressed
the will of Sir William Johnson. But they were closed institutions. An aspiring planter could gain a seat on the bench
only by the governor's appointment, and the governor would
never name a new justice unless the men who were already
on the court gave their consent. Only if a planter held a
court seat might he dare to stand for the Burgesses, and
again the chief men of the county would consult among
themselves and decide whom to support. But a favored young
man could move rapidly from private life to public power.
This was Richard Henry Lee's course, for he became a justice

of the peace in 1757, only five years after he returned from school in England. When he entered the Burgesses a year later, he was only twenty-six years old.

Virginia's eighteenth-century situation was perfect, if one was white, rich, and untroubled by slavery. Even if one was not rich, life was not bad. But in the mid-1760s men like Richard Henry Lee found themselves increasingly troubled, on three fronts. They were bothered by ever-increasing evidence that Britain was becoming a threat to their world. The most obvious instance came with the Stamp Act, and the impassioned response that the Burgesses made to it was one major element in America's campaign to frustrate the act and have it repealed. We will examine the act and the American response in a later chapter. But to Virginia planters the Stamp Act came after a long series of little causes and debates. No one of them was critical in itself, but all indicated that Parliament and the church were capable of taking steps which could weaken the planters' power. One instance came in the mid-century "Parsons' Cause," which erupted when the House of Burgesses cut clerical salaries. The clergymen mounted a challenge that went all the way to the Privy Council in London, and won. This action posed a frightening dilemma for the planters. The myth they had made for themselves told them that they were English gentlemen overseas. Yet here were two pillars of their Englishness turning against them.

But equally important were two developments within Virginia itself. Both turned on matters of religion and morality, not on politics, and both betokened a weakening of the position of men like Lee. One began when Lee demanded an investigation of the affairs of the late John Robinson, longtime Speaker of the Burgesses and treasurer of the colony. Robinson had been using his public position to make illegal loans to his fellow planters. After his death, rumors that his estate was in trouble began to circulate, and the Burgesses' investigation revealed so widespread and so complex a mess that it was all hushed up. But the affair became fairly common knowledge, and it helped convince men like Lee that moral rot was setting in among them.

More importantly, the planters had good reason to be worried about the growth among Virginians of the Baptist and Methodist Churches. Anglicanism was Virginia's established faith, protected by law and funded by the government. Its rituals, both within the chancel and in the congregation, were in accord with the planters' social vision. Its clergy, usually second-rate men without security in their pulpits, were, until the Parsons' Cause, little more than servants of the local planter community. The vestrymen who controlled each parish were, like judges of county courts, the leaders of the planter community. Virginians were not High Church men; Richard Henry Lee, a good Anglican, spoke for most of them when he insisted in 1772 that Virginia had no need for bishops and church courts. But Anglicanism was an organic part of his world.

When Baptists and Methodists appeared, however, they challenged virtually everything for which planter Anglicanism stood. In place of stately ritual, they offered emotion and enthusiasm. In place of social hierarchy, reflected even in the way that people entered the church building to worship, they offered an equality of brothers and sisters. In place of conspicuous self-display, they offered self-effacement. Most dangerous of all, they welcomed blacks. The basis of the planter synthesis was the wedge they had so carefully driven between slaves and lesser whites at the end of the seventeenth century. African slaves, poor whites, and rich planters lived in close proximity in Virginia, and that wedge of racism and power kept the poorer whites and the slaves apart. The evangelicals were no abolitionists. But their teaching and their practice threatened destruction of everything the planters had so painfully achieved.

There were probably a fair number of planters who, like Lee, said that they found black slavery detestable and that they wanted the slave trade ended. Such men understood that their way of life provided an endless contradiction to all their rhetoric about liberty. Jefferson spoke for them once when, with his usual vivid eloquence, he drew the image of having a wolf by the ears and not daring to let go. But Lee himself had no qualms about either living on the labor of slaves or buying and selling them. Small wonder that planters sometimes broke up evangelical meetings by force. The Baptists and Methodists challenged their way of life, not just their way of worship.

Richard Henry Lee stands out from the rest of his kind, both for the militance he displayed throughout the Revolution and for his personal austerity. But most Virginia planters made the Grand Cause of America their own, and most, like Lee, became committed republicans. In this they were different from two other elite groups, the landed aristocracy of New York and the merchants of the port towns, both of which broke into Tory and patriot wings. Virginia as a whole was unique, as well, for alone among the thirteen provinces it did not face armed internal dispute during the revolutionary era. The political skill of men like Lee had much to do with that. As they entered the revolutionary crisis, they were fully aware of the potential disruptions that their society faced.

Our last portrait is of Sam, enslaved to another Southern gentleman, Charles Cotesworth Pinckney. Pinckney became a prominent leader of the Revolution. A member of both South Carolina's constitutional convention in 1776 and the convention that wrote the federal Constitution in 1787, he eventually became a Federalist politician at the national level, and ran against Jefferson for the presidency in 1804. But Pinckney was a rice planter, not a tobacco grower. Whereas Lee inherited a force of some forty slaves, some two hundred belonged to Pinckney when the war began. The British confiscated everything Pinckney owned when they invaded South Carolina in 1780, but afterward he acquired an equal number of slaves.

Sam was born in 1757. He learned the carpenter's trade, which gave him a privileged position among blacks. Unlike Rebecca Alford, whose ancestry can be traced to the time of the *Mayflower*, Sam's known genealogy reaches only to his father, Old Anthony, of whom the records say little. They say so little, without question, because the nightmare that established slavery in South Carolina lay much closer to living memory in Sam's time than the nightmare that established servitude in Virginia. As Timothy Breen has shown, one difference between New Englanders and Virginians was that New Englanders were anxious to recall their past and Virginians were eager to forget theirs. How much more so for Carolinians. Rice became an important cash crop in South Carolina in the first half of the eighteenth century. In the 1720s and the 1730s, Carolina planters were buying blacks as fast as they could, working them to death, and then buying more. The province's black population barely grew over those two decades, despite massive importations. By Sam's time, Carolina had probably settled down, the way that Virginia settled down in the mid-seventeenth century. But the lowlands remained an overwhelmingly black region, "more like a negro country," as one observer put it. When blacks tried in 1739 to take advantage of their superior numbers by rebelling, the result was vicious repression. White Carolinians were not, of course, unique in this; white New Yorkers did the same thing when their slaves rebelled in 1712 and again in 1741.

By the time of Sam's youth, South Carolina had produced a planter class to rival Virginia's. The two societies had, however, significant differences. Unlike Virginia, South Carolina had a city, Charleston. Planters retreated to the town in the feverish summer months, believing that the Africans whom they left behind were less liable than they to come down with the terrible diseases of the region. In Charleston, the planters found two social groups leading lives different from theirs, merchants and artisans. Both groups were ultimately beholden to the planters, of course: Charleston's merchants dealt in the rice and the indigo that the plantations produced, and its artisans turned out goods in the hope that the planters would buy their wares instead of English imports. Nonetheless, Charleston had an autonomous urban life unlike anything to be found in Virginia. Moreover, at least some of Charleston's artisans were, like Sam, black.

Life was different for blacks and less-important whites, too. A black enslaved to Richard Henry Lee had to deal constantly with his own master's family and with countless other whites who came and went. Neither race could escape the other. It may have been different for Sam. When South Carolina's masters made their exodus during the fever season, their slaves came close to a situation of self-control. Carolina's poor whites did not intermingle with the planters the way poor Virginians did. Rather, they lived far to the west, beyond the pine barrens that separated the rich lowlands from the equally fertile Piedmont. The groups even had different origins. The planter group began with a massive migration from Barbados early in the eighteenth century, but most of the poorer whites had drifted down the long interior valleys of the Appalachian Range after entering the colonies at Philadelphia or Baltimore. There is no reason to think that these settlers were hostile to slavery; few whites of the time were. But they were not growing crops that required slave labor; that would come later, when tobacco and then cotton came to dominate the economy of South Carolina's interior. The settlers were German evangelicals and Scotch-Irish Presbyterians, while the planters were largely Anglican. The two groups shared neither the direct economic interest nor the close neighborliness and cultural patterns that made Virginia whites an organic group.

Instead, the people who ruled Sam's world squabbled, bickered, and fought among themselves. When the lowland planters gathered in their Commons House of Assembly to make laws, they were harmonious enough. But there was no one among them to represent the Charleston mechanics, let alone backcountry farmers. In the interior there were no courts to see that the law was enforced, and when people there formed a Regulator movement to impose some order, the lowlanders sent out militia units to crush it. The uplanders' "crime" was trying to enforce a law that gave them no protection.

Whether this made any difference to Sam, or to the thousands who shared his fate, is doubtful. Where he stood when white South Carolinians confronted the British and one another cannot be determined. His position certainly cannot be inferred from the patriot stance of his master, Charles Cotesworth Pinckney. Like Rebecca Alford, he stood outside the great debates of the era. Yet, again like her, he would live through great transformations, and would find by the Revolution's end that his own situation was markedly different from what it had been at its beginning. These people and others like them would have a hand in shaping those differences.

IV

Though both were obscure, Sam and Rebecca Alford were very different people, and the Revolution's course of human events took them in quite different directions. Richard Henry Lee was born to prominence; he lived his whole life in public and perhaps achieved his greatest fame as a leader of Virginia anti-federalism in 1788. Abraham Yates won equal prominence, eventually rising as high as the Continental Congress. Like Lee, he took a leading role in the struggle against the Constitution, and the two probably got to know each other well. For both of them, the Revolution took place in committee chambers and in the meeting halls of conventions and congresses. George Robert Twelves Hewes, however, won prominence only by the accident of his living to an extreme old age. If Yates typifies the artisan on the make, transcending his situation, Hewes typifies the artisan who made himself, becoming a proud equal citizen while still working with his hands. It was men of his sort who prevented stamps from being distributed in 1765 and who dumped tea into Boston Harbor in 1773. It was his kind, together with farmers like Alexander Alford, the son of Benedict and Rebecca, who seized Fort Ticonderoga from the British in 1775 and who fought at Saratoga, Trenton, Cowpens, and finally Yorktown. But Hewes's Revolution was not just a matter of fighting redcoats. He confronted arrogant Tory officials, learned that he need not bow to John Hancock, and conversed with General Washington. His Revolution taught him that he was as good as any of them. When men like him supported the Constitution in 1788, as they overwhelmingly did, it was from their own choice and judgment.

For Rebecca Owen Alford and for Sam, the Revolution would be far less public. Neither slavery nor the subordination of women would end. But by 1788 both slaves and women would be more of a problem for white males. Tens of thousands of former slaves would be free, whether as a result of their own actions or because of patriot masters' realization of how hypocritical slaveholding was. Black America would be taking the first steps toward making a people of itself, and Sam would be among the people taking those steps. Women like Rebecca Alford would have far more knowledge than their mothers had of what their men owned and did and of the larger world.

These six lived in very different communities, and their particular experiences are important because they tell us something about very different groups. Such people lived through the Revolution and took part in shaping it in their own ways, and no single "leader" could lead, no single "spokesman" could speak for them all. We must understand the interplay, the coalition-making, and the conflict that went on among them if we are to understand either the Revolution's fine texture or its large pattern.

Yet, as of roughly 1765, one thread does run through all six lives: disturbance. Hewes lived in a stagnating town where street violence was a way of life and where political rhetoric was always hot. Yates was confronting a class system and learning that his own frustrations were tied to it. Alford and her husband were on the point of leaving a town where their families had dwelt for more than a century. Beekman's business was falling off and his town was economically depressed. Lee was vexed and troubled by almost everything he saw. Sam, only eight years old, was learning the hard lessons that had to be learned if he was to survive in slavery.

The land, of course, was far from empty. It was occupied by people of many sorts, who were facing different situations and problems. But unsettlement was a fact of life that they shared. It was expressed in religion, in politics, and in the crowds that so frequently rioted, whether in the town or in the country. Between 1765 and 1775, the separate crises of town, of country, and of empire would merge in a general upheaval.

· 2 ·
British Challenge, Elite Response

George Grenville was an unlikely man to begin a revolution. When he became the king's first minister in 1763, he inherited a financial mess and his immediate goal was to straighten it out. Britain had spent itself close to bankruptcy defeating France in the Seven Years', or French and Indian, War. Now it stood supreme from America to India. But someone had to pay, and in Grenville's view the North American colonies had delayed paying long enough. It was time for them to assume at least the costs of their own administration and defense. So, with the approval of young King George III, Grenville launched Parliament on a program of imperial reform.

Daniel Dulany was equally unlikely for the role. A wealthy Marylander, he knew that the British Empire had been good to him. In 1776, when choices became final, he would choose that empire rather than America. But as he studied Grenville's reforms in 1765, Dulany felt himself not only aggrieved but insulted. He saw through the hollow arguments that Parliament's propagandists were making, and he decided to say so publicly. The pamphlet he wrote bore a windy eighteenth-century title: *Considerations on the Propriety of Imposing Taxes in the British Colonies, for the Purpose of Raising a Revenue, by Act of Parliament.* Learned, somewhat pedantic, and intense, it was written for men of Dulany's kind. But the colonies had many men like Dulany, men who were very privileged and who saw in Grenville's program the worst threat their privileges had ever faced. Such men could tell both themselves and their world that their cause *was* their world's, and they could do it with conviction.

Neither Grenville nor Dulany began the Revolution, of course. Grenville's importance lies in his temporary mastery of Parliament at a time when Britain's rulers had every reason to change the way they ran their empire. Dulany's lies in the way he expressed the first response of a large sector of the American elite. Understanding them and what they stood for is not the same as understanding the Revolution. But we cannot make sense of the Revolution unless we realize why and how Britain's rulers challenged American autonomy, and why and how America's leaders responded.

The main story is easy to follow. In 1764, 1765, 1767, and 1773, the British government forced the issue of the extent of its power over the American colonies. On each occasion, the fundamental problem was whether Parliament could tax the colonies or whether only their own assemblies had that right. Parliament's first attempt was ambiguous, and so was the American response. But on the other three occasions the result was naked confrontation, both in words, as heated debate raged in meetings and the press, and in deeds. Twice Parliament backed down, repealing its Stamp Act of 1765 after a winter of protest had rendered it unworkable, and its Townshend duties of 1767 after an extended boycott of British commerce by American merchants. The third occasion came in 1773, when Bostonians dumped East India Company tea into their harbor rather than allow it to be unloaded and have parliamentary duties paid on it. They thought Britain would back down yet again. When the British did not and insisted that Boston pay for the tea, the final rupture began.

Beneath the taxation issue, other problems festered and sometimes broke into the open. The presence of British troops and sailors proved a major irritant, first in New York City and, after 1768, in Boston. Customs men seemed to be everywhere, picking on one technicality after another to obtain condemnations on cargoes and ships. The colonial court system presented problem after problem. Should judges hold their posts for life, or only for as long as the crown wanted? Should some offenses be tried in courts of vice-admiralty, where no jury ever sat? Who would have the final decision if a case went to appeal? How far could a court go in assisting and protecting British officials? Could a servant of the crown expect a fair trial in an American courtroom? Problems like these became utterly entangled, and so did endless local questions. Unraveling them proved impossible until the question of independence cut through the knot and forced all colonials to decide which side they were on.

I

Only two other nations in modern history have savored world mastery as Britain did in 1763. One, briefly in the seventeenth century, was the Netherlands. The other, in the middle of the twentieth, was the United States. The end of the Seven Years' War marked more than the defeat of France. It ensured Britain's preeminence in Europe's trade with Africa and Asia. It gave Britain access to the riches of the Spanish Empire. It confirmed that London was the financial heart of the Western world. Perhaps the greatest sign of Britain's strength was that over the next fifty years it was able to lose the American colonies, fight the wars of the French Revolution, and still remain the world's foremost power.

But if Britain was victorious in 1763, it was also exhausted. The struggle with France had lasted half a century. It had been fought at sea and on battlefields in Europe, America, and Asia. The fleets and the armies had been expensive. Moreover, like any victorious imperial statesman, Grenville knew that troops and ships would have to remain on station to safeguard what had been won. The problem was how to pay for them.

The prime minister looked westward for an answer. The colonists in North America were Britons overseas, and no Britons had gained more than they from France's defeat. Ever since they had won their first footholds in the New World, the colonists had lived with warfare. They had fought the Dutch, the Spanish, the French, and, always, the Indians. Their goal, like that of Britain itself, had been mastery. In immediate terms they wanted control of the seaboard, the fur trade, and the vast rich lands of the interior. Now they had achieved that, all of it. In larger terms, some of them already saw a vision of their own potential strength. One sign had been the New England expedition of 1745 that captured the mighty French fortress of Louisbourg in Nova Scotia without help. Another came in 1754, when Benjamin Franklin proposed a plan of colonial unity to a congress in Albany, New York. A third, not long after, was the skill with which young Colonel George Washington saved himself and the Virginia militiamen he led from the disastrous defeat that the British general Edward Braddock suffered in western Pennsylvania.

Whatever their vision of the future, colonials of all sorts knew how high a price they had paid for Britain's victory. Frontier people had lived with terror, and had dealt in it themselves. Disease and battle had devoured men who went off to fight. Tax bills had soared. The colonists believed they had done their part. But George Grenville saw it differently. From his point of view, the colonials had won great gains at little cost. He knew that only rarely had the separate provinces managed to cooperate in the war effort. One colony might commit men and resources; another would hold back. Colonial ships supposedly carrying prisoners for exchange had in fact carried goods to sell. Fur traders in Albany had dealt with their French counterparts in Montreal. Sugar and molasses from the French and Spanish Caribbean had flowed freely to the distilleries and the refineries of New York and Boston.

Grenville also knew how difficult a task Britain's colonial administrators faced. Governors could not obtain their salaries unless they violated their instructions. Customs men could not convince American juries to convict smugglers. The White Pine Act, intended to preserve the best American timber for the use of the Royal Navy, could not be enforced. Nor could the Iron Act and the Hat Act, which were intended to render colonial industry subservient to British. Other powerful Britons held a similar view. Grenville's parliamentary colleague Charles Townshend recalled how he had had to deal with the land riots that plagued New Jersey at mid-century and how he had decided then that the Americans could not rule themselves. Powerful officials of the Anglican Church cursed New England for its Puritanism and Virginia for its insistence that parsons were merely the servants of planters.

Grenville had every reason to think he could do something about these problems in a way that everyone would accept. He knew perfectly well how the absolute monarchies in France or Spain would have handled them, but the French or Spanish way was not the British. Grenville was the king's first minister, but only because he could command the support of the Commons as well as the crown. Parliament was the safeguard of all Britons. Only with its consent could the king raise taxes or pass laws. No Briton need fear that an arbitrary monarchy would ever confiscate his property— Parliament existed to prevent that. It was a sacred British belief that the king could do no wrong. It was an equally sacred belief that Parliament could do no harm to the British Constitution. Ultimately, Parliament and its ways *were* the Constitution, so close was the tie between them. When the

Boston lawyer and pamphleteer James Otis tried to work out a way of separating them, all he got for his effort was more disturbance in his own already unstable mind.

The costs of the war, the looseness of the empire, the certainty that Parliament was the right institution to legislate a remedy; these formed the background to Grenville's decision to change the way the colonies were run. The immediate goal was modest. The colonists simply had to pay the costs of their own administration. Grenville proposed three steps to achieve that goal. He took two of them in the Revenue Act, or "Sugar Act," of 1764. First, the notorious inefficiency of the Navigation System had to be brought to an end. Wholesale smuggling and haphazard enforcement would stop. If colonial juries would not bring in convictions, let offenders be tried in courts of vice-admiralty, where the judge alone would hand down the verdict. If there were not enough petty officials to enforce the law, let more be appointed. If they faced damage suits when they could not make their charges stick, let the courts protect them with certificates of "probable cause." If the customs service was still not up to the job, let the Royal Navy help. Give customs men and sailors alike the incentive of gaining one-third the value of every ship and cargo on which they secured a condemnation. It made no difference that this was the same principle on which the navy operated against wartime enemies. Smugglers, after all, were the enemies of the imperial system.

The second step that the Sugar Act took built on practices that the Navigation System had long established. Sugar was the foremost American product, and in 1733 the Molasses Act had been passed to restrict British commerce to the produce of the British sugar islands. The act allowed sugar and molasses from places such as Jamaica and Barbados to be traded freely within the empire. But it imposed a prohibitive duty on the produce of the French and Spanish islands and of Brazil. On molasses, it was sixpence per gallon. The purpose of that duty had not been to raise a revenue but rather to secure British markets for British planters. Many of those planters lived as absentees in England, and some sat in Parliament. They had a way of seeing that the British government protected their interests.

But the tax on foreign molasses had rarely been collected in the colonies. Grenville's plan was to reduce it to three-pence a gallon, and to enforce the new rate rigorously. There would be new duties on other goods as well, including some on the intercolonial trade. Elaborate paperwork would have to accompany every cargo to guarantee that there was no fraud. The purpose was not to protect producers elsewhere in the empire; it was to raise revenue. The act's preamble said so. Despite some pamphlets written in protest and some resolutions by a few provincial assemblies, the act took effect. British officials enforced it as well as they could until war finally broke out a decade later.

Grenville's third step was more sweeping. The Sugar Act imposed duties to be collected at colonial ports, but the real goal was to reach into the heart of the American economy. The result was the Stamp Act. Grenville signaled his intention to introduce it as early as March 1764, but Parliament did not pass it until more than a year later. It was to take effect on November 1, 1765.

Using stamps to raise revenue was nothing new. Colonial assemblies occasionally had imposed stamp duties, and the British people were used to them; to this day, the British government has some in effect. The principle was simple. Before one could legally possess an object or carry out an action listed in the act, one had to buy the appropriate stamp from an official distributor. The act of 1765 imposed a host of stamp duties. All documents bearing on court cases, or on church matters, or on admission to public office would have to be stamped. So would bills of lading, letters of marque, deeds, other documents in land transactions, liquor licenses, wills, probate orders, bail bonds, and articles of apprenticeship. Passports and notarizations, dice and playing cards, newspapers and pamphlets, almanacs and calendars all would have to have stamps. There would also have to be a separate stamp for each sheet of a legal document and for each advertisement in a publication, and on publications that were not in English the duty would be doubled. The act set up sliding scales: the larger a land transaction or a book, the greater the duty.

The Stamp Act specified that these duties were payable in sterling. Americans would not be able to use the foreign coins, the paper currency, the bills of exchange, or the direct barter to which they were accustomed. The act would be enforced in vice-admiralty courts. These were special courts originally intended to deal with the technicalities of the law of the sea. Because of the kind of cases they decided, juries had no part in their procedure. Instead, a trained judge had the only say. Such judges were appointed by the government and were likely to enforce the law. That is why they were given jurisdiction in Stamp Act cases. A successful prosecution under the act would mean the confiscation of the goods or the land involved, with one-third of the booty each for the local stamp distributor, the provincial governor, and whoever had informed. The revenues raised would remain in the colonies, paying the salaries of officials and the costs of troops. But neither troops nor officials would be subject to colonial control.

The Stamp Act differed in important ways from all previous imperial legislation. One was its pervasiveness. Any colonist who bought or sold land, became an apprentice, went to church, married, read a newspaper, drank in a tavern, gambled, took public office, shipped goods elsewhere, or went to court would feel its effects. A second was its mode of collection: the taxes would be constantly evident, not paid once at a port of entry and then hidden in the overall price. A third was its requirement that payment be in sterling, with the threat of forfeiture if payment was not made. For people who rarely saw hard British coin, that threat was real. The act managed to offend everyone. The rich, the poor, producers, consumers, the powerful, the powerless, people of commerce, people of the fields, old people making their wills, young people planning to marry, pious people going to church, ribald people going to the tavern, all of them would feel it. Can there be any wonder that the colonists did not like it?

The movement that nullified the Stamp Act and forced its repeal was the first great drama of the Revolution. How that movement came about, who made it up, and how taking part in it changed the Americans themselves will be central problems discussed in this chapter and the next. The movement itself changed the issues. Colonial writers attacked the rationales that British spokesmen offered. They forced inconsistencies into the open; they made Parliament search for new ways to achieve its goals. Direct colonial action made whole policies unworkable. Despite the number of times the British backed down, colonial resistance stiffened England's determination to finally resolve the issue its way. The Sugar Act and the Stamp Act were simply the first expressions of a larger British policy aimed at establishing a new, firmer control over the colonies. It makes sense to look at that policy as a whole, rather than to take incidents one by one.

The central issue was Parliament's power to legislate for the colonies and to tax them. In strict theory, the two were not the same. Legislation meant requiring people to do some things and forbidding them to do others. Legally, it was an act of sovereign power. In Britain, "sovereign power" meant the king, the House of Lords, and the House of Commons acting together as the King-in-Parliament. But, in British tradition, taxes were another matter. They were the free gift of the people for the king's use. Legally, a tax was an act not of the government but rather of the people, through their representatives. That is why only the Commons, which represented the people, could initiate money bills and amend them. The House of Lords could do no more than say yea or nay to whatever the House of Commons produced.

Some aspects of the new British policy were clearly acts of government. The Proclamation Line that was intended to keep whites and Indians apart and thus prevent frontier warfare was one. So, too, was the decision to establish an American Board of Customs Commissioners and site it in Boston, and the decision in 1768 to deploy troops there for the commissioners' protection. So, too, was the decision in 1774 to organize a government on French lines for the conquered province of Quebec. Some of these actions, certainly, were statesmanlike. The Proclamation Line may have represented the last real hope that the Western Indians would be able to preserve their way of life. By recognizing the French customs and the Roman Catholic faith of the *Habitants*, the Quebec Act may have kept Canada from undergoing the agony that has tortured Ireland. Almost everyone in the colonies recognized that sometimes such acts were necessary and that the King-in-Parliament was the best means for carrying them out. By itself, none of these acts would have caused more than debate and mild protest before 1760. The Quebec Act probably would have led to more than most. It offended the land hunger of Virginians by taking the Mississippi Valley out of their control, and it offended the anti-Catholicism of New Englanders by recognizing popery virtually next door. But they would have had little ground to attack the principle that Parliament could pass such an act if it chose.

These acts caused more than simple debate because they became closely bound to the problem of taxation. Parliament itself made the confusion worse at a number of points. The first came in the spring of 1766, in the form of the Declaratory Act.

Parliament enacted this law as a gesture to its own self-image. The Stamp Act had proven unworkable in the colonies, and opposition to it was rising even in Britain. Grenville had lost both the king's confidence and his hold over the Commons and had stepped down. Central in the new ministry was William Pitt, the architect of Britain's defeat of France and a man who believed that the Stamp Act was a prime piece of foolishness. Pitt's French policies and his attitude toward the Stamp Act made him a hero to all Americans, but he also believed in Parliament's supremacy. The Declaratory Act asserted that Parliament had power "to make laws and statutes . . . to bind the colonies and people of *America* . . . in all cases whatsoever." It seemed straightforward, but it was a masterpiece of doublespeak. An Englishman could take "all cases whatsoever" to include taxation. A colonial could take it that "laws and statutes" and taxation were not the same thing. But, however one read it, it appeared at the time to be little more than a blustering afterthought, a gesture to Parliament's wounded pride at having had to repeal the Stamp Act.

It became clear in the following year, 1767, that it was more. Parliament had passed a Quartering Act to provide for the care of British troops stationed in the colonies. This law required that each colonial assembly appropriate money to house the troops and supply their needs. New York's assembly refused to comply. Parliament's response was stern. It passed an act that forbade the assembly to do anything at all until it voted the money the Quartering Act required. The assembly finally did what Parliament wanted, but people all over America saw the Restraining Act as disgraceful. Moreover, supply of the troops stationed in New York City would remain a political sore spot into the next decade.

A second problem with more general implications also broke out in 1767. It seemed to some British officials that the Americans had rejected the Stamp Act solely because of *where* the tax would be collected. They would accept an "external" tax, collected at the ports, but they would not accept an "internal" one, collected where they did business. Britons did have reasons for their confusion. One was the long submission of the colonists to the Navigation System, which used punitive taxes as a means of directing colonial trade where Britain wanted it to go. Another was that despite some murmuring and halfhearted protest, they also submitted to the Sugar Act, which was explicitly intended to raise a revenue. A third was ambiguity in some of their protests against the Stamp Act. According to one widely circulated report, Virginia Burgesses objected on the ground that they had always controlled their own "internal polity and taxation." Did that mean internal affairs and *all* taxation? Or would they accept a parliamentary tax if it was collected at the ports rather than within the province?

The objection seems purely technical, but throughout the colonial years technical questions had led to lengthy debates, usually between governors and assemblies. Now the Chancellor of the Exchequer, Charles Townshend, made a blunder that allowed the British government to be brought in. Townshend found himself obliged to raise more money, for he had allowed a massive drop in Britain's taxation of its own land. The seeming American distinction between external taxes and internal ones offered the chancellor a solution. He proposed that Parliament raise a colonial revenue by taxing painters' colors, glass, lead, paper, and tea as they entered colonial ports. These were among the duties that the newly created American customs commissioners were given the task of collecting.

Townshend's program failed. Though the taxes remained on the law books until 1770, collecting them proved impossible. The result was that once again Parliament's pride and the problem of colonial revenue became intertwined. When Parliament did repeal the duties, it left the tax on tea in effect. This, like the Declaratory Act, was a gesture to Parliament's own self-image. Whether there was any point in levying taxes when those taxes could not be collected seemed immaterial. It was important to assert the principle that Parliament could do what it wanted, when it wanted, to whom it wanted.

In fact, once the other duties were repealed, the tea tax was more or less successfully collected, at least on tea that was legitimately imported. In 1773, however, Parliament once again turned to the American colonies to resolve problems that had arisen elsewhere. Again it demonstrated that the Americans counted least as far as it was concerned. In 1733, the voices of West Indies sugar planters had rung loudest in the Commons, and the result had been the Molasses Act. In 1767, Townshend had taken a chance on setting off an American uproar in order to lower taxes for British landowners, and the result had been renewed resistance. Now it was the East India Company whose interests seemed most important; the result was the beginning of the final crisis.

Like the chartered companies that began American colonization, the East India Company tried to carry out both the private function of making a profit and the public task of governing a society. Like the colonization companies, it mixed these in a way that made it impossible to do either. Thanks to its ramshackle structure and to the ineptitude, or worse, of its servants, the company was failing either to return a profit to its shareholders or to consolidate Britain's hold on India. But the company's survival was important, both for British purposes of state and for the fortunes of the many well-placed investors who had money in it. Parliament decided to rescue it—the result was the Tea Act of 1773.

The act gave the East India Company two benefits. One was to allow it to market its tea directly to America, using its own agents there. Now it could bypass the network of auctions, wholesalers, and colonial merchants through which its tea previously had been sold. This was a straightforward rationalization of its business. It would give the company the same efficiency and economies of scale that multinational corporations seek in our own time. The other benefit was to free the company of duty on tea that it imported to Britain and then reshipped to America. Only the Townshend tax of threepence a pound would remain. The combination, ministers foresaw, would make taxed tea sold by the company so cheap that it could undercut both tea that was traded legitimately by American merchants and tea that was smuggled in, usually by the same merchants. The consumer would benefit, for tea would drop in price. The company would benefit, for it would find the revenue in America that it could not raise in Britain or the East. The treasury would benefit, for taxes would be raised. Parliament's pride would benefit, for at last the colonies would have accepted a tax that Parliament had imposed. No one in London thought very much about the American merchants who might be crushed by the East India Company's newfound strength.

The Sugar Act, the Stamp Act, the Townshend taxes, the Tea Act; these were the major mileposts along the road to imperial crisis. Had Parliament not passed them, there certainly would have been no American Revolution. What lay behind them? Was it mere blundering and happenstance, as many historians have thought? Was it conspiracy, as rebellious Americans came to believe? Or was there a logic built into the imperial situation that was working itself out?

It was not incompetence or simple accident. The men who made British policy—Grenville, Townshend, Lord Hillsborough, Lord Shelburne, Lord North, King George—were as capable of both wisdom and folly as anyone else. They did their work, however, within a larger framework of British needs, and they made policy to suit those needs. Despite colonial fears, that framework was not held together by conspiracy. Rather, it rested on the realities of power and development within the empire. British landowners, West Indies sugar planters who actually lived in England, and the East India Company all had louder voices in Whitehall than the North Americans. So, too, did the royal governors and placemen who filled their correspondence with reports of colonial "disorder." British policy responded.

In the long run, British policy would lead to stagnation and underdevelopment for the North American economy, and this was no accident. The Southern and Caribbean colonial economies suited British needs perfectly. The goods they produced had to be marketed in Britain. If they grew more than the metropolis needed, Britain would get the benefit of selling the surplus elsewhere in Europe. The wheat, corn, rye, and animals that Northern farmers raised were less necessary to Britain itself, so it let them be marketed more freely. But the Northern towns offered the possibility of complex urban economic development that would compete directly with Britain. Restraining that development was one thrust of eighteenth-century British colonial policy. The Hat Act and the Iron Act were not themselves serious restrictions, but they did point the way to further curbs on colonial industry. In 1764, Grenville's government followed the precedent those acts set when it forbade colonial assemblies to make their paper currencies legal tender. The Sugar Act, the Stamp Act, and the Townshend taxes were efforts to cream off what American development was producing. The Tea Act was a direct assault by the empire's foremost economic power on the merchants of the port towns. Whether anyone in Westminster or in the City of London, where financiers did their business, actually called for the subordination of the colonial economy is not the point. It *is* the case that in the very same years British domination over Ireland and India was leading to the long-term subordination of their economies to British needs. In those countries, local merchants and local trading networks were crushed as the British moved in. Local industry was stifled so British industry could prosper. Local agriculture was organized to produce staple crops for Britain to process, rather than mixed crops for local people to use. When Britain turned from "salutary neglect" to stricter control, it pointed its North American policy in the same direction.

The simple facts were these. The colonies were vibrant, dynamic, and only partly tied into the network of imperial control. Britain, more vibrant, more dynamic, was determined to organize the world for its own benefit. It had been willing to wage endless war with France and Spain for mastery. Now it was equally willing to do what was necessary in order to keep its colonies colonial. Given Britain's situation, its rulers would have been foolish to do anything else. But given America's situation, its people would have been equally foolish not to resist.

II

Britain achieved something quite remarkable in 1765: it brought its subjects in America closer together than they had ever come before. As we have seen, the colonials were not a united people. Part of the history of their Revolution tells how they created a common political identity. But other parts tell how they developed many separate identities, not only as Carolinians or Pennsylvanians or New Yorkers but also as merchants, planters, artisans, farmers, blacks, and women. Most of all, the Revolution's story tells how one coalition after another was built, what it achieved, and what became of it. The coalitions that came together in 1765 and 1767 and 1773 to oppose British policy were not the same as the one that formed in 1776 to win independence. Nor was either group identical with the coalition of 1787 that established the United States.

We must take each of these alliances on its own terms. What groups formed them? What did they share? In what ways did they differ? What did each group seek? How did they come to political consciousness? Asking such questions destroys the notion that we can simply speak of "Americans" or "colonists" or even "revolutionaries." It also destroys the notion that we can treat the Revolution as one group's exclusive property and then measure everyone else by that group's standard. Asking these questions enables us to understand much more clearly what the Revolution was. It enables us to see much more readily the changes that it brought to people's lives.

Throughout the era, Americans who would have called themselves the "better sort" were important. Sometimes they acted together. Sometimes they split apart. Sometimes they virtually decided what would happen. Sometimes they reacted to events thrust upon them. Sometimes these great planters, large Northern landowners, well-to-do merchants, skilled lawyers, and smooth politicians got all they wanted. Sometimes they did not. But there is no understanding the Revolution without understanding what they did.

Like everyone else, the rulers of colonial America confronted the crisis in terms of what they were. By the time of the Stamp Act, they had established a lively tradition of open political debate. For decades, they had been turning small problems into large issues, honing their constitutional principles and their political rhetoric to a fine sharpness. How, with whom, and over what they disputed varied, of course. New Englanders proclaimed how much they valued peace and proceeded to assail one another. In New York, New Jersey, and Pennsylvania, public life was endlessly factious. Farther South, slavery gave white rulers good reason to keep close together, but they never hesitated to open verbal fire on governors or on British officials. Ordinary people in all the colonies became used to the spectacle of the elite arguing loudly about its problems. They became used as well to the elite's insisting that whatever the argument was about, it made a difference to everyone. The most potent weapon colonial leaders held was their assertive language and their public style.

This tradition of debate and argument, in a press that was as free as any in the eighteenth-century world, helps to explain the sheer wordiness of the Revolution. Between the Stamp Act and the Constitution, American printers poured out political pamphlets, newspaper essays, broadsides, poems, sermons, songs, and doggerel. Town meetings, popular conventions, revolutionary committees, and regular assemblies passed endless declarations and resolutions. The "better sort" did not produce all this often-heated discourse. Watching ordinary people learn to think and especially to speak for themselves is one of the most exciting aspects of watching the Revolution develop. But except for Tom Paine and a few others, the major authors of the era either came from the upper class or hoped to join it. What they wrote tells us a great deal about how people of their kind confronted the crises and problems of their age. From 1763 to 1776, the prime problem was relations with Britain. Men who set out to write in opposition had two main tasks before them. One was to show what the real effects of British policy were. The other was to turn the crisis from a series of troubles and quandaries into a pattern that made sense.

Some elite writers saw the gathering problems in sharply material terms. One such was Governor Stephen Hopkins of Rhode Island, who published an "Essay on the Trade of the Northern Colonies" in 1764. Unlike any other province except Connecticut, Rhode Island elected its own governor. Most colonial magistrates came to their posts from Britain, but Hopkins was a Rhode Islander. He owed his high office to other colonials who chose him to fill it, not to the favor of distant great men. Providence and Newport, which dominated Rhode Island's economy, were trading towns, and Hopkins could see what George Grenville's policies would mean for them. He understood the realities of power in the imperial framework as well. He wrote his essay to show the real effects of the empire at work.

The governor's main argument was simple: the Northern colonies needed free trade, both with the non-British Caribbean and with the Old World. Hopkins slipped lightly over the way that slaves formed one of the most valuable commodities in which his people dealt. His major point was that, despite imperial theory, the restrictions that Britain imposed on colonial trade did not serve the commonweal. They simply served the interests of some, especially West Indies planters. Those privileged men enjoyed high prices in a guaranteed market, because the Northern ports could not get enough sugar and molasses. They also enjoyed a ready, cheap supply of foodstuffs and manufactured goods, because a constant glut in West Indies markets kept prices there low. What counted was simply the ability to get things done in London. These men had it, and the North Americans did not. In the short run, that fact would lead to stagnation for the Northern colonies. In the long run, it would create problems for Britain, because the colonies would not buy British manufactures if they could not pay for them.

Hopkins came as close as any writer to speaking for the entire colonial merchant class, but in 1769 a Charleston merchant, Henry Laurens, decided that the time had come to speak for himself. By then, Laurens and John Hancock of Boston were the foremost victims of the "customs racketeering" that plagued colonial administration in the late 1760s. The Sugar Act and the Townshend taxes had established so many technicalities and formal requirements for colonial traders to meet that a clever customs man could fleece them almost at will. One trick was to allow long-established ways of doing business to continue even though the law now forbade them, and then to crack down suddenly. Another was to make a minor technical violation the excuse for condemning a whole ship and cargo. Courts readily protected officials with certificates of "probable cause" even when the charge came to nothing.

Major merchants like Laurens and Hancock lost a great deal of property to customs men who operated this way. Boatmen taking small cargoes across provincial boundaries and seamen with small private ventures hidden in some corner on the ships they sailed became victims, too. In Laurens's case the hurt was especially galling, for the judge of the vice-admiralty court in Charleston was his own nephew, Egerton Leigh. Indeed, for a time Leigh not only

presided over the court where his uncle's ships were condemned but as attorney general of South Carolina also as-
sisted in bringing the prosecutions. Laurens finally decided
to let the world know what was going on, so he published his
Extracts from the Proceedings of the Court of Vice-Admiralty.
The pamphlet was not much more than a listing of the mis-
fortunes its author had suffered at the court's hands. But
the simple documentation filled a full forty-one pages, and
Laurens went on to discuss the general injustices that were
built into British customs procedure. By 1769, virtually anyone who had any reason to deal with the customs service
knew such stories. Like Hopkins, Laurens was reflecting on
the way that Americans lived as inferiors in the imperial
world. Merely to point that fact out was to bring its rightfulness into question.

Many other writers, however, made their case differently.
To understand what they were saying, we must confront the
language they used. We might compare the problems to be
found in reading them with the difficulties that someone
from another age might have with writing from our own
time. Such a reader would need to appreciate how figures like
Darwin, Marx, Freud, and Einstein have shaped our mental
world. They are not the only influences on us, of course:
Christianity and Islam are only two of many others. But to a
reader who did not understand what we mean by terms like
evolution, social class, personality, and relativity, our language would be gibberish.

The eighteenth-century literate elite lived in a different
mental world. They used terms that we also use, such as
liberty, virtue, and corruption, but they did not necessarily
mean what we mean by them. Their language, the reality
their language described, and the way their language shaped
their thoughts and actions have been the subject of intensive
investigation by recent historians, including Caroline Robbins, Bernard Bailyn, J.G.A. Pocock, and Gordon S. Wood.

What they have found is central to how we now understand the Revolution.

The roots of eighteenth-century political language lay in three very different historical experiences. The first took place centuries earlier in the Renaissance city-states of northern Italy. All over Europe, the power of the Holy Roman Empire and of the papacy was waning. So were the ways of life and the patterns of belief on which that power had rested. In Spain, France, and England, the result was the emergence of energetic new monarchies ruling whole nations. But, in places like Florence, Venice, and Milan, people turned instead to the idea of a republic, of a society where citizens ruled themselves. Breathing new life into traditions passed down from ancient Greece and Rome, they found in republicanism a better way of running their societies.

Yet their efforts failed again and again. Great Italian families like the Borgias and outside powers like France disrupted republican experiments repeatedly. It began to seem inevitable that a republic would fail and a despot would arise. Influential thinkers like Niccolò Machiavelli became preoccupied with the problem of why this was so. The result of their labors was a theory of politics and a theory of history. For the first time since the classical age, it became possible to see the world that people lived in as the product of human action rather than of divine will or mere chance. Their political theory held that a republic became possible only when its citizens thought of the whole, not of themselves. Central to it was the notion that the good citizen was a man of virtue. The word connoted not sexual morality but, rather, tough independence, physical strength, military courage, and public spirit. Virtue was impossible if a man owed his well-being to someone else. In consequence, thinkers concluded that a society of small producers was far more likely to generate a virtuous citizenry than one of masters and servants or landlords and tenants. Their republican theory of history told these same thinkers that even if men could establish such a society it was unlikely to last long. The very energy of hardy republicans would lead to conquest, accumulation, and eventually to luxury and decay. For these theorists, republicanism offered the best possible way to live, the only way, in fact, to be fully human. Yet, of necessity, it seemed, every attempt to live by it was doomed to fail. The books that developed this line of thought, such as Machiavelli's *Discourses on the First Ten Books of Livy*, became central texts for all political philosophy in the early modern world.

The second source lay in medieval England. There parliamentarians and jurists developed a body of law that consistently emphasized the rights of the individual rather than the power of the ruler. In this common-law tradition, a man could be sure he was free if he knew that his person and his property were his own. English common law did not presume that such freedom was a natural or a human right, only that it was a right of English subjects. It did not presume that all English subjects were equal, for class, sex, and age all made great differences in the amount of freedom a person could enjoy. But it did assume that someone who enjoyed freedom had every reason to hang on to it; and its technicalities, precedents, and procedures offered means to defend this freedom when it was threatened. The most obvious was the need to convince a jury drawn from a defendant's neighbors, rather than a judge appointed by the king, before a person could be convicted. What this had in common with the Italian tradition was the belief that liberty was good, that it could be enjoyed only in very specific social conditions, and that those conditions were easily lost. But, for the Italian thinkers, liberty was a public right that allowed a citizen to take part in running society. For common-law jurists, it was private, the right of a subject to be sure of where he stood.

The third source lay in the upheavals that England went through in the seventeenth and eighteenth centuries. The Puritan Revolution of the 1640s, the Glorious Revolution of

1688, and the gradual settling down that Sir Robert Walpole imposed in the 1720s and 1730s offered endless material for discussion. English people had deposed two kings, sending one to the scaffold and the other into exile. They had lived for more than a decade without a king or a House of Lords. They hobbled the restored monarchy with the Bill of Rights and subordinated it to Parliament. Diggers, Levellers, the Family of Love, Fifth Monarchy Men, and their heirs produced a popular radicalism that made Oliver Cromwell's look tepid. In the midst of it all, a long series of writers speculated on the history and the meaning of British freedom. The French social theorist Montesquieu celebrated Britain's eighteenth-century settlements as the perfection of political wisdom, and English thinkers, too, encouraged the world to believe that Britons were uniquely free. But from James Harrington and John Milton in the mid-seventeenth century to Richard Price and Catharine Macauley in the late eighteenth, "real Whigs" or "commonwealthmen" or "country" thinkers stressed how constant was the danger that freedom would be lost. Writing together as "Cato," the popular pamphleteers John Trenchard and Thomas Gordon insisted throughout Walpole's time that it virtually was lost. Their essays were more commonly read and more frequently imitated by colonials than any other English writings.

Drawing on all these traditions, American writers came to see the political world in terms of an unending struggle between liberty and its enemies. Sometimes they called the opposition to it power. By that, they usually meant a government's ability and desire to make people do what it wanted. Sometimes they called it oppression. By that, they meant the use of inordinate strength to take away the property of free men and turn them into cringing dependents. Sometimes they described it as corruption. This was not simple bribe taking or embezzlement. It was their shorthand for all the social entanglements and all the dependency that came with any way of life much more complex than simple farming.

When Virginia's planters responded to the Stamp Act, they brought their own experience and this language together. Spurred by the anger of a young member named Patrick Henry, they passed a series of resolutions against the act in June 1765. Widely and not always accurately reported, these resolutions declared Virginia's opposition to the act on four separate grounds. First, Virginia's founders had lost none of their English "Liberties, Privileges, Franchises and Immunities" when they emigrated. Second, two royal charters had confirmed their rights. Third, the right to tax themselves by consent of their own representatives was "the distinguishing Characteristick" of their *British* freedom." Fourth, they had always controlled their own "internal Polity and Taxation." As the Burgesses knew, the Stamp Act challenged them in two ways. First, it threatened the property of all colonials, for if Parliament could take anything, it could take everything. Second, it threatened the Burgesses' own position as privileged men, for if Parliament could tax Virginians, their own house would quickly fade to inconsequence. The Irish gentry had seen exactly that fate befall their Parliament in Dublin, and no Burgess wanted it to happen in Williamsburg.

Assemblies elsewhere followed the Virginians' lead. By the end of 1765, Rhode Island, Pennsylvania, Maryland, Connecticut, Massachusetts, South Carolina, New Jersey, and New York all had adopted similar resolves. In October, a Stamp Act Congress with delegates from nine colonies gathered in New York City. The congress adopted fourteen resolutions against the act. Making all the points the Virginians had made, it went on to defend jury trials, to protest the act's burdens, and to assert that America already contributed enormously to Britain's well-being. It finished its work with petitions to Parliament and an address to the king. Clearly, the leaders of the colonies were alarmed; they were giving their fellow colonials stirring guidance.

Yet many problems remained. Political representation was

a Briton's right, but Parliament said that *its* members represented the interests of all. The Burgesses asserted their control over "internal Polity and Taxation," but what did they mean by the phrase? If the colonials accepted that Parliament could legislate for them, how could they deny that it could tax them? What if Parliament passed a tax but called it a law? The Americans invoked the "ancient constitution," but Parliament itself was the heart of that Constitution. How, then, could Parliament violate it? These problems preoccupied many American writers through the decade of imperial strife. As they wrestled with them, writers destroyed not only the rationale for specific taxes and laws but also most of the rationale for the empire itself.

Daniel Dulany's historic moment came when he decided to address the first of these problems, Parliament's assertion that it stood for Britons everywhere. The claim was put strongly in the aftermath of the Sugar Act by ministerial spokesman Thomas Whately. In his pamphlet *The Regulations Lately Made concerning the Colonies and the Taxes Imposed upon Them, Considered,* Whately argued that whether or not a person could vote for a member of Parliament meant nothing. There were whole boroughs, like Leeds, Halifax, Birmingham, and Manchester, that sent no members at all. Not a single woman or child enjoyed the suffrage. Some important groups, like the merchants of London, had no immediate representation; others, like the universities at Oxford and Cambridge, did. Whately's point was that Parliament did not speak for particular interests; rather, its purpose was to determine the good of all. Like disenfranchised Britons, colonials all enjoyed "virtual" representation in the Commons. No British subject was "actually, all are virtually represented in Parliament, for every Member sits . . . not as Representative of his own Constituents, but as one of that august Assembly by which all the Commons of *Great Britain* are represented."

Dulany had no trouble destroying Whately's logic. That

there were English boroughs which had no members of their own did not mean that their people enjoyed no immediate representation. Every county in the realm had at least two members sitting for it, and a person did not have to stop living in Birmingham to vote for a member for Warwickshire. Even if he had no vote, he knew that the members for his county would have to pay the same taxes as himself and that they would know quickly if the burden became too great. But the only way a colonial could enjoy either a vote for Parliament or a seat in it was to move to Britain, and that meant that he would no longer be a colonial. Parliament might tax the colonies till they had nothing left, but its members would feel not the slightest pain. By the time Dulany had finished with Whately's argument, it lay in shreds. The British would not try to use it again.

John Dickinson succeeded Dulany as the foremost American pamphleteer. Though he was a wealthy lawyer from Philadelphia, Dickinson pretended in his writing to be a simple "Farmer in Pennsylvania." In December 1767, he began publishing a series of "Letters" in the *Pennsylvania Chronicle*. Other newspapers quickly picked them up, and by March 1768 all twelve had been collected in a single pamphlet. Like Daniel Dulany, Dickinson was a man led by both interest and temperament to a conservative view of the world. Unlike Dulany, Dickinson chose the American side at independence, but he spent so long making up his mind that many people believed he had become a Tory. His London legal education gave him close ties to Britain. His great fortune gave him much to lose. The world as it was had been good to him, and that showed in his choice of words. "This I call an innovation," he thundered in his second Letter. It was the strongest condemnation he could imagine.

In 1767, Dickinson found many "innovations" to worry about. One was the act suspending New York's assembly until it voted supplies for British troops stationed there, as Parliament required. By suspending the assembly, Parliament had posed the problem of the constitutional standing of the colonial legislatures. Assemblymen had long assumed that somehow they were both subordinate in the imperial system and the equals of Parliament in regard to their own societies. They opened their sessions with the same rituals; their members claimed the same immunities and privileges; they prefaced their statutes with the same legal formulas. But did they really amount to nothing more than local conveniences, comparable to an English borough council? Could Parliament suspend or change them at will? For Dickinson, the answer was clear: "The assembly of New-York either had, or had not, a right to refuse submission" to the Quartering Act. "If they had, and I imagine no American will say they had not, then the parliament had *no right* to compel them to execute it" or "to punish them for not executing it."

But Dickinson's great subject was the Townshend taxes. Charles Townshend had proposed them to Parliament with the firm belief that the distinction between an internal tax and an external one was silly. But he also thought that the Americans themselves had made it and that they ought to be prepared to live with the consequences. What, in fact, *did* the Virginia Burgesses mean in 1765 when they claimed control over their own "internal Polity and Taxation"? Were they conceding Townshend's point in advance? Or were they asserting the right to control all their internal affairs and all their taxation as well?

For Dickinson, a tax was a tax. Whatever its form, Parliament had no right to levy one on the colonies. No innovator, he fell back on a point the colonials had been making all along: "The parliament . . . possesses a legal authority to *regulate* the trade of Great-Britain, and all her colonies," but it had no right to tax the colonies in any way. Where and how a tax was collected made no difference. Parliament itself had announced that the purpose of the Sugar Act, the Stamp Act, and the Townshend taxes was to raise revenue, not to regulate trade. The British tradition that a tax was the free gift of the people either meant that the colonials taxed themselves or it meant nothing at all.

John Dickinson had the genuine conservative's acute awareness that one thing leads to another. "All artful rulers," he wrote, "who strive to extend their power . . . endeavor to give to their attempts as much semblance of legality as possible. Those who succeed them may . . . go a little further, for each new encroachment will be strengthened by a former. . . . A free people therefore can never be too quick in observing, nor too firm in opposing the beginnings of *alteration* . . . respecting institutions formed for their security." For him, as for the Burgesses or for Daniel Dulany, the task before the colonists was simply to hold on to a good state of affairs. They had learned well the lessons that their heritage had taught them. They knew how easily their liberty could be lost.

Yet Dickinson kept stumbling over the problem of the subordinate position that the colonials occupied. On the surface, he offered no objection: "He, who considers these provinces as states distinct from the British Empire, has very slender notions of *justice* or of their *interests*. We are but parts of a *whole*; and therefore there must exist a power somewhere to preside, and preserve the connection. . . . This power is lodged in the parliament." Yet the contradiction remained: "We are as much dependent on Great-Britain, as a perfectly free people can be on another." Was it really possible to be both dependent and free at the same time?

Being dependent meant that the colonials never could be their own masters. The theory of the British Empire rested on the belief that all its parts were interdependent, that within it all conflicting interests were balanced. Its laws were "calculated to regulate trade, and preserve or promote a mutually beneficial intercourse." But, as Dickinson could not help seeing, the reality was different. The colonies were underdeveloped, "a country of planters, farmers, and fishermen, not of manufacturers." What Americans needed, they had to buy. "Inexpressible . . . must be our distresses in evading the late acts, by the disuse" of British products. The cause lay in the imperial tie: "Great Britain had prohibited the manufacturing [of] iron and steel in these colonies . . . the *like* right she must have to prohibit any other manufactures among us." But why?

In 1774, Thomas Jefferson asked himself that question and decided that it had no answer, at least from the colonial point of view. Jefferson had been elected to Virginia's first revolutionary convention, and when illness kept him from attending, he drafted resolutions for it to consider. The convention took a less advanced stance than his, but his draft appeared in pamphlet form under the title *A Summary of the Rights of British America*. What he wrote marked one of the major intellectual milestones on America's road away from Britain.

The question of what Parliament could and could not do to the colonies had vexed many a writer. It bothered the Boston politician and pamphleteer James Otis so much that it contributed to the loss of his sanity. But for Jefferson it did not exist. Parliament could do nothing. The first settlers had taken with them not the legal rights and obligations of Englishmen but the natural rights of emigrants. Once in America, they were free to establish "new societies, under such laws and regulations as to them [should] seem most likely to promote public happiness." Britain had asserted no "claim of superiority or dependence" then, and the emigrants had accepted none. Nor had Britain borne the cost of settlement. The colonists' "own blood was spilt . . . their own fortunes expended . . . for themselves they fought, for themselves they conquered, and for themselves they have right to" the land they had won. At most, Parliament had lent them "assistance against an enemy," but accepting that aid had never meant that the colonists "submitted themselves to her sovereignty." Parliament's claim to authority over the colonies was no more than usurpation. The colonists had to live with the reality of dependency and subordination, but it had never been a matter of right. The Navigation Acts, the Hat and Iron Acts, even the act establishing an American post office were "void," for "the British parliament has no right to exercise authority over us."

Jefferson's view of American history cut through all the intellectual tangles that had grown up around British policy. The Stamp Act, the Townshend Acts, the New York Restraining Act, the Tea Act, and now, in 1774, the laws passed to punish Boston for the Tea Party offered good evidence that there was a concerted campaign to destroy American liberty. But in principle they were no different than the acts that had gone before. Parliament had never had the right to pass any of them. There was no need to worry about the difference between legislation and taxation, or between internal taxes and external ones. There was no need for elaborate explanations of why the colonists did not enjoy representation in Parliament or of what Parliament meant when it passed this law or that. There was no reason at all why "160,000 electors in the island of Great Britain should give law to four millions in the states of America, every individual of whom is equal to every individual of them."

Not much was left when Jefferson finished his demolition of the British theory of empire. All that still held it together was the person of the king. Jefferson drafted the "Summary View" in the form of suggestions for a "humble and dutiful" address to be "presented to his majesty." To that extent, he bowed to the polite formulas of his time. But, for Jefferson, George III had little about him of majesty. The king was "no more than the chief officer of the people, appointed by the laws, and circumscribed with definite powers, to assist in working the great machine of government." His power was for the people's "use, and consequently subject to their superintendance." The empire was no more than a network of separate republics, held together because they all shared the same constitutional monarch.

Jefferson still thought that that network might last indefinitely. It was neither Americans' "wish, nor our interest to separate." But no longer could the empire be based on the subordination of one part of it to another. Colonials would not cringe before the king: "Let those flatter who fear; it is not an American art." Nor would they accept that Britons could speak to him on Americans' behalf: "You have no ministers for American affairs, because you have taken none from among us." Nor would they grant any longer that their own economies existed for the good of Britain rather than for the good of themselves: let Parliament "not think to exclude us from going to other markets to dispose of those commodities which they cannot use, or to supply those wants which they cannot supply." Jefferson had stepped out of a world of hierarchy and subordination and into one of equality between men and between societies. Only two things kept the step from being complete. One was what little remained of Jefferson's acceptance that the king was his sovereign. The Virginian would deal with that problem two years later, when he wrote the Declaration of Independence. The other was his own sovereignty, far greater than any the king ever claimed, over the women in his life and over the slaves whose labor gave him the time to think his soaring thoughts and to write his elegant prose. That was a problem that Thomas Jefferson would never resolve.

Stephen Hopkins, Henry Laurens, the Burgesses of Virginia, Daniel Dulany, John Dickinson, and Thomas Jefferson: these were far from the only important writers of the imperial crisis. Some, like Martin Howard of Rhode Island, Samuel Seabury of New York, and Joseph Galloway of Pennsylvania, put the case against resistance. What they did took courage, for they suffered much more than the merely verbal wrath of their fellows for doing it. Others, like James Otis and John and Samuel Adams of Massachusetts, Alexander

Hamilton of New York, and Richard Bland of Virginia, made powerful points on the colonial side. Men and some women who are much less well known turned out an array of pieces, short and long, that often tell a different story from the writings of the major pamphleteers. But the writers we have looked at show in sharp relief what happened to the colonial elite as they confronted the crisis.

Dulany and Dickinson illustrate the doubts and fears with which many of them had to deal. Dulany was far from the only man who was profoundly alarmed in the mid-1760s by Parliament but who was even more alarmed in the mid-1770s by his fellow Americans. Dickinson was one of many who stood trembling on the edge in 1776, unable to make up his mind to live with what he had helped to start. Henry Laurens and the Virginia Burgesses show the wide range of arguments that the spokesmen for resistance used. For Laurens, the problems were hard and practical; for the Burgesses, they were matters of constitutionality and law. But for both, considerable self-interest was at stake. Laurens knew that he faced a debtor's prison if the customs service continued much longer to have its way with his goods. Colonial assemblymen knew that they faced a future without power if Parliament could just sweep aside the way things had "always" been done.

Yet, beneath the variations, there were parallel lines of development. One line led from doubt and uncertainty to militance. Tortured reasoning about laws and taxes and about internal taxes and external ones gave way to Jefferson's argument that Parliament could do nothing at all. Begging and petitioning gave way to the straightforward assertion of equality. Fawning on "the best of kings" yielded to bold advice that "the name of George the third" not "be a blot in the page of history." A second development was the growing realization of what it meant to be unequal. Jefferson's assertion that colonials were as good as Britons was new. But it marked the resolution of a problem that had plagued every single one of his predecessors.

Most important, these writers moved ever closer to an awareness that, whatever needed doing, they could not do it alone. Dulany reasoned in abstruse legalities; Laurens described endless technical procedures; Dickinson flavored his prose with Latin quotations. But Jefferson wrote in clear, polished, highly readable English. The difference is not simply between three writers whose style was indifferent and one whose style was superb. It is that Jefferson understood that debate was one thing and resistance another. He saw that people outside his own class would have to be the real source of resistance; indeed, that for a decade now that was just what they had been. Debating fundamental issues is an important part of the process of any revolution. When people begin doing it, that is one sign that something has gone profoundly wrong in their lives. But, intense as it was, the debate that Britain's policies provoked was only one of the elements that turned ordinary Americans from colonials to revolutionaries.

· 3 ·

From Rioters
to Radicals

Early Americans lived in a violent world. Colonizers from England, Holland, Spain, France, and Portugal waged endless violent struggles for dominion. Whites throughout the hemisphere used violence to drive Indians from the land and more violence to make blacks labor on it. Rulers employed the organized violence of the state to keep lesser people in their place. Puritan New Englanders used it against witches and Quakers, and Anglican Virginians used it against Baptists and Methodists. Drinking men in taverns settled their arguments with fists and knives. People in crowds threatened violence and sometimes turned to it to resolve problems that no one of them alone could handle.

These people were violent in eighteenth-century style. British colonials shared that style with Creoles in South America, with Britons who had stayed behind, and with people all over mainland Europe. That style was open and theatrical. A solemn judge pronouncing a sentence of death, the condemned man going to a gallows that stood in a public square, an army marching off to battle in its glittering glory, a master gathering his slaves and making them watch while the lash was laid on, a tavern braggart loudly asserting his superior manhood, all these were acting out rituals to be seen and understood. Such people were giving messages, and they expected that others in their world would act accordingly.

This was as true of crowd action as of any other aspect of
the violence of early American life.

Crowds or mobs or popular uprisings were central to the
public life of colonial and revolutionary America. By itself,
no single riot can ever make a revolution. In the eighteenth-
century world, rioting was often defensive. It was the act of
people who wanted to restore or protect something good, not
of people who were driven by a vision of change. But popular
upheavals were central to the way that British power in
America came to its end, and they were central as well to
the beginnings of republicanism. We can only understand
these revolutionary crowds against their colonial background.
But we must also understand that in the Revolution crowds
left that background behind. Beginning as a normal, almost
functional part of the old order, they played a major part in
bringing that order down. The consequence was that they
helped put an end to the very conditions of their own
existence.

I

Except for Virginia, each of the original thirteen states
experienced large-scale social violence between 1750 and
1800. In the two Carolinas, backcountry "Regulators" confronted low-country grandees through the late 1760s. In
Georgia, in Maryland, and on New York's western frontier,
the War of Independence became a vicious internal conflict.
Pennsylvania's interior erupted in 1763, when "Paxton Boys"
murdered peaceful Indians who lived nearby and then
marched on Philadelphia. It erupted again in 1792 with the
Whiskey Rebellion. Central New Jersey was torn apart in
mid-century by land riots. In New York's Hudson Valley,
tenant discontent simmered through the 1750s and boiled up
into a massive rising in 1766. Settlers from New England
and speculators from New York confronted one another in
the Green Mountains during the late 1760s and the early

1770s. Not just Massachusetts, but much of the rest of rural New England turned to violence in 1786.

Nor were the cities any quieter. The streets of Boston and New York witnessed violent and sometimes lethal strife during the imperial crisis. Philadelphians avoided such conflict then, but they opened fire on one another during the Fort Wilson riot of 1779. In lesser towns, too, people took to the streets, threw brickbats, tore down houses, and defaced property. We will not look at all of the upheavals of the period in this chapter. Some will be passed by, and some discussed later. But to list these few gives an idea of how important violence was during the revolutionary era.

Why was this so? Was it simply that "the mob" turned violent every time its tether slipped? Was it the expression of some vicious strain that has always disfigured the American soul? There can be no doubt that eighteenth-century crowds sometimes were bloodthirsty. Particularly in matters of racial strife, they helped to set ugly patterns that would reappear again and again in American history. But crowd action had a specific place in the early modern world. It did not usually lead to bloodshed, and when it did the authorities, not the crowd, were most often the cause. Sometimes crowds turned out at the urging and under the leadership of highly placed men. Sometimes they expressed the frustration and the anger of the "lesser sort" against their "betters." But almost always, crowd action rested on a clear understanding of what was right and what was wrong, what ought to be endured and what ought to be resisted. It also rested on well-developed ideas about how resistance ought to be carried out.

Crowd action came very close to being an institution in early American life. In some ways, the crowd became an institution of colonial society. Modern police departments did not exist, so crowds that were called sheriff's posses enforced the law; nor did modern fire departments, so crowds called volunteer fire companies gathered to save property and lives. Drawn into ranks and given officers, a crowd became a unit of the militia. Yet crowds that were less formal, less organized, and less recognized by officialdom were just as much a part of life. Sometimes they protected a community from a danger that faced everyone who lived in it. In places as far apart as Marblehead, Massachusetts, and Norfolk, Virginia, crowds kept smallpox victims from entering town, so contagion would not spread. When the Royal Navy sent a press gang into a port to kidnap men into service, it threatened everyone: prospective sailors, because life in the navy was appalling; merchants, because they dared not put their ships to sea; townsfolk and traders, because even small boats bearing food and firewood would not venture out on the harbor. Such a press threatened Boston in 1747, and the crowds that resisted it held control of the town for three days. In times of shortage, crowds kept merchants from exporting scarce foodstuffs. In times of moral outrage, they closed down houses of prostitution. In times of bigotry, they drove out sectarians. If inflated rhetoric, climbing to the heights of principle, was a prime social weapon of the elite, crowd action was a prime social weapon of the ordinary people.

Yet we cannot leave matters there, for eighteenth-century Americans knew crowds of many kinds. Again and again, even the most prominent people declared that crowd action could be perfectly legitimate, almost natural. Thomas Jefferson once said that "a little rebellion" was like a "storm in the atmosphere" and spoke of watering the tree of liberty with the blood of tyrants. John Adams used a similar metaphor, comparing "church-quakes and state-quakes in the moral and political world" with "earth-quakes, storms and tempests in the physical." Some linked American rebelliousness with British freedom. "Our happy constitution," said Josiah Quincy of Massachusetts, gave Americans "impatience of injuries, and a strong resentof of insults." Governor

Thomas Hutchinson of Massachusetts, whose sufferings at the hands of revolutionary crowds were intense, once observed that "mobs, a sort of them at least, are constitutional."

Men like these usually had crowds of a very specific sort in mind. Characteristically, such crowds drew their membership from the whole spectrum of colonial society. They might claim to be "the people," and they might all be wearing the long trousers and the plain hair of working people, rather than the knee breeches and powdered wigs of the gentry. But among the rioters there would be gentlemen as well as artisans, laborers, and apprentices, and everyone knew it. A "legitimate" crowd was usually urban and short-lived. Its members turned out, did what needed doing, and went back to their homes and employments.

Most important, a "legitimate" crowd acted within the "corporatist" political economy discussed earlier. In time of shortage, the rich had an obligation to help the rest; in time of trouble, the powerful had an obligation to help the weak. But if privileged men failed in their duty, lesser people might use violence to protect themselves. Poor people's right to a supply of bread at a fair price was more important than a merchant's right to seek his profit where he might. Usually the town fathers saw to that, by publishing an "assize of bread" that established prices and weights for the brown loaves that ordinary people consumed. But if they failed, the people might act for themselves, demanding what they needed and paying a fair price for it. The same principle held in other dimensions of life. A community's right to keep out smallpox was more important than the right of victims to wander in their misery. Its right to share out work among its members was more important than the right of outsiders to drift in, seeking jobs. Such crowd action was essentially defensive. It was also fairly easily controlled. It placed limits on the power of men who ruled, but it also provided a set of signals from people to their rulers. If the rulers heeded those signals and made just concessions, they could be fairly sure they would retain their power.

We will never know very much about who actually took part in most uprisings. Well-placed observers varied in their descriptions. They often used the phrase "the people"; it was usually a sign of approval. The term "mob" was used as well; it was short for *mobile vulgus* and it actually tells very little. If a crowd drew disapproval, it might be dismissed as a "rabble of Negroes and boys," whatever the color or the age of the people involved. But in broad terms we can distinguish crowds of two sorts. At times, virtually a whole community might rise. Boston's resistance to the Royal Navy's impressment of sailors in 1747 provides one example, whatever reasons different Bostonians had for joining in. At other times, people of a particular kind would act to protect themselves, whatever the rest of the community thought about it. The nighttime destruction of a market house that some Bostonians were building in 1736 was a sign of conflict in the community, not agreement. There were occasions when men with motives of their own manipulated crowds in order to get what they wanted. The violent Philadelphia election of 1742 seems a case in point. There were others when crowds themselves decided what to do. The mood of one crowd might have been fearfully serious; that of another might have been to celebrate with familiar rituals. During the Revolution, there was no "single" form of crowd action. Rather, the uprisings of the era drew on all these traditions.

II

Upheaval in the countryside was another matter. Throughout the eighteenth century, governments and upper classes responded to rural rebellion with hard repression. They called out the militia and regular troops: against the Regulators in both Carolinas, against Hudson Valley tenants in

1766, against Shays' Rebellion in Massachusetts in 1786, and against whiskey rebels in Pennsylvania in 1792. Their legislatures passed laws that condemned rioters to death without trial. One such was the "Bloody Act" that New York adopted against the Green Mountain Boys in 1774. It was modeled directly on Parliament's response to the Jacobite rebellion in Scotland in 1715. Courts likewise imposed gruesome death sentences: on Hudson Valley farmer William Prendergast in 1766; on Shays' Rebellion leaders twenty years later. The elite took up arms; even Quakers did so as the Paxton Boys approached Philadelphia in 1763. From their viewpoint, urban risings were one thing and rural rebellions were another. How can the difference be explained?

One answer lies in how rioters did what they did. Townsmen almost always went unarmed, except for stones and sticks. They acted and then dispersed. They organized quickly and posed no real challenge to institutions of power. Country people, however, were much more likely to be armed, if only because most farmers kept a gun or two for hunting. They were much more likely to attack the symbols of authority. They broke up courts; they kidnapped judges and sheriffs; they opened jails. Crowds acted that way in North Carolina during the Regulation, in New Jersey during the land riots, in the Hudson Valley in 1766, in the Green Mountains through the early 1770s, and in western Massachusetts during the Shays affair. These movements were strong and highly organized. Some of them lasted for years.

Unlike a traditional urban uprising, a rural rebellion offered a challenge to the whole social and political pattern. What that meant varied from place to place. The South Carolina Regulator movement developed as settlers with few or no slaves moved down the interior valleys and began to set up a small-farm society. A frontier can be a lawless, ugly place, and theirs rapidly became one. The settlers sought representation in Charleston and could not get it; they sought courts and sheriffs, and their petitions were denied. They finally realized that they had to look to themselves; hence the name they chose. All they wanted, they proclaimed, was to protect their lives. Yet they challenged the power of the governor, Lord Charles Montagu, who called them lawless. They challenged the planters in the Commons House of Assembly, who were more worried about their slaves and about the Stamp Act than they were about the backcountry. Though Montagu once sent the militia to put it down, the movement did not lead to pitched battle, but it did lay bare the differences between lowland and backland. Those differences would count in 1776.

North Carolina insurgents called themselves Regulators also, but their situation was much more complex. Their movement lasted from 1766 to 1771, when Eastern militia defeated a force of Western farmers at the Battle of the Alamance. At its height, between six thousand and seven thousand of the eight thousand farmers who lived in the piedmont counties of Orange, Rowan, and Anson were involved. As in South Carolina, part of the problem was simply tension between a frontier settled largely by small farmers and a seacoast that was becoming a plantation society. But more than simple regionalism was at stake. The issue was compounded by questions of land title, political power, economic development, and public symbolism.

Land became a problem for two reasons. First, like much of colonial America, North Carolina had boundaries that were ill defined. A farmer who lived near the South Carolina line might find himself confronted by tax demands and militia calls from both provinces. Worse, he might find that someone with a South Carolina title claimed the same land. Second, like much of the colonial frontier, the Carolina interior included enormous holdings that men of power had assembled. The English peer Lord Granville, descendant of one of the original Carolina proprietors, claimed a tract of 26,000 square miles. The immigrant speculator Henry McCulloh headed a combination that received grants in excess of 1,300,000 acres. Neither Granville nor McCulloh intended to run his land as a consolidated estate, but they did plan to make as much money as they possibly could. Whether that money came from quitrents, which were small annual payments due forever to the original owner, or from sales and actual rents was immaterial. These men had a great deal at stake, and they had no hesitation about using force against people who challenged them.

North Carolina frontier people did not suffer from an absence of government but rather from the kind of government they had. There were local courts, and the western counties had their delegates to the provincial assembly. But officials tended to be self-seeking adventurers who looked on public office as just one more way to improve their fortunes. One such was Edmund Fanning, a college-educated Northerner who worked his way into the confidence of two successive royal governors and who began to acquire post after post. Among these men, embezzlement, bribe-taking, and extortion were so rife that Regulators sang ballads making fun of their climb to wealth. Fanning and his sort, for their part, did their best to act like aristocrats. The provincial assembly spoke their minds when, confronted with public criticism, it refused to "be arraigned at the Bar [of lesser people's] Shallow Understanding."

The Regulators' quarrel was with the entire situation of their half-formed society. But the immediate issue that angered them most was the assembly's appropriation of £15,000 to build an elaborate dwelling for Governor William Tryon. Tryon's Palace was the scornful name it rapidly acquired. The issue was economic, since taxes had to be raised to pay for it. But it was also symbolic. North Carolina was not yet a society of rich planters, poor whites, and great slave forces, but men like Tryon and Fanning wanted to make it so. Imposing houses for the planters and a palace for the governor were symbols of increasing wealth, but they were also among the means that the rulers of such a society could use to dominate others. The Regulators developed a broad range of tactics, ranging from simple pressure on officials at one extreme to armed confrontation at the other. The fact that the movement ended with a battle between massed troops suggests that it grew out of the most fundamental issues.

The same is true of backcountry movements farther north. What the Paxton Boys of Pennsylvania did in 1763 to peaceful Indians who lived nearby was gruesome, and it was by no means the only such atrocity in the history of white America's conquest of its continent. But the frontiersmen's uprising and their march on Philadelphia were also signs of how wide the gap was that separated them from their rulers. Elsewhere, in the cases of New Jersey, the Hudson Valley, and the Green Mountains, tensions grew over the questions of who should hold the land and how it should be developed. In all three places, the result was movements that persisted for years.

Part of the problem was jurisdiction. In New Jersey, the area that surrounded Newark and Elizabethtown was claimed under a royal grant by a well-placed group of "proprietors." But it was also claimed under a direct Indian title by the descendants of New England migrants. In the Hudson Valley, the boundary between New York and its neighbors was uncertain. New York claimed to extend as far east as the Connecticut River in places, and Massachusetts claimed jurisdiction almost to the Hudson. New England townsmen pushed their borders west onto New York manors, and New York manor lords pushed theirs east into Connecticut and Massachusetts villages. Farther north, New York, Massachusetts, and New Hampshire all had long-standing claims to the mountainous country that lay between Lake Champlain and the upper Connecticut Valley. The Privy Council resolved the issue in New York's favor in 1764. But by then the New Hampshire government had made many grants to people who wanted to move up from the lower New England provinces.

Jurisdiction was not the only problem involved, however. The presence of New Englanders in all three conflicts is notable, but for reasons more complex than the simple fact that Yankees were one group and Jerseymen or Yorkers another. The real problem was that insurgents and their opponents had different social visions.

The Puritan settlers who came to New England in the seventeenth century were driven by the same powerful forces that tore old England apart in its "Revolution of the Saints." Both Puritans who fled to America and Puritans who stayed behind lived in complex relationship to the commercial society taking shape around them. In the end, their descendants would become that society's masters, on both sides of the Atlantic, but many seventeenth-century Puritans were repelled by their world's crude self-seeking. They were equally repelled by what was left of England's feudal heritage. Cromwell's Parliament abolished the House of Lords, and New Englanders wanted no lords among them. Instead, they founded a society of communal villages where, they hoped, they could live in peace, their lives controlled by a complex relationship of family, church, and town meeting. Some even tried to use the open-field agricultural system of the Middle Ages, with its requirement that a whole community do its work together. These people were not democrats in our sense. They did not believe in human equality. But they were still attempting a utopian experiment on a remarkably large scale. In good measure, their experiment succeeded. New England's greatest achievement was the social peace its settlers by and large enjoyed for almost a century.

But the Puritans paid a high price, part of which was their morbid belief that their jealous, wrathful God watched everything they did, ready to deal out punishment for the least transgression. Another part grew out of their very success. Their population expanded rapidly in the first few generations, thanks to longevity and fertility rates unknown in Europe. By the middle of the eighteenth century, they were running out of space, and that simple fact was forcing their synthesis apart. As land grew short and lost its fertility, the conditions of life changed. The birth rate fell and the death rate climbed. Town meetings turned rancorous. Congregations split. Fathers lost control over their children. As many grew poor, some found in business the chance to become very rich. But the old vision remained, and when new towns were founded to the west and north, they were modeled on the older ones to the south and east. Nucleated town centers, village greens, and town-meeting politics all signified that these people wanted to continue their old ways. Their greatest single fear continued to be that they would lose their farms and descend to the status of tenant under the dominion of a great landlord.

The New Jersey proprietors and the rulers of New York were heirs to a different tradition. There was more than a hint of feudal ways in the founding of much of North America. Proprietorships in the Carolinas, Maryland, Pennsylvania, and New Jersey all reflected the union of economic and political power that lay at the heart of feudalism. The philosopher John Locke even drafted plans for a fully structured colonial nobility at the request of the Carolina proprietors. Many an early New York land grant carried the hereditary status of manor lord. This never added up to a full-blown feudal society. Locke's Carolina constitution was abandoned; only the Penns retained their colonial governorship and passed it down through the family; New York landlords never held court. Yet the enticing vision remained, and it was clear by the mid-eighteenth century that what was left of feudal practice offered a route to enrichment. By then, many a landlord enjoyed a permanent tenant-based society over which he could rule, and others looked forward to establishing one. Some of them were nostalgic for old ways, some paternalistic, and some unashamedly exploitative. Most such men held frontier speculations that they planned eventually to sell off, but they maintained large home estates that they intended to pass on intact to their heirs. They looked on their land as the basis for large-scale gain, gain that someone else's labor would produce. They also enjoyed great political power, as colonels in the militia, council members, and judges. For three New York manors, Rensselaerwyck, Livingston, and Cortlandt, there were even special seats in the provincial assembly, seats that the manor lord or his nominee invariably filled.

The landlord's dream was the New Englander's nightmare. In some, but not all, cases it was also the tenant's distress. By the mid-eighteenth century, there was more and more frequent conflict. Landlords had the power of the New Jersey and New York provincial governments behind them, and they used it. But their opponents knew about fraudulent titles. They loathed the way life was lived on the great estates. They had political resources of their own. Where Massachusetts met New York, border settlers and insurgent tenants enjoyed the active support of the Boston government. In the Green Mountains, people who held New Hampshire titles established towns, courts, and their own militia, despite New York's attempt to impose its form of county government on them. Even in central New Jersey, far from any disputed border, land rioters "built a goal back in the woods," established their own tax system, elected their own militia officers, and "erected Courts of Judicature."

These movements were closer to insurrection than to riot. Like urban rioters, the people who took part in them chose their targets carefully: Abraham Yates during his term as sheriff of Albany County; jails where arrested rioters were held; settlers claiming the land under title granted by landlords; justices of the peace enforcing landlord law; sometimes the landlords themselves. Only the Green Mountain movement was successful. During the decade before independence, it became impossible for New York courts to function there and for would-be landlords to build their estates. After a brief reconciliation with New York revolutionaries in 1775, the movement finally established the state of Vermont. By contrast, the New Jersey movement fizzled out in mid-century and the New York tenant rising was suppressed by military force in 1766.

But, from the banks of the Pee Dee River to the shores of Lake Champlain, these rural risings exposed the lines of stress that ran through late-colonial rural life. Nineteen of every twenty people lived in the countryside in the 1770s. Their problems, like those of townsfolk, gave shape to their era and to the Revolution they helped to make.

III

From 1765 to 1774, however, the main story of the Revolution was acted out in the towns. It was urban interests that were most threatened by the Sugar Act, the Stamp Act, the Townshend taxes, and the Tea Act. Townspeople, not farmers, had to deal with inquisitive customs men and with the constant harassment of redcoats among them. Except for the Virginia planters, it was town writers who worked out the rationale of American resistance. Townspeople turned that rationale into action. What did they do? How and why did they do it?

Without crowd action, there would have been no resistance movement. Crowds made it impossible to enforce the Stamp Act; they gave power to the non-importation agreements that merchants adopted against the Townshend taxes; they dumped East India Company tea into more than one harbor. Crowds confronted customs men and soldiers, sometimes at the risk of their members' lives .They captured and destroyed British customs vessels. They forced officials to resign high positions; they gathered in huge, sometimes illegal meetings; they paraded with effigies; they tore down elegant buildings, disrupted concerts, and erected liberty poles. Individuals opposed these crowds at their peril. Some found their property destroyed or defaced. Others found themselves tarred and feathered or ridden on rails. In the end, some suffered not just broken windows but broken lives.

This enduring militance sprang from people's anger about what the British were doing, but it was more than spontaneous wrath. The energy that drove it had its sources in domestic as well as imperial problems. This militance gained discipline and direction because of a group of men whose commitment and organization made them, in effect, a revolutionary party. These were the Sons of Liberty.

Let us look at some of the major points of action and conflict. The first two events happened in Boston in August 1765. On the fourteenth day of that month, Bostonians awoke to find that some of their number were presenting a vivid dramatization of what the Stamp Act would mean. Effigies of stamp distributor Andrew Oliver and of a huge boot with a "green-vile sole" and a devil peeping out of it were dangling from a tree near Boston Neck. The boot and its sole were a pun on the names of the hated figures of Lord Bute and George Grenville. Men were waiting by the tree to collect a mock stamp duty from every passerby. They continued all day as carts with goods and foodstuffs rumbled back and forth between town and mainland. No one who passed could fail to learn the lesson: the Stamp Act would make a difference in everyone's life. Estimates of how many did pass by and gather to watch vary from 2,500 to 5,000, and toward evening people who had been standing around paraded with the effigies, marching to a small brick building that Oliver had under construction on the waterfront. Believing it to be the stamp office, the crowd demolished it and then proceeded to Oliver's house. They smashed some windows and tore down some fencing and then entered the house, seeking Oliver himself. At that point Lieutenant Governor Thomas Hutchinson, who was the stamp man's brother-in-law, arrived with the sheriff. The rioters met them with a "volley of stones" and then went their ways.

Twelve days later, another crowd gathered, again in the

evening. Marching on the houses of two British officials, it did some minor damage, just as the earlier crowd had done to Oliver's. The goal was the same, to force the officials to resign their offices, as Oliver in fact had done. One of them rapidly did. Then the crowd went to Thomas Hutchinson's elegant mansion, and for him there were no half measures. By the time the night was over, the house was a shell, its cupola torn off, interior partitions pulled down, and Hutchinson's property scattered in the street.

On the evening of November 1, a New York City crowd treated another elegant dwelling in exactly the same way. The Stamp Act was about to take effect, and the crowd had gathered to demand that the city's stamps be locked away and that the stamp distributor resign. It assembled outside Fort George, at the foot of Manhattan Island. The people knew that the fort's guns had been turned to face their town rather than out to sea. Again there were effigies, this time of the devil and Lieutenant Governor Cadwallader Colden. The crowd broke into Colden's carriage house, took out his sleigh and carriages, and burned them and the effigies on a bonfire. Then it marched to a mansion called Vauxhall, occupied by Major Thomas James of the British Army. What happened to Vauxhall was just about the same as what happened to Hutchinson's house, and by the time the night was through, it was nothing more than a wreck. This was the first of many times that winter that New Yorkers took to the streets, and in May 1766 they invaded and destroyed another building, a newly opened theater. After driving out the patrons and actors, the crowd leveled the house and then carried the wreckage to the fields, where an enormous bonfire consumed it.

These uprisings took place at the time of the Stamp Act, but if we look at the same two cities four years later, we find a different pattern. Now British soldiers have become the focus of action.

In January 1770, in New York, a week of street fighting

broke out between redcoats and civilians. It centered on two places. One was a tavern that faced across the fields to the barracks where many of the soldiers were quartered. Until just before the brawls, a stoutly constructed liberty pole, encased in iron, had stood in front of the drinking house. The other place was Golden Hill, where grain sometimes turned the streets yellow as it spilled from the wagons that were bearing it to the mills and granaries there. Not much more than sore heads resulted from the fighting, and New Yorkers did their best to forget this Battle of Golden Hill. But, two months later, similar tensions erupted in Boston, with tragic and lasting results. On March 5, a crowd gathered in King Street to confront troops who were guarding the customs house. Someone began to throw snowballs, and the soldiers panicked. Someone else—his name has never been established—shouted the order to fire, and a minute later five Bostonians lay dying. Many more were wounded. This was the Boston Massacre, and for the next thirteen years Bostonians would gather each March 5 to commemorate it. Only when the Peace of Paris brought the final guarantee of American independence would they begin celebrating July 4 instead.

For our last two instances, let us look again at these same two cities, this time in the winter of 1773–74. Late in November, the ship *Dartmouth*, bearing East India Company tea, entered Boston Harbor. Among the merchants to whom the tea was consigned were two sons of Thomas Hutchinson, who was now governor of the province. Other places had refused company tea, New York's ship turning around at Sandy Hook and Philadelphians sending theirs back down the Delaware. But the *Dartmouth* tied up, with twenty days to make its customs entry, pay the Townshend duty, and unload. Hutchinson and the consignees refused demands that the ship be allowed to sail with its cargo unbroken, and the governor let it be known that cannon on navy ships and at Castle William would open fire if the *Dartmouth* tried to put to sea.

The demands that the ship depart had come from an extraordinary continuous meeting that called itself simply "the Body." Thousands of Bostonians were gathering nearly every day to consider what to do, and after days of fruitless negotiation the body's moderator, Samuel Adams, announced that the meeting could do nothing more "to save the country." This was a signal, and immediately some one hundred Bostonians donned Indian disguise, boarded the ship, hauled out the tea, and dumped it into the harbor. Among these "Mohawks" was the diminutive shoemaker George Robert Twelves Hewes.

Another tea party took place in New York in March 1774. New Yorkers had forced their first tea ship to turn back, but when a vessel called the *Nancy* tied up, they found there was company tea on board. They set out to follow the Bostonians' example, so a mass meeting debated the issue while a party of Mohawks prepared themselves. But while the "Indians" were still donning their warpaint, a crowd from the meeting surged onto the ship, found the tea, and disposed of it. Then the crowd paraded with the empty chests to the fields and burned them. It was very much like the parade that another crowd had conducted with the wreckage of the theater eight years before.

By no means is this all that crowds did during the crisis. By no means were Boston and New York the only places where uprisings broke out. But these are among the most striking events, and they show us the range of what happened. We can begin to understand them by looking at what they had in common. Then we can ask how crowd action developed and changed between the Stamp Act and the several tea parties.

Most obviously, in every one of these instances except the sacking of the theater, the target was tied to British policy. Andrew Oliver and the sons of Thomas Hutchinson were doing the ministry's work. Hutchinson himself opposed the Stamp Act behind the scenes, but in public he supported

British authority and denied that people had any right to question or thwart it. Major James was the officer who had been responsible for turning the guns of Fort George so they faced New York City. Lieutenant Governor Colden, a miserably unpopular man, had the task of enforcing the Stamp Act in New York. The soldiers were stationed in the two cities to see that the will of British officials was done. In ways that were different but that were highly visible, all these people symbolized the change that had come over colonial relations after 1763.

Yet there is another dimension, one to which the attack on the theater points. Eighteenth-century Americans did not look kindly on playhouses. The Continental Congress voted a ban on plays as part of its association in 1774, and this was only one of many in the era. Part of the reason may have been a lingering Protestant mistrust of fiction of any sort, but most people disliked the theater for what it symbolized, not for what went on in it.

To colonials who knew they looked dull and provincial, theaters stood for European culture, sophistication, gaiety, and wit. Even for Americans with great privilege, Europe had qualities that both attracted and repelled. A political operator who was ruthlessly self-seeking by the standards of Philadelphia might come back from a trip to London relieved that he did not have to remain in so corrupt a world. An arrogant Virginia planter might find himself at once thrilled and terrified to hear a young minister who was fresh from Cambridge mouth fashionable unorthodoxies. Many an aspiring writer did his best to keep up with European literary fashion, but he always knew that his work was derivative and that London coffeehouse intellectuals would pay it no heed. So, too, with the theater. Even its patrons had reason to doubt that it was right for them to be where they were, despite the *Song in Praise of Liberty* that was on the playbill that New York opening night.

Something more was at stake, though, than provincial morality. The coming of peace in 1763 had brought an end to the overheated war economy which brought prosperity to many colonials. Imports and exports fell; the poor rolls increased; ships lay idle in the harbors, and tools lay unused in artisans' shops. But in the midst of this depression, some still thrived. The good fortune that Andrew Oliver and Thomas Hutchinson enjoyed was glaringly visible in Boston, where the economy had begun to stagnate as early as 1750. The year 1765 was a bleak one in New York as well, but privileged people still saw fit to grace their summer evenings with outdoor concerts in the Ranelagh Gardens, named after a fashionable London gathering place. Others drove about town in expensive imported carriages, like the ones that the crowd took from Colden's coachhouse. They accepted invitations to dine at houses like Vauxhall. That, too, was the name of a place in London where the lights were bright.

The Chapel Street theater represented, in other words, glittering ostentation and callous unconcern in a time of distress and shortage. The same was true of the Ranelagh Gardens concerts and of the whole way of living signified by large houses, silver plate, fine furniture, and good wine. A New York writer who styled himself "A Tradesman" made the point in unmistakable terms in 1767. Why, he asked readers of the city's most radical newspaper, had its coverage of "our distressed situation" lessened? "Are our Circumstances altered? Is Money grown more Plenty? Have our Tradesmen full Employment? Are we more frugal? Is Grain cheaper? Are our Importations less?—Not to mention the Playhouse and Equipages which it is hoped none but People of Fortune frequent or use." Bostonians had similar things to say about Hutchinson and Oliver. As early as 1749, when Hutchinson was involved in a scheme to end the easy circulation of paper currency, his house caught fire. Instead of rallying to put it out, bystanders shouted, "Let it burn!" We know of that incident from Hutchinson himself, but Oliver was never aware of his worst humiliation. It came with the cheering of people watching the onetime stamp man's body being laid in its grave.

This was class resentment, not class warfare. Despite the fears of some highly placed observers, such as Francis Bernard, governor of Massachusetts in 1765, it did not betoken open struggle between rich and poor. There were rich men, like John Hancock, who either joined crowd action or cheered it on. There were poor and middling people who took no part. But what these crowds did makes little or no sense unless we realize they were acting as crowds had long been expected to act in a corporatist society. The likes of Oliver, Colden, and Hutchinson made themselves enemies of the community because they served as British minions, and they made themselves enemies of ordinary people because they were profiting greatly in a time of severe distress.

Similar tensions lay behind the strife between soldiers and civilians. Colonials had many reasons to resent the presence of redcoats. All political theory told them that a standing army was the greatest danger a people's liberty could face. New York had had a small garrison ever since it was taken from the Dutch, but Boston traditionally had none. When the size of the New York garrison was increased at the war's end, when Parliament insisted that New Yorkers supply it and suspended their assembly for refusing, and when a large force was sent to Boston, it all seemed to point in one direction: tyranny. The military itself did nothing to allay such fears. Officers were gracious enough about asking prominent townspeople to dine; such townsmen were glad enough to accept the invitations and to bid for supply contracts. But in New York and in Boston the day-to-day presence of the troops became an endless aggravation. In Boston, especially, the needs of the soldiers clashed with the ways of the townsfolk. The garrison had to have a place to stay when it arrived, so it pitched its tents on Boston Common and then commandeered one public building after another. It needed to drill, and when better than a Sunday morning, when trumpets, drums, and shouted orders were sure to disturb the Puritans as they prayed. Soldiers deserted and vanished into the interior, so guard posts were established where people would have to answer a challenge from a foreign sentry in their own streets.

Worst of all, in each town the garrison made the depression's effects even worse. By tradition, off-duty soldiers and naval sailors could seek part-time work where they were stationed. Their own pay and conditions were wretched, and such work made all the difference between bare survival and some comfort. The jobs they took were the ones no one else wanted, and the pay they accepted was less than an American needed to live on. In the prosperous war years, it made little difference to colonials. But now depression had made every job valuable, and there were far more military men competing with the townsfolk for what work there was.

All these tensions fed into what happened on Golden Hill and in King Street. In New York, civilians were complaining as early as 1766 about how sailors from ships that were wintering over were taking away work. Local people tried to keep soldiers and sailors out of their taverns and markets. Civilians broke into the ranks as soldiers paraded in the streets. Military men responded in kind. Among themselves, officers dismissed Americans as "boorish peasants," and there were times when local people were beaten up and stabbed with bayonets. Throughout the late 1760s, the soldiers made it a point of honor to cut down a liberty pole each time the locals put one up.

In the immediate background to both outbreaks, ideological, symbolic, and economic issues fused. In New York, two inflammatory broadsides appeared at the end of 1769. One hammered away at the point that the soldiers were the tools of tyranny and accused the province's rulers of betrayal by finally voting supplies. The other addressed daily reality. "Whosoever seriously considers the impovrished state of this city," it said, "must be greatly surprised at the Conduct of such . . . as employ the Soldiers, when there are a number of [city people] that want Employment to support their distressed Families." It called for a meeting at the liberty pole in the fields. Immediately afterward, soldiers destroyed the pole and piled the pieces provocatively in the workingmen's tavern that faced their barracks. This was the incident which brought about the Golden Hill riots.

Precisely the same issue helped bring on the events that led to the Boston Massacre. Boston was already tense at the beginning of March 1770, for the previous month a well-hated customs informer, Ebenezer Richardson, had fired into a crowd demonstrating outside his house. His shot killed a young boy, Christopher Sneider. Thousands attended Sneider's funeral on February 26. Only a few days later, a soldier seeking work went to a south end ropewalk. One of the ropemakers taunted him, offering him a job cleaning his outdoor toilet. The soldier went for his comrades and a brawl rapidly developed. At its height, as many as forty soldiers were trading punches with workers from several ropewalks.

The people who started to throw snowballs at the customs-house sentries a few nights later were men like the ropeworkers, and they were responding to their whole experience with British soldiers since 1768. Challenges by sentries in their streets, bands marching past while they worshipped their God, soldiers at work when Bostonians could not find it, a son of the town shot dead at the age of eleven; these were memories that stung, and snowballs were a mild enough way to express them. But the soldiers themselves were young men, sent far from home to serve in a place where they were despised for what they were. They were the dregs of Britain, serving under aristocrats who paid more for their commissions than a private would ever see in his life. Many things came together in their heads as well, and what the guard detail saw that night was a vicious, irrational mob, not an outraged citizenry. When they heard the order to fire, they did not pause to ask who gave it or why they were there at all. They did what they were told.

IV

Colonials who took part in these events knew that they were confronting Britain and the people who served it. But they were also confronting their own situation. We can see in these uprisings the heritage of protest that people carried in their minds and hearts. Crowd action during the Revolution was often angry, but it was never anarchic. Disguises, liberty poles, the carrying of effigies, tarring and feathering, bonfires, even tearing down houses were all well understood in the eighteenth-century world. Colonials turned to them because they were familiar acts.

Now, however, several things were different. The first was the British issue. The second, reflected in the ostentation of Governor Hutchinson's house and in the violence of what happened to it, was the belief of an increasing proportion of the elite that the old ways were of use no longer, that they had no obligation to sacrifice in a time of distress. A third was the presence, in and with the crowds, of men who called themselves Sons of Liberty. From South Carolina to New Hampshire, the Sons took shape spontaneously in 1765 and 1766. They derived their name from a well-publicized speech that was given in Parliament by Colonel Isaac Barré, who was sympathetic to the American cause, and there were times when the term was used to mean virtually any American who was involved in resistance. But in New York City a core of committed radicals made the name their own, and they called on men of similar spirit to establish like groups elsewhere. Such groups were already taking shape; the one in

Boston called itself the Loyal Nine. Their foremost modern student, Pauline Maier, has found organized Sons of Liberty in at least fifteen places, and there may have been more. Some of the groups, though not all of them, were knit into an intercolonial correspondence union. It centered on the New York Sons and on their secretary, the instrument maker John Lamb.

Three sorts of men were central to the Sons: dissident intellectuals, small intercolonial merchants, and artisans. The intellectuals among them lived by their knowledge, valued ideas, and enjoyed political argument. Perhaps the best-known and most important was Samuel Adams, in Boston. A Harvard graduate and a long-serving petty town official, Adams had drunk deeply both from classical learning and from his Puritan heritage. He dreamed of making Massachusetts a Christian Sparta, a place where hardy, self-denying, God-fearing people would think of the public, not of themselves. There were radicals who shared the Christian element in that vision, such as the Philadelphia physician Benjamin Rush. Other radicals, like Tom Paine and the wandering revolutionary Dr. Thomas Young, emphatically did not. But whether they thought in secular or religious terms, these intellectuals understood that they had to work together, and that whatever divided them was less important than the cause which they shared.

Artisans and intercolonial merchants had a great deal in common as they faced the imperial crisis. Most of all, they shared an interest in making the American economy strong. Intercolonial traders enjoyed the protection of the Royal Navy, but they were less tied than transatlantic merchants to the network of trade, credit, and legality that formed the empire's sinews. They had no friends in Parliament, or correspondents in British ports, or sisters who had married into the British aristocracy. Some artisans, especially in the ship-building trades, were partly dependent on exports to the Old World, but all knew that what they produced had to compete with goods that the great merchants brought in from Britain. Whether they turned out humble necessities, such as the shoes of George Robert Twelves Hewes, or elegant luxuries, like the silverware and engravings of Paul Revere, these men knew that their personal welfare and their community's welfare were bound together. This is one major reason why these people supported the non-importation of British goods in response to the Townshend Acts. For the great merchants who organized it, it was a burden to be borne—and to be shed as quickly as possible. But for artisans and small traders, it was an opportunity to be seized. It offered the hope that colonial producers and the traders who dealt in their goods could produce a new prosperity for themselves.

Isaac Sears and Alexander McDougall of New York City were small-merchant Sons of Liberty. Both were first-generation New Yorkers, and both came from humble backgrounds. Sears was the son of a Cape Cod oystercatcher. He had married the daughter of a tavernkeeper who ran a bar where merchant seamen drank. McDougall's father was a Scottish immigrant who made his living delivering milk. Both men had experience at sea, commanding small vessels with tiny crews and earning not much more than an ordinary sailor would receive. Both had sailed on privateers during the Seven Years' War. Each bore the title "captain," in recollection of those days, rather than the more prestigious "Mr." or "Gent." or "Esq." By the 1760s, these men could approach the places where the elite gathered. McDougall had the spare time and the inclination to sit in the gallery and watch the provincial assembly as it deliberated. But such a man could have no expectation that he would ever cross its bar and become a member himself. That was for the Livingstons and the De Lanceys and others like them, who enjoyed everything that McDougall lacked.

Paul Revere of Boston can stand for the artisans. Like Sears and McDougall, he came from an obscure background. His family were French Protestants; the name had been anglicized from Rivoire. As an aspiring mechanic, Revere had climbed the ladder from apprentice to journeyman to master craftsman. Now, as owner of his own shop, he was a small businessman. But, as a master of his trade, he still worked side by side with his own journeymen and apprentices. A successful artisan could lead a comfortable life. Though no mansion, Revere's house in the north end of Boston was spacious enough. Around 1768, Revere commissioned a portrait of himself by the renowned John Singleton Copley. Despite the depression, the silversmith was doing well, and the portrait celebrated that. But it celebrated his way of life as well as his increasing wealth. He had Copley paint him in his leather work jerkin, with his tools lying in front of him, while he fingered a teapot of his own making. Fame came to Revere long after his death, when the poet Henry Wadsworth Longfellow gave immortality to the ride he made to Concord in 1775 with the warning that the British were on their way. But Revere's real importance does not lie in that one spectacular exploit. Rather, it lies in the increasing pride and self-assertion that he and men of his kind took in their own lives.

Such men could organize a popular resistance movement because they occupied a place between the elite and genuine plebeians. As men of some sophistication and occasional leisure, they could understand the abstruse political arguments that elite pamphleteers put forward. Samuel Adams, in fact, always dressed in gentlemanly style, a practice shared by Maximilien Robespierre, leader of the radical Jacobins during the French Revolution. When *he* posed for Copley it was in a frock coat with his hair powdered and a scroll representing the provincial charter in front of him. But whatever they wore, the Sons knew the ways of ordinary people and the pressures those people lived under. Their great task was to turn traditional crowd action toward the British question and to generate new political consciousness among ordinary

Americans. They were not master manipulators, bent on forcing an issue about which most people did not care. Nor were they tribunes of the oppressed, using the problem of relations with Britain as a way to bring internal change. Rather, they began the job of fusing the imperial issue and domestic problems into the one grand question of what kind of place America would be.

How they did so varied, for the situation in Boston was not the situation in New York, and neither was it the same as the situation in Charleston or Philadelphia or Albany. In Boston, the Loyal Nine used several means to generate Stamp Act resistance in 1765. One was to contact a cobbler named Ebenezer MacIntosh, who was the acknowledged leader of one of the crowds that traditionally gathered on November 5, "Pope's Day." This was the day when English Protestants celebrated the discovery of the "Gunpowder Plot," in which seventeenth-century Catholics had schemed to blow up the Houses of Parliament. Even now, people all over England call it Guy Fawkes Day, after the plot's leader, and celebrate with fireworks and bonfires. At the center of each fire, there is an effigy of Fawkes. Colonial Boston celebrated with parades by people from the north and south ends, carrying rival effigies of the Pope and the devil. Those effigies would likewise be burned, but often it was not before there had been a brawl about which side's was the best. Partly it was just an excuse for a fight; partly it was a way of saying that Bostonians, too, were British. But the tradition also preserved folk memories of the town's revolutionary Protestant heritage, and these acquired new life in 1765. With the encouragement of the Loyal Nine, MacIntosh rallied his followers to support the open-air political theater of August 14. The devil's effigy that hung in the Liberty Tree was familiar from many a Pope's Day celebration, but now Satan had Andrew Oliver and George Grenville for company. When the crowd took to the streets that evening, MacIntosh was in front, wearing a gaudy uniform, general for a day. Questions of ritual and memory, class and culture, and imperial politics had come together to start Boston on the road to revolution.

New Englanders invoked many other such memories between 1765 and 1776. Calls for action by the "Committee for Tarring and Feathering" were signed by "Joyce, Jr." The name referred to Cornet George Joyce, the low-ranking Roundhead officer who captured King Charles I during the English Civil War and who supposedly stood on the royal scaffold. People called up the ghost of Oliver Cromwell; the Loyal Nine themselves were among the first to do so. Cromwell's memory was a horror to orthodox Whigs, who were committed to the political solution established by the Glorious Revolution of 1688. But New England's founders had known and supported Cromwell, and they had given shelter to regicides fleeing England after the Stuart monarchy returned. Their descendants kept those memories alive; even George Washington once found himself being addressed by a Massachusetts farmer as "Great Cromwell." As Alfred Young has pointed out, a Yankee then might have spoken of "Oliver" in the same respectful tone that a black American would now use to speak of "Martin" or "Malcolm." Both the name and the tone in which people invoked it carried the same heavy symbolic burden.

Boston's radicals made the most of this consciousness and these issues. They knew perfectly well what stagnation and poverty meant in their town. But they insisted, in public at least, that local issues should not come to the fore. Their newspaper, *The Boston Gazette*, carried on an endless campaign against the British administration, its policies, and its servants in Massachusetts. Their campaign led to a state of permanent hostility between two successive governors, Francis Bernard and Thomas Hutchinson, and the Boston Town Meeting. When Bernard was recalled in 1769, he sailed away from the humiliating sight of a town that had illuminated its buildings and that was ringing its church bells to celebrate his departure. But by then Ebenezer MacIntosh, who perhaps had presented the possibility of genuinely lower-class leadership, had lost his prominence. By 1770, MacIntosh was in debtor's prison, and no Son of Liberty would go to his aid.

In New York, the Sons operated differently. The Boston Sons made plain their disapproval of the sacking of the Hutchinson house, and they took careful steps to prevent anything like it from happening again. But the New York Sons showed no shock at all when crowds destroyed Colden's carriages and Major James's mansion. Admittedly, Colden and James were associated much more visibly with the Stamp Act than Hutchinson was. But neither did the Sons show any opposition to the disruption and leveling of the Chapel Street theater. In fact, Sons of Liberty led it, and members of the crowd cried "Liberty! Liberty!" as they carried the wreckage to the fields. New York's most radical newspaper, the *New York Journal*, dramatized the British issue, but it also carried essay after essay attacking the evils of high rents, rising prices, and short employment. It told of popular risings in London to resist the engrossment of grain. It castigated fashionable youth who would not give up their finery. It opposed the imprisonment of debtors. For both the leadership and the people of New York, domestic issues were part of the crisis.

Other groups operated in other ways. In Charleston, the Sons of Liberty developed out of a volunteer fire company. In Connecticut, their roots lay partly in sectarian bitterness left over from the Great Awakening, partly in disputes about paper money, and partly in conflicts among speculators. In some places, the "wealthiest gentlemen and freeholders" provided leadership; in others, such as Annapolis, Maryland, and the whole province of New Jersey, it came from men now lost in obscurity. In Philadelphia, no group emerged at all at the time of the Stamp Act, largely because the artisans themselves were divided. Never, in other words, was there a single pattern. Each group of Sons operated in its own way within its own community. But the Sons of Liberty maintained contact with one another and pledged mutual cooperation. They disbanded their formal organization at the end of the Stamp Act crisis, thinking their task was over. But the radical leadership that had sprung up among them remained important throughout the era.

Leaders are nothing, however, without followers. Neither the colonial elite nor the Sons of Liberty could have done anything serious against British policy without enormous popular support. It was people in crowds who turned what was happening from a debate to a movement. Crowd action was a fact of life in the whole eighteenth-century world, and the American movement built on all the traditions and customs that made it up. But the sustained popular political militance on a great political issue that developed in America's towns was something very new.

· 4 ·

Independence and Revolution

During the eight years that followed the Stamp Act, Britain tried again and again to make the colonies serve its interests. The result, however, was the opposite. Laws and policies proved unworkable. Colonial writers demolished the rationalizations that British spokesmen put forward. Colonial people made it impossible for British officials to do their jobs. Twice the British sought a way around colonial objections. The Townshend program distinguished external taxes from internal ones in the hope that Americans would pay one even if they would not pay the other. The Tea Act used the lure of lower prices in an outright appeal to consumer self-interest. But each time the result was new forms of resistance.

In the two years that followed the Boston Tea Party, Parliament turned to stronger measures. The colonists had to be taught that they were truly subordinate, that Britain could alter their charters, close their ports, change their rules of law, and billet troops on them as it chose. If need be, it could and would use its immense military strength to make them submit. The Intolerable Acts that were passed to punish Boston for the Tea Party and the appointment of General Thomas Gage as governor of Massachusetts established these points. These acts needed and received no elaborate rationale; they were a resort to naked force. But the result was not to end contention—it was to rip apart the empire. As the empire was sundered, colonials found reason and opportunity for thoroughgoing political revolution.

I

The internal revolution and the destruction of the empire began when the people of Massachusetts decided to resist rather than pay for the tea. People in other provinces rallied to them. From New York to the Carolinas, local communities established committees of correspondence to keep abreast of events. Up and down the coast, people loaded vessels with supplies for the relief of the "poor of Boston." By the summer of 1774, colonials had decided that they needed a Continental Congress to give direction to their movement. It met in Philadelphia in September, the first "official" gathering of delegates from the different provinces since the Stamp Act Congress nine years before. Some of its delegates were chosen by provincial assemblies, some by local meetings and committees, some by illegal conventions. The members from New York and Pennsylvania quickly established reputations for moderation. As events were to show, this was a reflection of their own fear of upheaval, not opinion in the provinces. Virginians and Massachusetts men formed a coalition that pressed for strong measures. The Southerners could afford upheaval; they were confident that they could control their own province. The New Englanders needed it; they were in the greatest immediate trouble. Following their leadership, the Congress defeated Joseph Galloway's attempt to offer an "Olive Branch" petition to the crown. Instead, it adopted the Continental Association, with its call for a boycott of British trade, for internal discipline and sacrifice, and for committees everywhere to oversee both. The first steps toward destroying British power and toward creating a revolutionary government had been taken.

In their earlier struggles, the Americans had been aided

by support in Britain and by turbulence in Parliament. Crowds had rioted in London as well as in New York and Boston, and both Americans and Britons had recognized the connection between the uprisings. John Wilkes, the radical parliamentarian in whose support London crowds had turned out in the mid-1760s, became an American hero. In turn, he encouraged the American cause. The colonials enjoyed support from moneyed men in the City of London as well, and that also helped convince Parliament to retreat. Political instability was an additional factor. Through the 1760s, ministries rose and fell as George III searched fruitlessly for leaders able to control the House of Lords and the Commons. At least part of the reason for the repeal of the Stamp Act was that George Grenville, the act's father, was out of office.

But now, in 1774, matters were different. Though Wilkes had become Lord Mayor of London, the crowds were quiet. In Frederick, Lord North, the king finally found the prime minister he needed. Plodding and reliable, North would serve faithfully until 1782. He held a "courtesy" title, not a real one, which meant that he sat in the House of Commons rather than in the House of Lords. When Britain's tiny electorate went to the polls in 1774, North won an unquestionable majority. There were angry speeches attacking his policies, but he won every vote. The Americans had to stand alone.

When the First Continental Congress adjourned in October 1774, it called for a successor, to meet the following spring. All it expected the new Congress to do was consider how well the association had worked, but by the time it gathered, General Gage had redefined the issue. Aware that arms had been secreted at Concord, not far from Boston, he dispatched a column of infantry to seize them on April 18, 1775. Even had Paul Revere not made his ride, the Concord farmers would have been ready, for the coming of the troops could not have been kept secret. It may be that all the farmers intended was a symbolic confrontation, before allowing the British to take the few supplies that had not been hidden. But, like the troops, these Minutemen were armed. Whoever fired the first shot, the skirmishing there and at Lexington and the sniper fire that the redcoats endured as they marched back to Boston marked the end of words and the beginning of war.

What happened in Massachusetts transformed the task of the new Congress that had just convened in Philadelphia. A pickup army of New Englanders quickly surrounded occupied Boston. The high price they made the British pay before they were dislodged from Breed's (Bunker) Hill, overlooking Charlestown, demonstrated their ability to fight. Cannon that were brought from Fort Ticonderoga, on Lake Champlain, and placed on Dorchester Heights gave them considerable strategic advantage. The capture of the fort itself by a backwoods force under Ethan Allen and Benedict Arnold gave them momentum and encouragement. The new Congress understood that its first task was to broaden the army's base. Supplies had to be organized and men and officers found outside New England. The appointment of George Washington to the supreme command was a recognition as much of Virginia's political importance as of Washington's talents. Similar considerations lay behind the way that Congress distributed the lesser generalships that it created at the same time.

From our point of view, the rest of the story seems almost preordained, and we can only ask why Congress took so long. More than a year passed with the colonies and the metropolis in open warfare before Congress finally declared independence. Britain, meanwhile, announced that the colonies were in a state of rebellion, sent thousands of troops including German mercenaries to put it down, ordered the closing of all the colonial ports, and dispatched a mighty navy to blockade them. When the redcoats withdrew from Boston in March 1776, it was only for tactical reasons; everyone knew that a massive new blow would fall soon, most likely at New York. Congress, for its part, declared to the world its reasons for taking up arms, opened American ports to the commerce of all the world save Britain, and began secret negotiations with France for arms and credit. Yet, until the end of 1775, the word "independence" remained almost unspoken. Even when cutting the tie became a real possibility, it took the whole first half of 1776 for Congress to make up its mind. The situation was almost like the one that many a divorcing couple must face: bitterly antagonistic, facing different directions, the two partners still seek to hold on.

British interest lay in maintaining the mastery of the Western world, including the colonies, that they had won over half a century of conflict. But why did it take the colonies so long to make the break? Part of it was that Americans did not believe what was happening. They had long thought of themselves as Britons overseas, as heirs to the full, proud tradition of British freedom. Their heritage, their history, their identity were important to them. That was so even for colonists whose actual ancestry ran back to the original Dutch settlers of Nieuw Amsterdam, or to French Protestants who had fled Louis XIV, or to Germans, or to Sephardic Jews. Many colonials, especially those who picked up their pens and tried to work out what was going on, still believed that the only problem was an aberration in an otherwise commendable state of affairs. They turned readily to the idea that the source of their troubles lay in a conspiracy of evil men, not in the existence of the British Empire itself.

They were not paranoid. Rather, as the historian Gordon Wood has argued, they were trying to work out an explanation in human terms for the course of the human events that were swirling around them. An earlier generation might have tried to understand its tribulations in terms of witchcraft, or God's punishment for sin, or Satan's malevolence. Many Americans did think exactly that way, but by 1776 an increasing number of people did not. To them, the notion of conspiracy offered a way to make sense of their troubles. Who the conspirators were remained something of an open question. Some blamed evil ministers surrounding and duping their "best of kings." Among such, they thought, were Lord Bute, the Scot who was George III's earliest adviser; George Grenville; Lord Hillsborough, who oversaw colonial affairs after 1768; and Lord North.

Others looked closer to home. New York's lieutenant governor Cadwallader Colden, who supposedly had supported the Jacobite rising in Scotland in 1715, was one favorite target for suspicion. Thomas Hutchinson of Massachusetts was another, especially after his call to London for a curb in the colonies on "what are called British liberties" was discovered and published. Even the Declaration of Independence carries overtones of this fear of conspiracy in its recital of how "a long Train of Abuses and Usurpations, pursuing invariably the same Object" had shown "a Design to reduce [the colonies] under absolute Despotism." But conspiracy can usually be rectified: find the evil men, throw them out of office, undo their work, and all will be well again. By itself, the suspicion of conspiracy could have produced neither independence nor revolution.

What was needed was a radical breakthrough in Americans' understanding of what the British Empire was and meant. By 1775, people had been moving toward that breakthrough for ten years. The distance between the hesitant half-acceptance of subordination that marked Daniel Dulany's writing in 1765 and the sharp self-assertion that runs through Thomas Jefferson's in 1774 is one measure of how far they had traveled. Another, as Pauline Maier has argued, lies in people's understanding of where the much-feared conspiracy lay. Initially, suspicious minds located it among ministers and placemen. But gradually its compass spread until it included most of Parliament and finally the king. That is why it is the monarch who receives the blame in the Declaration for "a History of repeated Injuries and Usurpations, all having in direct Object the Establishment of an absolute Tyranny over these States." Even the British people did not escape, for the conviction grew that they were so corrupt that they could not save themselves from their rulers.

Yet it was not in Jefferson's eloquent prose that the most radical American insights found their voice. Rather, it was in Tom Paine. Paine published his great pamphlet *Common Sense* in January 1776, nine months after war first broke out. The reception that Americans gave it is the fullest proof that it said what needed saying. Paine's predecessors among American pamphleteers might have been lucky to sell a few thousand copies of their work. But *Common Sense* was reprinted and reprinted, in place after place. Perhaps as many as 150,000 copies came off the presses, and Paine himself exulted in this "greatest sale that any performance ever had since the use of letters."

Part of the reason for Paine's success was the way he wrote. Even the crystalline purity of Jefferson at his best could not match Paine's combination of passion, insight, and vivid yet straightforward prose. Paine's medium was part of his message. He deliberately wrote for people who would tolerate no condescension but who made no pretense to high learning. What he said, however, was as important as how he said it.

Paine attacked not one policy or another but the whole structure of Britishness, subordination, and monarchy within which colonial Americans had lived. The problem was not to explain what had gone wrong in a good system; it was to explain why the system itself was the problem. Addressing a people taught to revere the British Constitution, with its age-old balance of king and Parliament, Paine attacked the monarchy: "A French Bastard landing with an armed Banditti and establishing himself king of England against the consent of the nation, is in plain terms a very paltry rascally original." To a world that revered antiquity, he wrote of the absurdity of the past: "Monarchy and succession have laid (not this or that Kingdom only) but the World in blood and ashes." In a world built on subordination, he showed where inequality led: "America is only a secondary object in the system of British politics. England consults the good of this country, no farther than it answers for her own purpose." To people troubled as they had never been troubled before, he offered a task of worldwide significance: "Freedom hath been hunted round the Globe. Asia and Africa have long expelled her. Europe regards her like a stranger, and England hath given her warning to depart. O! receive the fugitive, and prepare in time an asylum for mankind."

Perhaps most important, Tom Paine offered more than just a vivid summary of what Americans were against. He gave them something to be for: a republic. " 'Tis the Republican and not the Monarchical part of the constitution of England which Englishmen glory in," he wrote. "It is easy to see that when Republican virtue fails, slavery ensues. Why is the constitution of England sickly? but because monarchy hath poisoned the Republic." The task before the Americans was not to restore a good state of affairs they once had enjoyed—it was to abandon their old ways so they could build a republic of their own.

Paine's call was exhilarating. *Common Sense* crystallized what events had been teaching Americans about themselves and their world since 1765. It changed the terms of American debate. No longer would the questions be how reconciliation might be won and how the British Constitution might be applied to American reality. Henceforth the issues were the coming of independence and the kind of republic it would bring. Those questions presented a frightening prospect for some. Paine's real power lay less in what he said than in the people for whom he spoke. He wrote *Common Sense* after two years of immersion in turbulent revolutionary politics in Philadelphia and after a lifetime of dissent in his native England. Paine's immediate audience was Philadelphia's

artisan class; by extension, it existed among the whole population of farmers and mechanics who were finding their
political voice in the Revolution. Many an American "leader"
shuddered at the points Paine was making and at the way he
was making them. They shuddered most of all at the thought
of power falling into the hands of the people whose voice
Paine had become. To understand both these men's fears and
other men's hopes, we must look at what the independence
crisis meant for the ordinary people who lived through it.

II

For eighteenth-century Massachusetts farmers, late August
and early September were a time to slow down. The hay and
the winter wheat were safely harvested; the spring wheat,
barley, oats, and peas were not yet ripe. It was a brief moment
of leisure in their endless cycle of work, but in August 1774
farmers in Worcester County made it a moment of intense
politics instead. They knew that soon the county court would
open for its new term, the first since the Massachusetts
Government Act had abolished the old provincial charter.
As if to provoke the people, the judges of the court had sent
a message supporting the act to Governor Gage, and in town
after town people gathered to decide what to do about it.
Fine resolutions would not be enough, for no one thought
that Parliament would pay any attention to them. Nor would
the old weapon of cutting off trade; Parliament itself had
already done that when it closed Boston's port. The only
choice was between defiance and submission.

The farmers chose defiance. Early in the month, a gathering of their committees of correspondence resolved in favor
of "wise, prudent and spirited measures" to keep the Intolerable Acts from going into effect. By the end of August, they
had decided what those measures would be. The "ordinary
course of justice" would be stayed. There would be a "convention of the people" to "devise proper ways and means"

of conducting public business. In the days before the court was to open in Worcester, towns voted to go there in whole bodies. Records of the town meeting in the village of Westminster tell us that command of the town's two militia companies passed to officers who would not acknowledge Governor Gage's authority; the same was happening elsewhere. When the judges arrived in their wigs and robes to open the court, Westminster farmers were there, together with people from every other town in the county. They were orderly, drawn into ranks on the Worcester town green. But they were also angry and armed, and the court did not open. Instead, by the end of the day the judges had resigned their posts, reading their statements aloud as they walked bareheaded through the townsmen's ranks. It was a humiliating ritual of submission.

This was Worcester County's moment of revolution, different from any experience American people had known before. Part of the difference was the massive presence of farmers. At last, after nine years, the American movement was no longer an affair of the seaport towns. A second part was the direct defiance of both British and colonial authority. Worcester's people were challenging not the rightfulness of any particular law but rather Parliament's legislating for them at all. The judges, the provincial councillors, and the militia colonels whom they were displacing were not Englishmen sent from outside to lord it over the colonials. They were successful sons of Massachusetts itself, basking in the rewards that a lifetime of achievement had brought. Not many New Englanders ended by choosing the king's side, but a disproportionate number of the ones who had enjoyed high favor did.

Perhaps the most important difference lay in the popular committees that organized this defiance. Since as early as 1772, towns throughout the Massachusetts interior had been picking small groups of men to correspond with the world outside and to keep track of political events. These committees of correspondence had no legal standing. They enjoyed no more mandate than the vote of a town meeting. But now they were taking power, acting as if they, not the courts, were where authority lay. As judges faced down committeemen, as militia officers who acknowledged Governor Gage confronted militia officers who did not, as the General Court itself barred its doors to the governor's secretary with a proclamation dissolving it, Massachusetts found that two sets of institutions and rulers were competing for the people's loyalty. One set rested on old teachings, long-standing customs, well-established habits, and the belief that some people deserved to rule others. The other set was still forming, as people cast off what they had "always" believed, called up seventeenth-century radical memories, and began to act as if all men were created equal.

Political scientists call such a situation one of "dual power" or "dyarchy." It is intolerable to any working government, but it is at the heart of the process of political revolution. By the end of that summer, Gage's writ ran no further than his troops dared to march. In name, the whole upheaval was for the sake of keeping the Massachusetts Government Act from going into effect. In name, the committees, the new militia officers, and the defiant General Court did all that they did for the sake of preserving their old provincial charter. But, in reality, the old order was collapsing and something very different was taking its place.

Country people joining in, popular committees taking power, old rulers being displaced, and confrontation politics: these were the elements that changed a limited movement of resistance into a popular movement of revolution. They came together all over America between 1774 and 1776, but how and when this process happened varied from place to place. Though knowing the course of events in Massachusetts may provide us with questions to ask about what happened in Virginia, we will have to turn to Virginia for its particular answers. Everywhere, however, people found they had to face the same problems that the farmers of Worcester County faced that August and September.

Let us look at three instances. The first is a frontier county in New York. The second is Philadelphia, which was the greatest city in British America. The third is the province of Virginia. Tryon County, New York, had been created only in 1771. It was named after William Tryon, who had been transferred that year from governor of North Carolina to governor of New York. The county sprawled west of Albany, along the Mohawk Valley, and the people who lived in it were farmers, fur traders, and Iroquois Indians. For decades the Mohawk Valley had been the unquestioned domain of Sir William Johnson, but late in 1774 a small group of men began meeting secretly to challenge his family's rule. Among them were small freehold farmers, perhaps resentful of the manorial way of life he had built on his estate of Kingsborough. There were also petty traders, unhappy at the strict control Johnson exercised over commerce with the Iroquois. Farmers and traders alike probably would have been glad to get rid of the Johnsons, their Catholic Scottish tenants, and the Iroquois, and to appropriate the rich lands on which they lived, but the immediate idea was to organize help for Boston.

The Mohawk Valley revolutionaries emerged into the open in May 1775, in response to the news of fighting in Massachusetts. A county committee of thirty-two men was elected, but it and what it stood for met the determined opposition of Sir William's heirs. These were Sir John Johnson, who had just succeeded his father as baronet, and Colonel Guy Johnson, who had inherited Sir William's post of Indian Superintendent. Like the confrontation on Worcester Green, the face-down in the Mohawk Valley was public and dramatic. However, unlike what happened in Massachusetts, it pitted evenly matched forces against each other and brought tragic results. The Mohawk baronet had been good to his tenants and to the Iroquois, and his heirs could count on support from both. In June 1775, Sir John chanced upon a popular meeting "to choose a Captain agreeable to the resolution of their committee." In the words of one of Johnson's friends, "One Mr. Visher who was a candidate" for the captaincy "became so very impertinent that Sir John could not bear it—but gave him a hearty Horse-whipping . . . and then very cooly got into his carriage and drove [off]." The next month, news began to spread that Sir John's county sheriff had arrested a prominent rebel. A crowd of about one hundred men gathered at Johnson Hall, which had been fortified with light artillery. After some shots were exchanged, the ranks of both defenders and besiegers swelled to about five hundred. The rebels sent to Albany for cannon of their own, but the committee there sent negotiators, who arranged a truce. It lasted only until the autumn, when the Johnsons and their allies fled to the Niagara frontier. Their flight marked the beginning of seven years of civil war.

In Philadelphia, events took a different course. The Quaker City had been noticeably quieter than other port towns through the 1760s, but in 1774 "radical resistance leaders" won "their hesitant, divided community . . . to a determined opposition to London's new imperial policies." The city never had a Sons of Liberty organization, but now a committee movement took shape. As Richard Alan Ryerson's detailed study has shown, the radicals who founded and developed the committee system had to overcome the determined hostility of Philadelphia's traditional leaders, especially its Quaker mercantile elite. Pennsylvania's old rulers had two bastions. One was the Corporation of the City of Philadelphia. The city was ruled by a small group of men accountable only to themselves. They did not have to face either town meetings, as leaders did in Boston, or open elections, as in New York. Instead, Philadelphia's city fathers decided among themselves whom to invite to join them. The provincial assembly of Pennsylvania was the old rulers' other bastion. Unlike Virginia's Burgesses and the Massachusetts

General Court, Pennsylvania's assemblymen had steered a course that kept them well apart from the resistance movement. In 1765 they passed some resolutions against the Stamp Act, but they never courted dissolution by defying royal orders and they never transformed themselves into an illegal revolutionary gathering. Instead, the assemblymen simply tried to keep business going as usual. Governor John Penn followed much the same policy.

But, after the Intolerable Acts, most Philadelphians accepted that they had some sort of duty to support Boston. After all, they had refused company tea themselves. On May 20, 1774, a meeting of the city's leaders voted a boycott of British commerce and named a committee of nineteen to enforce it. Among the nineteen were a number of men who wanted to go slowly, but there were only two who became outright loyalists. Already the hold of the city's genuine conservatives was slipping. As they became less influential, "official" institutions like the assembly came under the control of men like John Dickinson, who believed in resistance but shuddered at the idea of revolution. Dickinson and other "moderates" did well in several assembly elections between 1774 and 1776. But they rapidly lost influence in the city's growing committee movement. There, men of different social background and of a different cast of mind were coming to power.

As Ryerson notes, Philadelphia's committee system went through two phases. First came a "revolution of the elite," and then a "revolution of the middle classes." The first brought to the fore several dozen men who had stood outside the charmed circle of the old order. In general, they were prosperous enough, but they did amount to "a new elite for a new society, chosen (and self-chosen) to perform unprecedented public services." The second phase mobilized several hundred lesser people: German immigrants, Scotch-Irish Presbyterians, and "obscure mechanics in shirtsleeves and leather aprons." Here, says Ryerson, was "a birth of modern American politics."

The confrontation in Pennsylvania was not just between the colony and the mother country; it was also between committee and assembly and between people who stood for one order and people who were coming to stand for another. It finally came to a head in June 1776, when the Philadelphia committee organized the overthrow of the old assembly. Within little more than two years, Philadelphia and the whole of Pennsylvania with it had been transformed. From a city of hesitation, led by men determined not to lose their comfortable control, it had become the most thoroughly radicalized place in all America. We will look later at the consequences to which that led.

Virginians entered their Revolution in yet another way. The Old Dominion had not known serious internal strife since Bacon's Rebellion, a full century earlier. But its leaders were aware both of the decay of their own civic virtue and of the challenge posed by militant evangelical Protestants. So serious was it that at times planters dealt with Baptists and Methodists in the same way that Sir John Johnson tried to deal with Mohawk Valley revolutionaries. In Virginia, even more than in Massachusetts, the top echelon of leaders chose loyalism; 57 percent of the councillors and high administrative officials ended up on the king's side. But save for men who stood at the very pinnacle, most of Virginia's elite chose the Revolution. As a result, similar to the one in Massachusetts, the provincial assembly became a core of resistance, confronting the governor above it, not the committees below. Lord Dunmore dissolved the House of Burgesses at the end of May 1774, for voting a day of "Fasting, Humiliation and Prayer" against the Intolerable Acts. But its members simply reconvened as a provincial congress. Then they set in motion a campaign to win the backing of lesser Virginians, inviting them to join in rituals of virtue and commitment. Virginians of the "middling and lower classes" stood patiently at county court houses while condescending orators explained how "on the virtue . . . of the people . . . does it depend whether we shall be happy or miserable." Others turned out in good order for ceremonies like the return from the Continental Congress in 1775 of Peyton Randolph, its president. As one account, noted by Rhys Isaac, put it, they surrounded "the FATHER of his COUNTRY, whom they attended to his house, amidst repeated acclamations, and then respectfully retired." Virginia's whites entered their Revolution as something close to a united people. The committee movement that grew there reflected the existing order, rather than either a desire or a need to subject that order to change.

That does not mean that no change came. The crisis demanded sacrifice: of food, so Boston's poor would not starve; of private pleasures like horse racing, dancing, and gambling, so austere virtue could be demonstrated; of private dissenting opinions, so the world would see a united Virginia front. As Virginians armed to resist Britain, they changed the terms on which they dealt with one another. The change from ceremonies of hierarchy to ceremonies of commitment gave lesser men the chance to narrow the distance between themselves and greater ones. Politics became more contentious, though hardly as much as they were in Philadelphia. But much of the narrowing took place at the symbolic level. The best example was when great men bowed to public pressure, doffed their habitual elegant costumes, and agreed that a plain hunting shirt and a tomahawk would be the emblems of commitment to the cause. The reality of power in Virginia did not alter; it remained a society organized around the needs and interests of its planter class. But the planters did not retain their power simply because there was no pressure from below. They held on to it by symbolic accommodation to pressure which, if not explicitly political, was still very real.

These examples show us the immense variety in what happened; they do not show us everything. Worcester County's response was like that of most of the rest of Massachusetts, but the Mohawk Valley's was not like that of the rest of New York. Elsewhere in that province, the people of some counties plunged wholeheartedly into involvement, the people of some were divided, and the people of others remained overwhelmingly loyal. New York City's Revolution was very much like Philadelphia's. That is not surprising: the two cities were similar in many ways. But Maryland's Revolution was unlike that of either Pennsylvania, to its north, or Virginia, to its south, despite the fact that the province had elements in common with each. Though Virginia planters kept control of lesser whites, Carolina planters did not. Backcountry people there were still bitter in the aftermath of the Regulator movements, and when the British invaded the lower South in 1779, the whole Carolina interior broke into vicious civil war.

It would be wrong to be deterministic, to say that this factor or that decided what people would do. Once raised, fundamental questions are not easy to answer, and from 1774 to 1776 prominent and obscure people agonized about what they should do. People of very similar background decided with great pain that they had to go in different directions, and not all were John Dickinsons or Joseph Galloways. One of the most poignant examples comes from a band of frightened farmers who gathered in 1776 in the forbidding Helderberg escarpment, west of Albany, New York. Most of them were tenants, already alienated from their landlords, and they had retreated to the hills so they could decide in privacy what to do. Nonetheless, a spy was among them. It is thanks to his testimony that we know how one of them, John Commons, finally put the question. "Those who thought Congress was in the right," Commons said, "should go and those who thought the king was right should stay." But to put the question was one thing, to answer it was another, and Commons himself "did not know who was right." Independence may have been both necessary and justified, but it was also frightening. Despite Paine, Jefferson, and a decade of crisis, the step into it was not an easy one to take.

In these stories of challenge and struggle and upheaval, we can see why Congress took so long to declare American independence. The alliance of Massachusetts Puritans and Virginia grandees, so strange on the surface, begins to make sense when we realize that Massachusetts was in serious trouble and that white Virginia, with very little in its way of life to hold it to Britain, was close to being a united society. The foot dragging by the rulers of the middle colonies likewise becomes understandable. Why should a Hudson Valley landlord like Robert Livingston, Jr., have been quick to risk new upheaval among his tenants? Why should a Philadelphia lawyer like John Dickinson have been any quicker to throw down the last barriers that kept artisans, or men who were even more humble, from taking control of public life? Neither Dickinson nor Livingston was enamored of Britain. Both chose independence, but not until they had to. They did not actively seek it.

Congress finally accepted the need for independence in the summer of 1776. On July 2, it voted in favor of a "resolution of independence" that Richard Henry Lee had offered almost a month before. The resolution proclaimed "that these United Colonies are, and of right ought to be, free and independent states, that they are absolved from all allegiance to the British Crown, and that all political connection between them and the State of Great Britain is, and ought to be, totally dissolved." Two days later, Congress approved the Declaration, which a five-man committee led by Thomas Jefferson had been drafting since early June.

Independence could not have come earlier. Breaking the emotional, political, economic, and intellectual ties that held colonials to Britain took time. For many, the ties were never broken. Loyalists never formed a large percentage of the American population, all in all, but in a few places, such as the area surrounding New York City, they were an overwhelming majority. In others, including the Hudson Valley and Maryland's Eastern Shore, they were strong enough to wage extended guerrilla resistance. In the Carolina and Georgia backcountry and on New York's western frontier, they were so numerous that the Revolution became a war of American against American. When "one people" broke the "political bands" that had "connected them with another," a fair-sized minority of that people dissented.

What, however, did Congress declare? Two major historical studies have considered the problem. One, written long ago by Carl Becker, was based on the assumption that when Jefferson wrote the Declaration he translated the ideas of the English philosopher John Locke into political reality. In Becker's view, both Locke and Jefferson rested their whole argument on individualism. Some men would always try to take or destroy the life, health, liberty, and possessions that other men enjoyed. Threatened with the loss of what was rightfully theirs, individuals joined together to protect their separate interests. The "pursuit of happiness" of which the Declaration speaks came close to being the pursuit and preservation of property. The other book, written much more recently by Garry Wills, points out the contrasts between what Jefferson wrote and what Congress finally adopted. Wills makes a powerful case that Jefferson owed most of his ideas not to Locke but rather to a group of eighteenth-century Scottish thinkers. All of them stressed the importance of sociability over self-seeking. If Wills is correct, what Jefferson wrote declared the right of a people to find a way to live together rather than the right of individuals to look out for themselves. Happiness meant a shared state of affairs, not a private enjoyment of what one owned.

The Declaration became possible only when virtually every other option was closed. Britain opened warfare and declared the colonies in rebellion. The Americans opened their ports, formed an army, and overturned all that was left of British authority. Now foreign aid was necessary. The French were already giving it under cover, but only independence could bring them in openly. That was an important reason for the Declaration. But it was not the only one.

The Declaration is divided into three parts. The first proclaims high principles: that all men are created equal, that they all have unalienable rights; that among these are life, liberty, and the pursuit of happiness, whatever happiness may be. The second declares why the Americans are altering their political order: King George's whole history had convinced them that a plan to establish tyranny over them was under way. The third proclaims the sundering of the tie: the former colonies are now "free and independent states," entitled to do everything "which independent states may of right do."

Most of us who live in the modern world would agree that the most important right of any sovereign people is to rule itself, on whatever terms it may choose. This belief was already commonplace in 1776; the Declaration announced nothing new when it said "that whenever any Form of Government becomes destructive of these Ends, it is the Right of the People to alter or to abolish it, and to institute new Government, laying its Foundation on such Principles, and organizing its Powers in such Form, as to them shall seem most likely to effect their Safety and Happiness." The greatest immediate consequence of the Declaration was that it gave the people of the former provinces their chance to make such a choice. Independence was only the beginning. The question of what people were to do with it is just as important as the problem of how they seized it at all. It is a question to which the revolutionaries gave many answers.

III

Only two things were certain in 1776. One of them was that the new America would be republican. The Revolution was not like its "glorious" namesake in England in 1688 or like the Jacobite uprisings in Scotland in 1715 and 1745. It did not replace one monarch or one ruling house with another; rather, it abolished monarchy and ruling houses altogether. To accept independence was to state one's confidence that free people could govern themselves. The other certainty was that the new states would have written constitutions. In metaphorical terms, the colonials killed their king in 1776. In very real terms, they destroyed the whole ancient pattern of institutions, beliefs, habits, and usages that had comprised the British Constitution in America. To replace it, everyone agreed, there would have to be special, solemn documents laying the basis for future public life.

With that, agreement stopped. As Americans set out to shape their new ways and institutions, they debated intensely. What was at stake was not just ideas; it was also power, interest, property, and the course of the future. The struggles that developed around the making of the state constitutions reveal the internal lines of stress in the revolutionary coalitions. They show how groups and individuals who had agreed there had to be a break with Britain were divided and in conflict about what should follow.

Fourteen states—including Vermont—adopted constitutions between 1776 and 1780. But the documents that were produced in Pennsylvania, Maryland, New York, and Massachusetts show the range of argument and the problems to be overcome. Pennsylvania's constitution established a simple democracy in which "the people" came very close to being their own rulers. Maryland's created complex, restrictive institutions designed to keep citizens and rulers as far apart as possible. New York's constitution of 1777 represented the second thoughts and the cool deliberations of men with much to lose. The Massachusetts constitution of 1780 was very similar. But in its creation we can see the working out of procedures that would become standard practice, not just in America, but in many other post-revolutionary nations.

It would be a mistake, however, to say that "the people" of any one state were either "radical" or "conservative." It would also be a mistake to say that "public opinion changed" between 1776, when Pennsylvania wrote its constitution, and 1780, when Massachusetts wrote its version. In every state there were some people who wanted simple democracy and some people who feared it. Each state constitution reflected the balance of power at the time of its writing as well as the honest search of men trying in good faith to find the best way. People across the political spectrum were exhilarated by the good fortune that had made them the founders of a new order. We can best understand what they produced by looking at their struggles and debates as they produced it.

Radical democracy triumphed in Pennsylvania because men of moderation were routed there. Letting fear turn into panic, they forfeited leadership precisely at the moment of independence. Some, like the colonial political leader Joseph Galloway and most of the Philadelphia Quaker elite, moved into outright loyalism. Benjamin Franklin, once Galloway's firm ally, chose independence, but he was busy with Continental matters. The spokesmen for the center were men like John Dickinson, whose fear grew as the crisis deepened, the wealthy merchant Robert Morris, and the rising lawyer James Wilson. Though they knew that independence was bound to come, they would have been happy to delay it indefinitely. With the genuine loyalists already gone, centrists made the provincial assembly their power base in 1775 and early 1776, and this proved a disastrous mistake. In the spring of 1776, radicals in Philadelphia, aiming at internal change, united with radicals in Congress, aiming at independence, to undermine them. When Congress called in May for the abolition of all institutions that still accepted royal authority, they were aiming at Pennsylvania's moderates. The people of the province responded, bringing the assembly down. Neither genuinely Tory nor really revolutionary, the moderates suddenly had no place to stand.

The consequence was that Tom Paine's people found themselves in control. Paine himself did not take part in writing the 1776 Constitution, but the plan he sketched in *Common Sense*—"Let the assemblies be annual, with a president only"—was in perfect harmony with it. Among the authors of the Constitution were a number of Paine's friends, including James Cannon, a teacher and scientist from Scotland; Timothy Matlack, a disowned Quaker and the son of a brewer; Christopher Marshall, a retired druggist; and Dr. Thomas Young, a radical physician who had practiced medicine and politics in Albany, Boston, and Newport before coming to Philadelphia. They wrote their document under the authority of a convention that had been chosen at polls open to every adult militia member. The militiamen had a program of their own, which they announced through their committee of privates. They wanted as much equality as possible between men and officers; they wanted the officers to be elected, not appointed; they wanted no exemptions from service, whether for Quakers with conscientious objections or for the wealthy with money to buy substitutes. Most of all, as James Cannon put it in a broadside that was published in the privates' name, they wanted no man in power "who would be disposed to form any rank above that of freeman." The radical coalition had its own lines of stress. One ran between the free thought represented by Young and Matlack and the stern piety typified by Marshall, who maintained his Quaker faith despite his revolutionary politics. Not everyone who had been militant in bringing down the old government liked either the new constitution or the policies the new government adopted. But the major point is that in the summer of 1776 Pennsylvania's old elite abdicated, allowing new men representing new constituencies to take its place.

The state's democratic constitution emerged out of that situation. It established no governorship and no upper house at all. Instead, an executive council under an annually elected president would administer affairs, without taking any part in the making of law. The House of Representatives would be elected annually as well, and every adult male taxpayer who had lived in the state for one year would be eligible to vote. The only qualifications for election to the House were to be "noted for wisdom and virtue," to have two years' residence in the constituency, and not to "hold any other office except in the militia." To keep officeholders from developing into a separate caste, no man could be elected to the House for more than four years in any seven. Perhaps the most startling provision was the constitution's attempt to bring Pennsylvania's people directly into the process of making laws. Once a bill was considered by the representatives, it was to be "printed for the consideration of the people" before it was "read in general assembly the last time for debate and amendment." Except "on occasions of special necessity," that final reading would take place at the assembly's next session. In the interval, the people would have the chance to let their representatives know what they thought of their work, if necessary by refusing to reelect them.

Maryland was led into independence by its great planters. The land-holding and slaveholding families there were comparable in wealth, in sophistication, and, as events showed, in political skill to the Carters and Lees of Virginia. However, Maryland's planters were a much less secure and self-confident group. The Calvert family, which held the proprietorship of the colony and among whom the title Lord Baltimore descended, retained enormous economic power through the whole colonial era, even though they lost political control. Some Maryland planters, such as the Carrolls, were Catholics, disqualified by their faith from pre-revolutionary public life. Perhaps most important, white Maryland was never the united society that eighteenth-century Virginia became. Slavery, tobacco growing, and the social ways of the planter class were major facts in Maryland life, but they did not bind the province's whites together. The Eastern Shore, between Chesapeake Bay and the Atlantic, was much more a farming economy than a planter one, and the farther north one went, the more likely one was to find free labor, both black and white, producing wheat, rather than slave labor producing tobacco.

Unlike Virginia, Maryland knew serious problems of "disaffection" and outright loyalism during the Revolution. The militia proved unreliable; Tory guerrilla bands roved freely; state courts could not open; blacks and poor whites talked of making common cause. While popular loyalism gathered force, other Marylanders were generating an intense republican radicalism. In July 1776, for instance, the militia of Anne Arundel County put forward its members' ideas about government. The militiamen wanted a two-house legislature, each house to be elected annually under a broad suffrage. There would be a governor, rather than a president as in Pennsylvania, but he would have no power to veto laws. Local officials would be elected, not appointed. The tax system would be based on "a fair and equal assessment in proportion to every person's estate." The militia were not alone in their radicalism. In August, almost nine hundred freemen of the same county instructed their delegates to write a constitution along the same lines, adding that the suffrage ought to be open to every taxpayer. In the state's revolutionary convention there were figures such as John Hall and Regin Hammond who spoke for such men.

It was in the face of all this that Maryland's planter-revolutionaries adopted the constitution they chose. Their correspondence, largely centered on Charles Carroll of Carrollton, reverberates with tones of danger and near-panic, and so does their constitution. Its most striking quality is the distance it tried to place between the people and their government. Both in its procedures for choosing men to office, and in its requirements about who could be chosen, it gave Maryland's people very little control over their rulers. Only once in three years would they get a chance to vote, and then only for county sheriffs and the members of the lower house of the state legislature. Their connection with the rest of the government would be indirect. The state senators would be picked for seven-year terms by a college of electors, which would stand between them and the voters. The governor would be chosen for a one-year term by the senate and the lower house together. There would be high property requirements for office. To sit in the assembly or to be an elector for the senate, a man had to be worth £500; to be a sheriff, a senator, a congressman, or a member of the executive council, the sum was £1,000. To become governor, one had to have a fortune of at least £5,000. Ronald Hoffman's careful research has demonstrated what this meant in reality. Taking Maryland's adult white males county by county, the percentage eligible for the lower house ranged between 7.2 and 15.3, with a state average of 10.9. The percentage eligible for the upper house hovered between 3.2 and 13.3, with a state average of 7.4.

New York's old elite of merchants, professionals, and landowners faced as many problems as the Pennsylvanians did. The New Yorkers, too, broke apart along lines that had been etched by a long history of internal dispute. They, too, had to face enormous popular discontent. But their patriot wing handled the situation with considerably more skill, and it survived to write a constitution that both reflected its own beliefs and interests and proved acceptable to the state's citizenry.

The elite patriots were helped by two elements beyond their control. The first was that from 1768 to 1775 the provincial assembly was in the control of their class's other wing, the men who were moving toward outright loyalism. This group was centered on the De Lancey family of New York City. The elite patriots were comprised of the Livingstons, the Van Rensselaers, and the Schuylers of the Hudson Valley, together with urban figures like John Jay and Gouverneur Morris. Like Pennsylvania's moderates, these people were in no hurry to win independence; however, they were in no position to use the assembly as a means of staving it off. When the assembly collapsed during the winter of 1775–76, it took with it only the Tory wing of the old ruling group. The patriots had already shifted operations to provincial congresses, where they mastered the art of delay. They were also aided by the British invasion of New York City in August 1776. The coming of the redcoats scattered the artisans and the Sons of Liberty of New York City, ending their power as a radical force. Moreover, the invasion forced all New York revolutionaries to see their problem as one of survival rather than one of internal dispute.

The leadership that emerged centered on John Jay, Gouverneur Morris, the ambitious merchant William Duer, and Robert R. Livingston. The latter was not the Robert Livingston who was lord of Livingston Manor, but a young landowner and lawyer, one of many men in his family who bore the same first name. He and his associates made the most of events. As their correspondence shows, they appreciated the magnitude of the task that confronted them. As early as 1774, Morris, watching the election of a revolutionary committee, compared "the mob" to "poor reptiles" basking in the morning sun. Ever the pessimist, he was sure that " 'ere noon they will bite." But between then and 1777, these men used, in Livingston's words, "well-timed delays, indefatigible industry and minute . . . attention to every favourable circumstance" to prevent the fate of their Pennsylvania counterparts from becoming their own. Heeding the warning of their loyalist mentor, the jurist William Smith, they understood that the place for men of property was "rather to the Cabinet than the field." When it was all over, Duer reminisced to Jay about their labors on the "Council of *Conspiracy*." Livingston, meanwhile, was summing up both their methods and their goals with a metaphor of "swimming with a stream it is impossible to stem" and of yielding "to the Torrent" in order to "direct its course." Plenty of signs did appear to show where the torrent might have gone otherwise. In May 1776, the organized mechanics of New York City demanded that the people have a chance to ratify any state constitution that might be written. They also wanted the constitution to allow the election of popular committees whenever people might want them. The first draft that the New York revolutionary convention produced pointed toward a constitution like Pennsylvania's. It called for a president, not a governor, and for direct election of most officials. One observer, a future popular politician, called it a "child of heaven." But another, making up his mind to be a loyalist, feared the power it gave to "the peasantry."

The document to which the "conspiracy" led was realistic, not reactionary. It created a two-house legislature. The assemblymen would be elected annually in county delegations and the members of the state senate would be chosen at staggered three-year intervals to represent four "districts," apportioned roughly by wealth. The governor would also be chosen for a three-year term. Except for the assembly's exclusive right to initiate money bills, the two houses would have equal powers. A "council of revision," made up of the governor and highest judges, would have a veto on laws unless two-thirds of each house voted to override. Patronage would be in the hands of a "council of appointment," made up of the governor and four senators. There were no property qualifications for office, but a freehold worth £40 or a renthold valued at twenty shillings was necessary to vote for the assembly. A freehold worth £100 was required to vote for state senators or for the governorship. This constitution placed a premium on order rather than involvement, but it erected no imposing barriers. Perhaps the men who wrote it would have liked to do more. Proposals did circulate for a qualification of £10,000 and a New York City residence to sit in the upper house, but men from most of the political spectrum joined John Jay, the main author, on the drafting committee and sat in the convention that finally approved and proclaimed the document. Using a physical image different from Livingston's "Torrent," Jay observed that "another turn of the winch would have cracked the cord." The upper-class patriots had gone far enough. Moreover, they had no doubts about who would fill the state's high offices: themselves.

Massachusetts took longest. Its old order dissolved in 1774, but it was not until 1780 that a new state constitution was written and put into effect. During those six years, people argued incessantly about the shape their government ought to take. A good part of the argument turned on procedure. The revolutionized General Court, having defied the governor's order dissolving it in 1774, simply pretended that it was upholding the old royal charter of 1692. But far to the west of Boston a group of mountain dwellers who became known as the "Berkshire Constitutionalists" began to insist that the commonwealth needed a firmer basis. These were the people who started Massachusetts toward the constitution it finally worked out, just as the mechanics of New York City were the first to broach the idea of popular ratification. While the legal standing of the government was in doubt, people who were worried about losing their land had a good excuse for keeping the courts closed. Throughout the interior, they learned to make do with arbitration under the auspices of their county conventions and of their town committees. In some places, this experience led to proposals for a permanent order. The towns of Ashfield and Middleborough and an anonymous pamphlet called *The People the Best Governors* all proposed that simple, direct institutions rather than complicated, balanced ones be adopted. Elections would link the people to almost all their officials, and there would be no property requirements for voting. There would be no real power higher than the one-house assembly; a council might exist, but only to advise, not to take part in making the laws. In Ashfield's plan, as in Pennsylvania's constitution, the voters would have the right to pass judgment on the assembly's actions. In that plan and under *The People the Best Governors*, judges would be elected, not appointed. Middleborough's plan made no proposal for courts at all.

But Massachusetts ended up with a settlement of a very different sort. In 1778, the interim government wrote a constitution and offered it to the towns. From Boston to the Berkshires they rejected it, partly because of its content, which was like Maryland's, and partly because the temporary rulers had no authority to write it in the first place. In 1780, a convention that was elected with special powers wrote another constitution. Under it, a man had to have a freehold worth £60 to vote. Assemblymen would represent towns, but the state senate would be apportioned according to the value of property in any district, not according to population. Senators would have to possess at least £300 in real property or £600 in personal property, and to become governor a man would have to be worth at least £1,000. The governor would enjoy considerable power, both in appointments to public office and in a qualified veto over laws. The convention offered this document to the towns as well, and this time it was accepted. This mechanism of a special convention to write a constitution and a special popular vote to ratify it was the real breakthrough in Massachusetts, for it made it possible to distinguish the constitution from ordinary law. The special solemnity of convention and popular vote made the constitution the expression of the will of a sovereign people, able to be altered only in the same way it had been created. There was an element of mythmaking and some fakery involved, of course. The Harvard historian Samuel Eliot Morison showed long ago that the towns actually rejected the document and that the convention, desperate to establish a permanent government, juggled the figures so it could declare ratification. But Massachusetts worked out a procedure that resolved a problem which had plagued constitution writers in every state. The special conventions and the plebiscites on which post-revolutionary political orders have been founded ever since have their beginning here.

All these problems and debates echoed and reverberated throughout America. The clearest example of how ideas traveled comes from Vermont, where the Green Mountain Boys found at the moment of independence their chance to break free of New York and its hated land system. As Ethan Allen's brother Heman put it to a town meeting, "If we submitted to the mode of Government now forming in the state of New York . . . we could not get off in a future day." Being "without law or government," it was up to the Green Mountain people to create their own forms as they saw fit. Vermont did not receive "official" recognition until after 1790. But, from 1777 onward, its existence was a reality that even New York could not ignore. Vermont's winning of independence was the only time in the eighteenth century when backcountry rebels got the chance to do everything they wanted. They chose, with very minor changes, to adopt Pennsylvania's radical democracy.

They did so at least partly at the suggestion of Dr. Thomas Young, whose career illustrates the ties that could make of American radicalism a coherent force. Young had grown up in New York's Hudson Valley, where he had confronted the system of landlord and tenant in his daily life. In the early 1760s, when he was living near the Connecticut border, he made friends with Ethan Allen, who was running an ironworks just across the line. Together they talked about the evils that great landed estates brought and about deeper issues as well. They discovered that neither believed in Christian revelation or in the power of the church, and they began to write a deist tract. When the book was published decades later, it would become known as *Ethan Allen's Bible* and it would make Allen's name hateful to orthodox ministers all over America. Young moved to Albany, where he was practicing medicine at the time of the Stamp Act, and then on to Boston, Newport, and finally Philadelphia. He threw himself into the resistance movement wherever he went; his name comes first on a roster of Albany Sons of Liberty that was drawn up in 1766. In Philadelphia he associated with Tom Paine, with whose ideas he had a great deal in common, and he helped to draft the constitution of 1776. When the Vermonters declared their independence from New York, he published a broadside offering it to them as a model, calling it "as near perfection as anything yet concerted by mankind." Even then, Young was still berating the "men of some rank" who wanted to re-create in America "the system of Lord and Vassal, or *principal* and *dependent*." It is as if Thomas Young was drawing on not only his own experience but the whole experience of all the people among whom he had lived. The Vermonters certainly thought so, and they followed his advice.

Even titles of office took on significance. The word "president" turns up again and again: in New York's first draft; in Tom Paine's call to "let the assemblies be annual, with a president only"; in the actual state constitutions of Delaware, New Hampshire, and South Carolina, as well as that of Pennsylvania. The choice was deliberate. Unlike "governor," the word carried no overtones of distant monarchical power. It suggested that the job of the officer who bore it was to preside rather than to rule. The people of Ashfield, Massachusetts, had the same point in mind when they announced that they wanted no governor save the "Goviner of the Univarse." It is a phrase that also turns up in the Pennsylvania constitution. The people who used it did not see their God as either a father or a king but rather as a republican magistrate. Their Revolution had taught them to think of themselves not as sinners in tearful exile but rather as citizens of the grandest republic the mind could imagine.

We can see, then, how tangled was the process of destroying the remnants of the British Empire and erecting the first structures of the American republic. At the point of independence there was only one question to answer: which side was a person on. But Americans came to that point by joining in coalitions that linked regions, interests, classes, and individuals, all with their own points of view, their own fears, and their own visions. That the coalitions started to come apart as soon as independence was declared should not be surprising. That the shaping of the state constitutions was affected by questions of balance and tactics within each state should not be surprising, either. Their shared commitment to independence and republicanism gave the Americans something to agree on. But their differences were many and, naturally, gave them something to argue about. The arguments would continue well after the new state governments had begun to function.

· 5 ·

Fourteen States

Careful, self-controlled, always pondering consequences, John Adams was not a man to let himself go. But in May 1776, when Congress called on the people to create new state governments, his joy knew no bounds. "It is independence itself," he exulted in private, and in his pamphlet *Thoughts on Government* he crowed over his generation's immense privilege. "How few of the human race have ever enjoyed an opportunity of making an election of government," he wrote, "more than of air, soil, or climate for themselves or their children." Adams and his kind would be the fathers of a new order. History would speak of them as it did of the great republican founders of the city-states of the ancient world.

Yet exultation was not the only mood in Adams's heart. He knew that cutting the tie with Britain meant cutting many ties between Americans. When crowds closed courts, towns elected committees, militiamen debated with their officers, and Tories took flight, Adams was appalled. With characteristic clarity, he defined the problem and worked out a plan to resolve it. "To contrive some Method for the Colonies to glide insensibly from under the old Government, into a peaceable and contented submission to new ones" was "the most difficult and dangerous Part of the Business Americans have to do in this mighty Contest."

If we stand back far enough, it looks as though John Adams's plan worked. States wrote their constitutions and put them into effect. Congress became the center of a national system of sorts and finally gave that system form in the Articles of Confederation. Together, they won the war. When postwar problems grew too large, a suitable enduring remedy was found in the federal Constitution. Not for Americans, it would seem, the agonizing disorder that has plagued so many other peoples seeking to emerge from revolution.

But it was not so simple. The long struggle over the formal shape of the new governments only began to resolve the question of what independent America would be like. During the war years, from 1775 to 1781, and the Confederation period, from then until 1788, American society confronted immense problems. Raising and disciplining an army was hard enough, for the surge of military enthusiasm that followed Lexington and Concord tapered off quickly. Finance was worse. Congress had no taxing power at all, and the states had little, so the only recourse was to borrow abroad and print paper currency at home, with the promise that someday it would be redeemed. The new governments had to deal as well with loyalists and neutrals, enough of them in some places to make it impossible for revolutionaries to exercise any real authority.

Most important, in practically every state people debated about how, for whom, and by whom, the new order would be run. This great, decade-long debate took place in many arenas. It went on in legislative chambers, in the rooms where popular committees met, and at polling places. It went on in newspapers, in broadsides, and in private correspondence. It also went on in city streets, where people sometimes rioted, and in the fields of western Massachusetts, where people finally rose in arms ten years after independence. Shays' Rebellion, as this backcountry uprising was called, was no aberration. Rather, like Pennsylvania's democratic constitution, it marked the most extreme aspect of a general conflict.

I

From the outbreak of fighting at Concord to the surrender of Lord Cornwallis at Yorktown, the first problem was to keep Britain's military might from destroying the American movement.

The war dragged on for seven long years. The first theater of conflict was New England, where farmer-soldiers besieged British-occupied Boston until the redcoats withdrew in March 1776. After regrouping at Halifax, the British invaded lower New York State in August 1776, with the greatest seaborne army the modern world had seen. They would hold New York City until the end of 1783. Washington's skill at retreating as the British came on kept defeat from becoming disaster and kept the American army in existence to fight again. Preserving the army, fighting only when he could be sure of victory, and retreating whenever he had to would be the core of his strategy until the war's end. In 1777, the British came close to cutting the country and the rebellion in two when General John Burgoyne led a massive column south from Montreal along the Champlain and Hudson Valleys. He was defeated at Saratoga, north of Albany, by Americans under Horatio Gates, and a lesser British force coming from the west was stopped in a frightfully bloody engagement at Oriskany. The failure of this attempt to cut New England off provided the French with an opportunity to enter the war as open allies of the colonies. The British occupation of Philadelphia that winter meant humiliation and terrible suffering for the American troops encamped not far away, at Valley Forge. But the Revolution had not been split in two, let alone defeated.

Then the action shifted to the South, as Sir Henry Clinton mounted and led an invasion of Charleston. From 1779 to 1781, the Southern backcountry was the main scene of conflict, with Nathanael Greene emerging as the foremost

American commander there and Lord Cornwallis eventually replacing Clinton. Marching north into Virginia, Cornwallis finally let himself be trapped between the James and York Rivers by a land force under Washington's direct command and a French fleet under Admiral de Grasse. The surrender at Yorktown marked the effective end of the war, although the making of peace and British withdrawal took two more years.

The warfare itself had revolutionary qualities, as the historian John Shy has argued. He and other recent military historians, such as Piers Mackesy and Charles B. Royster, have noted that the virtuous American self-image of a nation of citizen-soldiers putting aside their plows and picking up their guns does not, in fact, stand up. After an initial burst of martial enthusiasm, most people went back to their farms, shops, and countinghouses, and the officers and men of the Continental Army came to think of themselves as a caste apart. In some places, the war these people fought went by the rules as eighteenth-century gentlemen understood them. British officers were gentlemen by definition, and many American officers decided that their rank made them gentlemen, too. But by no means did all of them behave as their code required, and for many "lesser" men the rules never held. The Massachusetts farmers who sniped at redcoats marching back from Lexington and Concord set the pattern. They were more interested in survival than in glory, and they knew that firing from behind a rock or a tree made their chances of survival a lot better. In places as far apart as the Georgia and Carolina backcountry and the western frontier of New York, the war became a vicious guerrilla struggle. In those places, the devastation and the bloodshed were frightful, and the British, the revolutionaries, and the loyalists all bore a share of the responsibility.

But simply keeping the army intact was as important as winning battles. This, in the face of enormous adversity, was George Washington's great achievement, but he did not do it alone. Part of his problem was internal discipline and organization. After Lexington, farmers all over New England dropped what they were doing and joined in the siege of British-occupied Boston, but this haphazard, informal army could not last long. It took years of effort, experiment, frustration, and mistakes before Washington genuinely commanded the army of professionals he had wanted from the start. It also took the services of a host of other officers. The generals, whether Americans like Nathanael Greene, Horatio Gates, and Benedict Arnold, or foreigners like Friedrich von Steuben, Charles Lee, or the Marquis de Lafayette, are the best-known. But there were many lesser men—colonels, captains, and lieutenants—who also came to think that they were the Revolution's heroes. Most of all, however, it took the willingness of thousands of very ordinary men in the ranks to put up with disease, danger, physical conditions that often were horrifying, and discipline that grew steadily more severe, all in a war that must have seemed as if it would never end.

The other problem that Washington had to face was supply. Shoes, clothing, food, firearms, ammunition, tents, cooking equipment, all these and more had to be found on a massive scale. The French provided some help. At first they sent it under the guise of business dealings by the fictitious firm of Hortalez et Cie., of Bordeaux. After 1777, when Louis XVI recognized American independence, it came openly, as aid to an ally. But the vast bulk of supplies had to be provided by the Americans themselves. How to do it was the first great problem that confronted the revolutionary conventions, congresses, and committees. The complications to which the task led formed a great continuing problem that plagued the state governments.

From the start, the question was more than just one of physically finding supplies. Bad enough in the first stages of the war, the problem worsened and became more complicated in 1777, 1778, and 1779. One reason why it worsened was people's loss of initial enthusiasm. Another was the demands of three armies, French and British as well as American, creating a vastly increased market for what American farmers and artisans could produce. A third was the fact that the two foreign armies could pay with hard coin, gold and silver, whereas the Americans had none. Instead, both Congress and the states paid their bills with paper money, which people had less and less faith in. At first the inflation was slow, but by 1779 it had run away, leaving the Continental Dollar virtually worthless. It is not that long since the phrase "not worth a Continental" could be heard occasionally in American speech.

The armies' demands and the British blockade of the coast brought real shortages: of meat, grain, and salt; of cloth, shoes, and gunpowder; and of imported goods like tea, spices, and rum. But in good part the problem was politics and distribution, not absolute lack. Washington's army froze, starved, and bled at Valley Forge over the winter of 1777–78. But twenty miles away the British troops who had occupied Philadelphia were enjoying a season of festive indulgence with their American collaborators. That was by no means the only time when the army starved while men in a position to profit took what they could.

Civilians faced the same problem. All over the Northern states they could not get what they needed, not so much because it was not available, but because their dollars could not buy it. To make sense of what was happening, and to find a way of dealing with it, they turned to their long-standing tradition that the good society was cohesive and "corporate." Merchants who played the market or held back goods and speculators who depreciated the currency became "monopolizers" and "hoarders." Crowds, often made up largely of women, gathered and acted out the rituals of popular price setting that people of their time knew so well. Hearing that a trader had a supply of tea or salt, the crowd would visit him, offering a price its members thought just.

Only if the trader refused would his store be sacked, and even then the "just price" would be left behind. It happened in Ulster and Dutchess Counties, New York, in the Connecticut Valley, and in seacoast Massachusetts towns like Beverly, Salem, and Marblehead. In Boston, a figure who called himself "Joyce, Jr." led crowds of up to five hundred people that carted monopolizers about town and enforced price controls. The same name, with its echoes of the seventeenth-century Puritan revolution, had been signed a few years earlier to calls for action by the "Committee for Tarring and Feathering."

Crowd action of this sort rested, as we have already seen, on an ethos that looked backward. It was one in which the community as well as the owner had a say in the disposal of property. If the government did not act to see that property's use did no harm, a crowd could. This ethos expressed people's longing to return to a genuinely just and organic society that may never have existed, save as a vision and a dream. It had always been perfectly compatible with a real society of great inequality. But now something very new appeared: the union of this old tradition with the power of popular committees and with the radical politics of equality and involvement that they embodied. As Richard Ryerson and other students of the committee movement have shown, the committees were the means by which people who once would have joined crowds now moved to the center of political affairs. The difference was very real: a crowd could act, but a committee could set and execute a policy; a crowd would dissolve, but a committee could adjourn. One unfortunate New York State storekeeper learned the difference in 1777, when he was visited for the second time by angry women bent on seizing his stock. When he protested, they told him that "they had orders from the Committee to search his house."

People founded the committees to resist Britain, not to change America. But resistance and corporatism went together. People's response to the fact of war in 1775 was to unite, to submerge self into community. The great nineteenth-century historian George Bancroft put it in the most romantic of terms with an account of the news from Lexington echoing from hill to hill and valley to valley. If we make allowances for Bancroft's overblown rhetoric, he was close to the mark. Records exist that show towns and counties meeting as soon as they heard what happened. They elected new committees, created new militia units, and started raising supplies. Military associations passed from hand to hand, and the worst punishment a non-signer could face was the contempt of the community. Men laid lesser quarrels aside. Perhaps the most striking example was the appearance of the Green Mountain leaders Ethan Allen and Seth Warner before the New York provincial congress in 1775. Both men stood condemned to die for leading their people's insurrection against New York, according to a law passed only the year before by the same province's assembly. Now Allen and Warner pledged cooperation.

In this heady atmosphere, it was easy to do what needed doing and to announce that the burdens would be shared as equally as possible. But to the extent that slogan became reality, it was because of pressure from below. The militiamen in Virginia and in Philadelphia who demanded plain hunting shirts as standard uniform understood that. So did committeemen, who were insisting as early as 1775 and 1776 that for the good of the community they had to control the price and the supply of necessities. As we have seen, the Pennsylvania constitution summed up the political experience of the committee movement, insisting that it was good that "more men . . . be trained to public business." It likewise summed up the movement's political economy, noting an expectation of times when the government would have to "lay embargoes, or prohibit the exportation of any commodity."

Most people probably expected that the committees would

fade away when new regular state governments appeared.
New York's constitution said as much, calling the committees "temporary expedients . . . to exist no longer than
the grievances of the people should remain without redress"
and condemning the "many and great inconveniences" that
they brought. But that state's new government swiftly found
that it could not do without the committees, and they persisted there until well into 1778. More important, when the
inflation reached its worst in 1779, people spontaneously
revived their committees all over the Northern states. The
revival began in Philadelphia, and it spread from there to
Boston, to the New England interior, and to the Hudson
Valley.

Throughout the North, the late 1770s saw people linking
patriotism, direct involvement, and corporatist economics.
"As soon as the authority of your committees ended, knavery
showed its head, villains of every class came forth and practiced with impunity," said a New York writer in 1779. A
Massachusetts almanac reminded its farmer readership of
"how you asserted your rights as freemen" against the British.
It contrasted that heroic record with "the vile practice of
extortion" that now seemed rife, and it called monopoly
and hoarding "incompatible with private interest and public
liberty." In Philadelphia, a broadside signed "Come On
Warmly" showed contempt for a few "overbearing merchants, a swarm of monopolizers and speculators, an infernal
gang of Tories." All were enemies of the commonwealth. A
general meeting of Philadelphians resolved that public control of the marketplace was the very "spirit of liberty."
Bostonians issued a circular letter that linked "the many
happy consequences which have been derived from the
appointment of committees" with the Revolution itself.

Clearly, this was a resurgence that the Revolution's leaders
dared not ignore. Governor George Clinton of New York, a
man of undistinguished background who owed his high
office to the votes of farmers and soldiers, knew as much. He

went out of his way in 1779 to call the state legislature's attention to the "sense that your constituents loudly express of applying some suitable remedy" to the currency crisis. In Pennsylvania, a club formed to support the constitution of 1776 made acceptance of corporatist economics one of its conditions of membership. But there were other people, some in positions of great power, who saw the committees and the attempt to control the marketplace as foolish, or worse. We cannot understand what went on in the sovereign states unless we understand what these men stood for and the ways they responded to the popular movement.

II

By the time of the American Revolution, corporatism had been under ideological attack for the best part of a century. The most powerful statement came in 1776, when the Scottish thinker Adam Smith published *The Wealth of Nations*. Smith summed up objections to a controlled economy that had been taking shape since the time of Thomas Hobbes and John Locke. He presented a powerful argument that a society of free individuals, all seeking what was good for themselves, would offer the best way to achieve the good of everyone. Smith's vision was exhilarating and, in its time, profoundly liberating. Tear down controls, set individuals free, let them strive for what they wanted, and all of society would gain. This was not abstract speculation. It was the intellectual fruit of the enormous, transforming burst of energy that the modern age was setting loose in the Atlantic world. Nor was it necessarily coldhearted. Smith believed that men of sociability and good will could achieve what they wanted without hurting their fellows.

Merchants, politicians, and other thinkers came around increasingly to this position, but ordinarly people did not necessarily see things the same way. The consequence was struggle between people who had decided that corporatism was archaic nonsense and other people who saw it as a necessary means of self-defense. In England, that struggle took place over many decades; in America, as later in France, it was compressed and intensified by the heat of revolution.

In the first enthusiasm of 1775, loyalists were virtually the only people who rejected the dictates of committees and congresses. Some were outspoken in their insistence that the community had no right to tell the individual what to do. The New Englander Timothy Ruggles invited signatures to an association in defense of "our undoubted . . . liberty, in eating, drinking, buying, selling, communing and acting what, with whom and as we please." In New York, one Tory wrote that "no man can be in a more abject state of bondage, than he whose Reputation, Property and Life are exposed to the discretionary violence . . . of the community." A Philadelphian, meanwhile, was calling the committees "gigantic strides to set the resolves of the populace above the law." Loyalism was many things. It was black slaves who thought that the king's banner, not Congress's, offered them real freedom. It was small farmers who wanted no part of a revolution led by great landlords. It was Quakers who rejected the movement on the ground of high principle, and it was port-city merchants who could not bring themselves to break with the empire that had made them rich. It was officeholders whose hearts had been bought for a colonelcy or a mayoralty or a judgeship. Like the Revolution itself, loyalism spoke with many voices. But here it was one of its most powerful.

As early as 1776, some men were beginning to separate corporatism from American commitment. In April, as Eric Foner notes, ninety-odd Philadelphia merchants "petitioned the Committee of Observation and Inspection, denying its power to regulate prices and announcing their intention to refuse further cooperation." A month later, the committee of Albany, New York, hauled a trader before it on a charge of raising his prices. His sly defense was that the prices of his goods had remained the same and that the two shillings he now asked in addition were "for his trouble in weighing." By the late 1770s, such opinions were hardening into a political position, which combined three separate principles. First, committee power and interference in the marketplace had to end. Second, the best way to combat inflation was by unremitting taxes to dry up the excess money. Third, complex, balanced political institutions offered the best means to achieve sound social policy.

From the northern Chesapeake to New England, men who held this position faced the same problem. How they dealt with it, however, differed from state to state. In Pennsylvania, the question of the shape of the institutional structure became central. Pennsylvania's men of property loathed their state's democratic constitution, and they worked to put an end to it even as they worked to end committee power and to secure a free market. In Massachusetts, similar men had everything they wanted after 1780, both in institutions and in policies. But the reaction to their policies proved so strong that it became a reaction against their institutions as well. In Maryland and New York, however, the story was different. There the men who had built the new institutions realized that the task before them was to make those institutions take hold. They learned swiftly that it could not be done by simple force or by pushing too fast.

It was in Maryland that the revolutionary elite learned this lesson most swiftly and with least cost to themselves. As the last chapter showed, while the planters were working out their elaborate political system, other Marylanders were showing their dislike for both it and them. Blacks and poor whites who were moving toward each other, the failure of courts to open, and militant loyalism all showed how weak the position of the planters was. Even people who accepted the Revolution were in an uproar. Some militia captains led their own men in salt riots, on one occasion seizing what they needed from a member of a revolutionary convention.

In other units, men deserted rather than serve under officers they disliked. One such officer, a Captain Watkins, had earned his men's hostility by physically beating them. In Queen Annes County, militiamen, "induced to believe they ought not to submit to any appointment but those made by themselves," refused the officers named over them. In Anne Arundel County, questions of class and of military service came together when militiamen complained of their "Captain and Ensign speaking in public Company against the poor people in general." The captain in question, Richard Chew, had said that "no poor man was entitled to a vote, and those that would insist upon voting . . . should be put to death." Chew's brother had observed that "a poor man was not born to freedom but to be a drudge on earth." There may have been a time when poor Marylanders put up with such arrogance, but that time had passed.

The most astute member of the planter leadership, Charles Carroll of Carrollton, came fairly early to a recognition of "the wisdom of sacrifice." He understood that if men of his kind did not make substantial concessions they might find themselves losing everything they had. He realized as well that the most important thing an intelligent conservative could hold on to was his ability to influence events. Ronald Hoffman's account of Maryland's Revolution shows how Carroll argued his case in endless correspondence with men of his kind, and most notably with his father, Charles Carroll of Annapolis. The younger man's analysis pointed to major concessions on matters of taxation and finance, and the sacrifice that he called for was real. The new tax system that he helped work out placed greater burdens on the rich than they had ever borne. The cheap paper currency that he advocated would let debtors pay back far less than they had actually borrowed and still call the debt clear. For the older Carroll, these policies surpassed "in iniquity all the acts of the British Parliament against America." But the son realized that "great revolutions" did not "happen without much partial injustice and suffering" and that some things had to be endured. "I entirely agree with you as to the injustice of the law," he wrote to his father, "but I can not follow your advice to withdraw: where should I withdraw?" In the end, the younger man proved right. Once the government demonstrated that it was not in the business of oppressing its citizens, disaffection tapered off, the militia became reliable, and popular loyalism started to fade away.

In New York, both the situation and the solution were similar, but each was more complicated. When the constitution of 1777 was proclaimed, it was over a broken state. New York City, Staten Island, Long Island, and the southern part of Westchester County were held by the British. The western frontier was at war with itself. Two counties and part of a third had gone their own way to form Vermont. In the Hudson Valley, armed loyalists roamed at will. Some twenty-three hundred men there had been disarmed for loyalism and "disaffection." And the committee movement refused to put an end to itself.

New York had its men who recognized the dimensions of the problem and who knew that resolving it would not be easy. At the center of the group stood the young, highly educated landowners and lawyers who had written the constitution, such as Robert R. Livingston, Egbert Benson, and John Jay. These men had found a political identity in their brilliant holding action of 1776 and early 1777. Now they commanded the high courts, with Jay as chief justice and Livingston as chancellor. Benson, elected to the assembly, was certain that he could control it as well. But already they had overreached themselves. Their first setback came when the landowner Philip Schuyler, their candidate for governor, lost the election to the much more plebeian George Clinton. Though surprised, they were still confident. "They may chuse who they will, I will command them all," Schuyler boasted in private. But over 1777, 1778, and 1779 he learned otherwise.

Initially these men thought that asserting authority was all that was needed. Tories had to be controlled, so there would be a political police, called the Commission for Detecting and Defeating Conspiracies. Taxes had to be raised, so there would be laws to do it with as little threat as possible to the property of the rich. The power of the committees had to end, so Jay, Livingston, and Benson insisted that the laws of the state make no mention of it. But the Tory problem remained, taxes were not paid, and the committees would not go away.

In 1779, when the committee movement boiled up again, the state government made a series of dramatic and highly visible changes in its policies. It stopped trying to control the loyalists and began to punish them instead. The most important step was to pass a law confiscating the estates of some seventy of them, whom the act named. The families that lost their property included some of the greatest names of the colonial era, such as the De Lanceys of New York City, the Philipses of the lower Hudson Valley, the Johnsons, and Philip Skene of the northern frontier. The act made it easy for the state to seize the property of others as well. This was the start of what became a massive body of anti-Tory legislation, so large that it filled a sizable volume when it was collected and published in 1784. The government responded to the state's other problems as well. It enacted price controls and imposed an embargo on the export of scarce goods from the state. It drastically altered its system of taxation. No longer would personal property and land held empty for speculative gain go untaxed. Instead, elected assessors would decide what a person owed on the basis of "circumstances and other abilities to pay taxes, collectively considered." The new system was anything but elegant. It would be the cause of endless debate over the coming years. But it proved popular. For the first time in New York's history, its landowning elite would face tax bills that reflected what they really owned.

The picture is much like the one in Maryland: by adopting

radical policies, conservative institutions were able to take hold. Loyalism started to diminish; the popular committees faded away; taxes began to be paid. There was, however, one big difference: New York had no Charles Carroll of Carrollton, able to grasp the wisdom of sacrifice and to force others of his kind to accept it. Instead, the pressure for the turn-about came from Clinton, the outsider who had become governor, and from the obscure committee veterans who were entering the state legislature. These men did not come to power with any collective self-awareness, or with any great sense of hostility to other patriots. In 1776 and 1777, when they were trying to rule a state torn to shreds, internal bickering was a luxury they could not afford. But by 1779 they were beginning to acquire their own consciousness. Coalition was giving way to conflict, for people like Jay, Livingston, Schuyler, and Benson resisted the turnabout as long as they dared. When they finally realized they could not win, they accommodated. The high judges who sat on the Council of Revision began to allow radical laws to pass. Benson, who had greater technical skills than any other man in the legislature, began to draft bills that he loathed on behalf of others. But these same men quickly began to pull out of a situation they no longer could control. By 1780, they would be gone: Jay to be the American minister to Spain, Livingston to be Secretary for Foreign Affairs, Benson to a seat in Congress. Other men, of much different background, would lead New York through the end of war and the coming of peace. When the elite politicians returned, it would be from the high ground of national affairs, a ground that by then they had made securely their own.

In Pennsylvania, the lines of confrontation were clearly drawn. Philadelphia's merchants and lawyers, its Robert Morrises and James Wilsons, had lost their political position in the spring of 1776, but by the autumn they were already regrouping. They were determined that the state's constitution should not endure, and they kept up their pressure until 1790, when they finally got their way. Fairly quickly, these men began to call themselves "Republicans," to signal the difference between them and their "Constitutionalist" opponents. By 1779, each group was organized as a formal "society."

Almost from the start, the Republicans were aided by men who had until independence stood in radical ranks. Perhaps their foremost recruit was Benjamin Rush, physician, politician, and writer of talent. Rush decided quickly that radical democracy was no way to run a republic, and he decided almost as fast that free-market economics worked better than corporatism. Others joined him, including to some extent Tom Paine himself. Paine did not give up on democracy. Nor, in contrast to Rush, did he pull away from Philadelphia's common people. But Paine had grown up in the same Britain that produced Adam Smith, and he came to agree more and more with Smith that economic freedom would lead to the liberation of all.

It took time, for Paine did become part of the effort to use committee power to control the economy in 1779. The movement emerged among artisans, sailors, and especially among the militia. Philadelphia's citizen-soldiers petitioned in May for price controls and they joined forces with the Constitutional Society to bring them about. Together they called a mass meeting that elected one committee to put controls into effect and another to investigate the dealings of Robert Morris. Paine, like Timothy Matlack, David Rittenhouse, and Charles Willson Peale, was named to both. Daniel Roberdeau, the militia brigadier general who chaired the meeting, summed up a position on which militiamen and Constitutionalists agreed: "Combinations have been formed for raising the prices of goods and provisions, and therefore the Community . . . have a natural right to counteract such Combinations, and to set limits to evils which affect themselves."

But Philadelphians had reached a point of serious division.

One did not have to be among the elite to accept the free-market case. The city's leatherworkers—tanners, curriers, and cordwainers—met and decided that price controls did them nothing but harm; they then published a broadside saying so. "Trade should be as free as air, uninterrupted as the tide," they wrote. Not everyone who worked in the leather trades joined them. One Whig shoemaker claimed that the broadside had originated among people who had collaborated with the British during their occupation of the city, and there were two shoemakers and a tanner on the price-control committee itself. The actual clash between the two sides came in October. Some twenty prominent free-market men, including Robert Morris, had gathered in the house of James Wilson, a man "obnoxious to a large portion of the community" for his various political positions. A unit of the city militia marched on the house and besieged it. It was not the first time such a thing had happened; late in July, a crowd of several hundred had surrounded the home of White-head Humphreys, a man of similar stance. Now matters went further, for someone inside the house fired on the militiamen. A serious riot was averted only when Joseph Reed, the president of Pennsylvania, and his fellow Constitutionalist Timothy Matlack arrived at the head of an elite militia unit called the City Light Horse. As Benjamin Rush noted, Matlack and Reed had drawn their swords against the very people they had long led.

With that confrontation at "Fort Wilson," the effort to control prices by popular action went into decline. It may have been the nakedness of the clash. It may have been the abandonment of the militiamen by Reed, Matlack, and other prominent radicals such as Charles Willson Peale. It may have been that a schism was opening between the artisan intelligentsia and ordinary people. Whatever the cause, the same decline was starting to take place in New York and New England. In Pennsylvania, the end of the movement to control the market did not mean the end of division. The Republicans and the Constitutionalists had in effect become political parties, and throughout the 1780s they would compete for control of the state.

Disputes and disorders went on longest in Massachusetts. Working out the system of a special convention to write a constitution and a popular vote to ratify it was a major achievement, but the state refused to settle down. The reasons were both economic and institutional. By the time Massachusetts debated the shape of its new order, both the first euphoria of independence and the perils of open warfare were fading. The British withdrawal from Boston in March 1776 and their defeat at Saratoga in October 1777 ended serious military danger. Instead, the great issue was the deteriorating economy. Controlling prices was as much on people's minds as whether to have a strong senate and whether the governor should have a veto on laws. Records of meetings in such towns as Upton, Westborough, Sturbridge, and Petersham show people debating both issues.

There is no doubt that the complicated, balanced government Massachusetts adopted marked a victory for the coastal port communities over the farming towns of the interior. The ports won a series of victories of another sort, first in the old General Court, which governed the commonwealth until 1780, and then in the new state legislature. Both institutions confronted the economic crisis with an unremitting policy of hard money and demanding taxation. After 1780 there was no legal tender in the state save gold and silver, which were impossible to find. Failure to pay either debts or taxes could lead, as farmers knew, to lawsuits, imprisonment, and, worst of all, the loss of a man's land. It was the very nightmare that the men of the interior had feared was taking shape as early as the time of the Stamp Act. Then they had blamed distant Britons and an elite whom the British had seduced. Now the cause lay in their own republican government.

Matters grew worse, not better, after the coming of peace.

Under the terms of the Treaty of Paris that ended the war in 1783, British creditors were free at last to call in their American debts. British merchants were likewise free to dump their goods on the American market. The result was a quick boom and then a deep depression, as credit contracted further and further. Even in states like New York, where soft money and anti-British laws gave people—some people—some protection, the effects were serious. In Massachusetts, they were devastating. Pressed by London, Boston merchants called in their debts from traders in county towns like Worcester and Springfield. These then demanded what was owed them by storekeepers in small villages. The storekeepers in turn told farmers and artisans to pay or face legal action. Meanwhile, those same farmers found themselves faced with impossible tax bills from their government.

For men who had built their lives on commerce and who understood its ways, it was all regrettable but unavoidable. But for farmers who traded mostly for necessities and who had no hard coin, it was disaster. With more time, with a different background, and perhaps with a little more money in their pockets, they might have mounted an immediate pressure campaign on their representatives. They might have persuaded the legislature to give them some protection by changing the laws. In terms of sheer numbers, the towns could control the lower house easily, but that smacked of partisanship, which was an evil word in these people's vocabulary. Moreover, each town had to pay its own representative, and if individual farmers could not pay their debts and taxes, how could the towns they lived in find the money to send a man to Boston? If they did send someone, he would be raw and green, no match for the eminent, self-confident figures elected in places like Salem, Newburyport, and Boston itself. And even if they could win the lower house, there was still the senate and beyond it Governor James Bowdoin, who was very much a hard-money man.

So they chose another way to protect themselves. Town

meetings and county conventions had served them well for more than a decade. Let them do it again. The resolutions that the farmers voted and the actions that they took rested on the good, classic republican principle that if a community acted together it could solve its problems. The interior people knew about the differences between poor and rich, and between men of agriculture and men of commerce. But they did not think of themselves as a group that had to do battle with other interests, or as a class that was locked in struggle with other classes. They did make some openly political points: they wanted the capital moved westward so it would be closer to them; some wanted an end to or changes in the state senate, with its special representation for property. But, most of all, they wanted to close the courts and work things out among themselves, so that they would not lose their land and sink into tenancy.

As the British historian J. R. Pole notes, their rebellion did not amount to much. But the state government repressed it with all the force it could muster. Though General Benjamin Lincoln, who commanded the troops that marched against them, was not interested in killing or destruction for their own sake, he did intend to show the farmers where power lay. Chief Justice William Cushing was more determined. His charge to the grand jury that indicted the rebellion's leaders and the sentence of death that he handed down on four of them were intended to terrify. "Instead of a due reverence to authority, and submission to government, enjoined in the holy Scriptures as indispensable duties upon all Christians," he intoned, "have you not endeavoured . . . to overturn all government and order, to shake off all restraints, human and divine, to give up yourselves wholly to the power of the most restless, malevolent, destructive, tormenting passions?" His fierce words had the effect he wanted. Over the winter of 1786–87, individuals and whole towns got down on their knees and begged forgiveness. "True it is that I have been a committee-man," wrote one, but "I can truly say that in draughting any papers of a publick nature, I have ever endeavoured . . . not to have anything therein . . . which might reflect upon authority, or strike at the dignity of government, and if any thing of that nature in fact appears, I am sincerely sorry . . . and hope it will be overlooked and pardoned." The pride and self-assertion with which such men had stood up first to Britain and then to their own rulers seemed lost.

Whether that pride was really lost is another matter. The state government backed off quickly from its policy of repression. Even the death sentences Cushing had imposed were commuted. Soon it was time for new elections, and the westerners took advantage of their right to vote. Three times as many people voted in the election for governor as had the year before, and James Bowdoin found himself replaced by John Hancock. Sixteen new men appeared in the forty-member senate. Two hundred twenty-eight towns sent members to the lower house, far more than in any previous session, and 60 percent of these were new men. This was not an internal revolution. Hancock, like Bowdoin, was an easterner and a man of commerce, and the government made no dramatic switch from hard money to paper currency. In fact, by the time the new legislature met, people's attention was focused not on Boston but on the federal convention that was about to meet in Philadelphia. But it was still a fact that Massachusetts had changed. A government that the rich had created largely for their own benefit had become something that lesser people could capture and try to use for themselves.

Four separate stories, four separate courses of events, four separate outcomes; one set of problems: this is what emerges from the records of Maryland, New York, Pennsylvania, and Massachusetts during the first years of independence. We could find the same problems in New Hampshire, Vermont, Rhode Island, Connecticut, New Jersey, and Delaware. Questions of ideology, of institutional balance, of power, and of economics intermingled in different ways, but with a single underlying trend. The wrenching experiences that had made up the revolutionary crisis were forcing people to think hard about who they were and to find new ways of dealing with the complexities of their world. Farther south the problems were different, but the transformations were just as real.

III

Events spared the Deep South the worst of the inflation of the late 1770s, but it was spared little else. Georgia and the Carolinas became the main theater of war after 1778, and by 1781 fighting had moved north into Virginia. These states had to endure the same problems of disaffection and militant loyalism that Maryland went through. But, except for Virginia, they felt them in a much more severe way. As in Maryland, questions of class, race, culture, and region contributed to people's decision that they would stay neutral or that they would fight for king rather than Congress. In Maryland, those elements came together most powerfully on the Eastern Shore, cut off by Chesapeake Bay from the realm of great planters and fundamentally different in its social structure. Farther south, it was in the deep interior that planter control was weakest, and it was there that the most serious trouble erupted.

When the British general Sir Henry Clinton took the war to the South, the coastal communities gave him virtually no opposition. They had little choice. The main American military force was far away, and there was no question of the planters arming their slaves to drive Clinton's troops back. When Congress suggested in 1779 that Carolina and Georgia blacks be made soldiers and given their freedom for serving, the state governments would not even think of it. Instead, the revolutionary governments fled and their people either joined the flight or knuckled under. In Charleston, whites of all classes signed a congratulatory address to Sir Henry in the hope he would let them get on with their lives. Artisans and shopkeepers soon found that stronger gestures, including joining the loyalist militia, were necessary, for the conquerors would allow only men who were overtly loyal to practice their trade. For all their assertive rhetoric during the imperial crisis, the lowlanders rapidly settled down to a life of submission.

The interior was another matter. Already soured in the aftermath of the Regulator movements, its people had not been enthusiastic about the Revolution even in 1775 and 1776. In South Carolina, a team of lowland political missionaries found themselves preaching their gospel of liberty to a largely uninterested audience. At one point, the team's leader, William Henry Drayton, had to negotiate a treaty to prevent a pitched battle between his supporters, numbering about one thousand men, and a larger force of the disaffected. In North Carolina, revolutionaries and loyalists faced one another under arms for the first of many times at the Battle of Moore's Creek Bridge in February 1776. It was not that the backcountry was united for the king; rather, the region was divided against both itself and the seaboard.

When the British invaders dealt with low-country grandees, they treated them as gentlemen. But when they dealt with the rough men of the interior, it was another matter. As Jerome Nadelhaft's study of South Carolina's Revolution shows, it was the British who released the backcountry's tensions and set off the immense wave of violence that swept through it between 1778 and 1781. A British officer, Sir James Beard, pointed the way early, when he ordered that rum privileges be taken from every soldier under his command "who [took] a prisoner." On one occasion, Beard slaughtered more than a dozen rebels himself, despite their surrender. Beard set a pattern that was followed through 1780 by such officers as Colonel Banastre Tarleton and Major James Wemyss. On one occasion, leading Clinton's cavalry, Tarleton chased a Virginia regiment and caught it at the Waxhaws. He paid no attention when the Americans tried to surrender and even had his soldiers pull apart piles of bodies so that living men at the bottom could be bayoneted. Tarleton's creed was clear: "If warfare allows me I shall give . . . no quarter." Wemyss, meanwhile, was devastating an area seventy miles long and as much as fifteen miles wide between Georgetown, on the coast, and Cheraw, well inland and near the North Carolina line.

Such brutality reignited passions that backcountry people knew well. Patriot partisan groups took shape under men like Thomas Sumter, Andrew Pickens, and Francis Marion, the "Swamp Fox." Tory guerrillas formed similar groups of their own under officers like William "Bloody Bill" Cunningham. Which side slaughtered more of the other cannot be said. Revolutionaries victorious at King's Mountain shouted "Tarleton's Quarter" and killed the loyalists whom they had captured. Cunningham's loyalists, for their part, once chopped to pieces twenty Whigs who fell to their mercy. These are only two of many instances. Nadelhaft's picture of the interior's agony reveals the worst suffering that any community in revolutionary America had to endure.

Virginia's strongest tension was between blacks and whites. As early as 1775, the royal governor Lord Dunmore took advantage of it by offering freedom to slaves who would rally to him. Not surprisingly, a sizable number did. Thomas Jefferson had that incident in mind when he tried to put into the Declaration of Independence some overheated prose that blamed the king both for forcing the institution of slavery on unwilling white Virginians and "that this assemblage of horrors might want no fact of distinguished die," for "exciting those very people to rise in arms among us." The final version simply charged the monarch with inciting "domestic insurrection."

But, as the war moved northward toward the Chesapeake, even Virginia saw outbreaks of white popular loyalism. It was strongest in the far southwest of the state, where Bedford, Henry, Montgomery, Pittsylvania, and Washington

Counties experienced genuine popular uprisings. Why the outbreaks happened is uncertain. It may have been that as Lord Cornwallis and his army drew near, people just wanted to be on the side that was winning; that had happened in northern New York, as General Burgoyne drove southward from Montreal in 1777, and in New Jersey, when Sir William Howe marched his troops through. It may have been simple proximity to the tortured Carolina piedmont. It may have been that the tensions behind Virginia's evangelical dissent were finally becoming openly political, Methodism certainly had a strong appeal in Maryland's loyalist-ridden Eastern Shore, and it was in the southwestern frontier counties that Virginia's own evangelical movement had first begun to take shape. Whatever its roots, however, popular loyalism came to far less in Virginia than in either Maryland or the Carolinas. Planter control remained strong, and Cornwallis's surrender to Washington at Yorktown firmly established which side had won.

With peace came new problems. As early as 1783, British merchants were beginning to regain control of Southern commerce. They had what planters needed: slaves and familiar goods to sell, markets for plantation crops, and credit to make up for the planters' lack of hard cash. Virginia never had had a merchant community of its own, and in South Carolina the planters used the power of the state to give British traders a privileged position. There was intense anti-British feeling in Charleston after the war, which took political form in the activities of groups like the Marine Anti-Britannic Society. Had such groups won the contest, artisans and local merchants might have become the basis for a pattern of development that did not depend fully on slavery. Charleston might have joined New York and Philadelphia on the course of differentiation and rapid growth that turned those Northern ports into great nineteenth-century cities. It had, after all, been very much like them in the late colonial years. Nor was it absolutely certain that the deep interior would become the heartland of slavery. Carl Bridenbaugh pointed out long ago that only in the Chesapeake and the South Carolina lowlands was slavery firmly established at the time of the Revolution. The small farmers of the piedmont and the interior valleys were different. Most of them were Germans and Scotch-Irish who had migrated down from Philadelphia; many of them were receptive to the evangelical appeal, with its insistence on brotherhood and sisterhood even across the gulf of race; most important, the way they lived did not require large numbers of slaves to do their work. It may not have been necessary for the Southern states to become "the South."

But slavery did triumph, spreading not only into the piedmont but all across what would become the Cotton Kingdom. The South Carolina government, under planter control, embarked on policies which effectively cut off any possibility of the state developing into a society of merchants, artisans, and free small farmers. Most important, it began, almost as soon as peace returned, to give benefits to British traders and manufacturers at the expense of local ones. It extended citizenship rights freely; it allowed aliens on trial before a Carolina court to have other non-citizens on the jury; it established a city government for Charleston which took as its first priority the crushing of anti-British action. All the planters really wanted was sure markets and cheap goods. They knew that British traders could supply these and that American traders could not. But what they did committed South Carolina to a course that would leave it a colony in everything but name. In 1850, as in 1750, it would be a society based on unfree labor, producing primary goods for people in places far away to process and to market. In 1850, as in 1750, Charleston would be a small port, serving its hinterland but enjoying little life of its own. The planters gained, immensely in some cases. But the society they ruled lost, for it would reap almost none of the benefits that rapid transformation would bring to the North. Whether or not the planters intended it, they were condemning their world to permanent underdevelopment.

They probably could not have done it had the interior not begun to transform itself in their image. By 1785 and 1786, tobacco culture was moving into the piedmont, bringing with it large-scale slavery and the plantation system. Even before Eli Whitney's invention of the cotton gin, the division of South Carolina into a lowland region of plantations and an interior region of small farms was coming to an end. With it also ended the structural basis for white popular movements against planter control. Carolina society had been wracked by the Regulation and then by the Revolution; now it would be united around the institution of slavery.

South Carolina thus left behind the tensions that had plagued it in the late colonial and revolutionary periods. Now it could become the center of pro-slavery feeling. It alone would allow the importation of slaves from Africa during the twenty-year interval in which the federal Constitution forbade Congress to prevent it. In the time of Andrew Jackson, it would be the state that forced the issue of the right to nullify a federal law. In the time of Abraham Lincoln, South Carolina would be the first state to secede from the union. The basis for all this was laid in the 1780s, as slavery triumphed over urban artisanship and commerce and backcountry free labor as the basis of the state's way of life.

Even policies which in the North might have betokened a small-farmer triumph marked planter gains here. The South was as troubled as the North in 1785 and 1786 by glutted markets and tight credit. There were places where Southerners took the first steps along the road to rebellion that backcountry Massachusetts farmers were starting to walk; in May 1785, for instance, popular action kept a judge in Camden, South Carolina, from trying suits for debt. South Carolina's government responded with a series of laws that reflected everything the Massachusetts farmers could have wanted. But their net effect was to benefit planters, not small farmers. A law that allowed debtors to tender property rather than money, as long as assessors agreed on the property's worth, is a good case. Rich men who owned useless land in the pine barrens had no trouble discharging their debts by offering it. The assessors were local men, and usually they would agree with the owner's exaggerated statement of its value. But people "without different kinds of property had to offer creditors something of value, at least to them," and they were likely to lose it. The act looked like populist legislation, but it was the planters who gained from it.

But, in the South as in the North, the Revolution brought marked changes in how rulers and the people whom they ruled dealt with one another. In the colonial period, people had either deferred or rebelled, and most often they deferred. By contrast, suggests Jerome Nadelhaft, in the 1790s people "did not politely or humbly request anything. . . . They described their condition and assumed simply that the people who were no better than they but who happened to sit in the legislature would act." "That," Nadelhaft argues, "was the Revolution." Something similar happened to Virginians. Their colonial social order had been organic and hierarchical. Its rituals, ceremonies, and patterns had served both to link people to one another and to show that some were above and some were below. But in the state's revolutionary settlement such structure and hierarchy disappeared. Rhys Isaac's portrait of Virginia's transformation suggests that post-revolutionary Virginians lived lives that were much more private and self-contained than had their forebears. Gone were the lavish hospitality for the whole neighborhood and the open display that had marked great-house life. Gone was the enforced Anglican worship that the planters had used on occasion to assert their own worth. Only court day and the militia muster remained as occasions for the community to gather.

As Isaac shows, the planters put an end to their effort to

force their own cultural patterns on people who were unlike themselves. Thomas Jefferson's act for establishing religious freedom, made law in 1786, marks the change. Virginia's greatest planters would remain immersed in a "proud, assertive culture," but other Virginians would not be obliged to share it. Lesser whites, in turn, would think of the planters as people who perhaps were more fortunate and powerful than they but not intrinsically any better. On that basis, their version of American republicanism would be built. On that basis as well, slavery and the society it produced would spread westward. Virginians, Carolinians, and other white Southerners would find it possible to think of themselves both as equal citizens in a republic and as members of a master race.

IV

As republican Americans confronted the problems of revolution, war, and peace, the ideology they tried to live by told them one set of things about their world, but the reality they were building told them another. All good republicans knew that the first duty of a citizen was to forgo selfish interests and to seek the common good. But experience was teaching them over and over that the common good was elusive, and that if people did not assert themselves, they would be crushed. What they were learning and how they were learning it found its reflection in political action. In the 1760s and early 1770s, people rioted. As we have seen, one major justification for crowd risings was the belief that if rulers forgot the public good the people would remind them of it. In the late 1770s, people formed committees. These, too, rested on the ideological basis that a single public good existed and could be determined. But now there was a difference. Instead of rioting in the hope that rulers would set matters right, they acted like rulers themselves.

Within both crowd action and the committee movement,

the notion of a single, clear public good was on the decline. The imperial crisis demonstrated that the old pieties about Parliament protecting the interests of Englishmen everywhere were false. Being a colonial Briton in America and being a real Briton "at home" were just not the same. A similar lesson slowly emerged from the attempts at radical democracy that followed independence. Some Americans had their doubts about simple democracy from the beginning. The complexity and the balance that these people tried to put into the state constitutions were needed, they thought, to protect different kinds of people from one another. Paradoxically, radical democrats began to learn a very similar lesson. Using committee power to stem the economic crisis did not work. Partly it was that the crisis was too great. Partly it was that the interests of traders, consumers, and different kinds of producers not only were not the same; they did not even seem reconcilable.

These hard-learned lessons explain why a very different form of political action began to take shape in the 1780s: open, competitive partisanship. It would be an overstatement to say that a fully formed party system was in place by, say, 1785. There were no national or state committees, no carefully worked-out platforms, and very little orchestrated campaigning. In only one state, Pennsylvania, were there party labels that men proudly wore. There was not even any real understanding that party politics offered a way for people to get what they wanted. Parties were "the dangerous diseases of civil freedom, the first stage of anarchy, clothed in mild language." Voters should "distrust men of violent party spirit," for they "would wish to split the state into factions." "The sooner we can effectually destroy the Spirit of Party in Republican Governments, the more we shall promote the Happiness of Society," wrote one observer. Let there be a time "when all Party and Animosity will be absorbed in the general and Generous Sentiment of promoting the Common Good," said another. Practically every voter and every officeholder agreed: political parties were Bad Things.

But, by the mid 1780s, such talk was one matter and political reality was another. From Georgia to New England, people with interests in common were learning that they would do well to act together and that they could expect opposition from others who were unlike themselves. The process moved more quickly in some places, especially New York and Pennsylvania, and less quickly in others, especially Massachusetts. But it was under way everywhere.

It happened fastest in Pennsylvania. There the Constitutionalist Society and the Republican Society amounted to political parties as early as 1780. During the war years, the Constitutionalists were a continuation of the coalition that had overturned Pennsylvania's old leadership in 1776. The group included Philadelphia artisans, backcountry farmers, and self-conscious radical politicians. It even recruited a few members of the old elite who at first had opposed the constitution of 1776. The party had an ethnic and cultural dimension as well, for it drew a great deal of support from evangelical Germans and Scotch-Irish Presbyterians. The Republicans began as little more than the patriot wing of the old elite. But they gained support, first among former radical politicians like Benjamin Rush and then, more slowly, among Philadelphia's working people.

Without doubt, there was a class dimension to the contest. Both sides said so often enough. But how they understood the world was also important. The Constitutionalists tried to hold fast to the classical republican belief that in a good society the only real interest was the public interest. That meant, for them, the interest of the small producers and small consumers from whom they drew their support. For the Republicans, however, commerce was as much the way of the world as productivity. In their eyes, it was just as legitimate to seek wealth by manipulating money as it was to seek personal independence by producing food and objects people could use. In 1784, Benjamin Rush actually used the phrase "productive property of this state" to mean money for investment rather than tools or land or draft animals.

One of the largest immediate issues that divided the two was the Bank of North America. Chartered in 1781, under the aegis of Robert Morris, it was the first bank in the United States. It was also the perfect symbol of the aggressive, commercial society that Morris and his sympathizers wanted America to be. It was the perfect means of furthering the interests of people who were close to its directors and whose reputations and policies the directors approved. Among the enemies that the bank acquired were some men who disapproved of banks on principle, seeing "enormous wealth in the hands of a society who claim perpetual duration" as a danger to the republic. There were others who were simply envious, or perhaps angry because their own applications for loans were refused. In 1785, the bank's enemies won control of the legislature and they repealed the bank's charter. The bank promptly launched a campaign to reestablish itself, hiring Tom Paine to make its case. Its friends, the Republicans, won the election of 1786 and soon the bank was back in business.

The affair of the bank illustrates the way that Pennsylvania's party system was changing by the middle of the decade. It was not just that the Republicans and the bank recruited Paine. It was also that their case seemed more and more appealing. They understood far better than the Constitutionalists that there were many sorts of Pennsylvanians and that the state's future would have to be built on that fact. Self-assertion, not self-denial, would be the basis of people's lives. The Philadelphia leatherworkers began the shift when they refused in 1779 to support price controls, and now others were following. The result was that the Constitutionalists became more and more a party of inland farmers, without significant urban support. Farmers were still the vast majority of Pennsylvanians, but the tide was running against the Constitutionalists. By 1790, they would be finished as a political force.

Let us look in detail at only one other state, New York. There it took time for parties to develop. The social elements were much the same as in Pennsylvania: artisans and small farmers for whom the Revolution was a political awakening, and the mercantile, landholding, and professional elite. But conditions were different. With New York City occupied by the British until the end of 1783, neither merchants nor artisans had a base from which to operate. As a result, a coalition of freehold and tenant farmers became the democratic core. When New York City artisans entered state politics in 1784, their alliance with upstate radicals would be only tenuous. A second contrast was that the state's institutions never became an issue, for almost everyone accepted the constitution of 1777. Nor were New Yorkers as quick as the Pennsylvanians to develop party labels. Historians sometimes write of "Clintonians" and "Anti-Clintonians," referring to the central position that Governor George Clinton came to hold on the democratic side. Clinton was reelected to his office repeatedly through the war and Confederation years, and that would not have happened if he was not a politician of consummate skill. But people of the time never used his name as a political label. The earliest use of any label at all came in 1787, when a farmer-politician named Henry Oothoudt described his own side as "the Republican party." What he meant by it was nothing like what the Pennsylvania Republicans meant, and he was using the phrase in private correspondence.

Labels are one thing; consciousness and organization are another. Partisanship first began to develop in the state legislature in response to the issues that came to a head in 1779. Confiscating loyalist land, controlling prices, taxing by "circumstances and abilities"—these were all policies that hurt someone. The elite's response to the fact that it could not stop them was to pull away, but that only opened the way for more. In 1782, 1783, and the spring of 1784, dealing with the loyalists was the prime issue. Under farmer and artisan control, the legislature put a stay on all Tory suits against patriot debtors. It allowed disputes to be settled by referees drawn from the revolutionary side, rather than by court trials. It discharged all wartime interest and allowed payment in cheap paper currency rather than in specie. Patriots who had fled the New York City region could bring damage suits against people who had used their property, even if the British occupying forces had authorized its use. Loyalists were burdened with double taxes. Anyone who suspected anyone else of trading with the enemy could seize the property in question and bring the person to trial, hoping to win half of what had been seized for himself. "Zealous Friends" of the Revolution who had "done Acts . . . not conformable to the strict Letter of the Law" were protected from damage suits by their victims. An act "to preserve the Freedom and Independence of this State" disqualified from voting or holding office anyone who had aided the British. At the war's end, the liberated Southern counties found themselves burdened with a special tax as "a compensation to the other Districts" that had carried the long struggle through.

By the autumn of 1784, the issues were shifting from retribution to reconstruction. Most especially, the popular party sought to reform the old elite's institutions. Trinity Church, the immensely wealthy Anglican congregation in New York City, came under attack. So did the city's chamber of commerce and King's College, later renamed Columbia. The men who wanted to reform these institutions were also likely to favor granting a charter of incorporation that the artisans of New York City sought for themselves. These years also brought changes in how the state disposed of public land. Before independence, land operations had taken place behind closed doors, and getting in on them had been a gentleman's privilege. Now sales were open, on the basis of clear surveys, and only minimal fees were due to the officials involved. Gentleman's privilege had become citizen's opportunity.

But most of the state's gentlemen had little liking for what was going on. By the mid-1780s, they were beginning to return to state-level politics, with a view to putting an end to it. At their center stood Alexander Hamilton. His own ascent from obscurity into New York's aristocracy showed that by no means were the aristocrats a closed group. When Hamilton left the army in 1781, he began to look hard at the state's affairs. In the many essays that he wrote for publication, and in the long letters that he wrote to others who shared many of his views, he worked out an analysis and a program. He wanted the easy readmission of loyalists to citizenship, especially if they had money and trading connections. He wanted the market, not the state, to determine "the prices of all commodities." He wanted an end to the state's "radically vicious" system of taxing. Most of all, he called on "all those who have anything to lose" to take steps so that "the power of government" would be "intrusted to proper hands." "For their own defence," the "principal people" had "to endeavour to put men in the Legislature whose principles are not of the levelling kind."

Hamilton got a good part of what he wanted. People in sympathy with his policies organized. They set out to win popular support, and they succeeded in forcing some of the radical politicians out of the legislature. In so doing, they were laying the basis for the Federalist movement, not just in New York State, but to some extent in the whole country. The success of that movement was to be their great triumph, and we will look at how they achieved it in the next chapter. What is immediately important is the change in the way New Yorkers were going about their public affairs. The issues were real; so were the divisions; so was the transformation of public life. People had learned two lessons in the course of the Revolution. One, the lesson of radical democracy, was that the public arena belonged to everyone. The other, the lesson of emergent capitalism, was that to get what they wanted people would have to organize and compete.

New York and Pennsylvania are the two states where the new politics of the 1780s has been most fully studied. But the massive body of writing that the historian Jackson Turner Main has produced on the war years and the Confederation era demonstrates that what happened there was happening in most of the other states as well. New men poured into the state legislatures. They were veterans of popular committees, former crowd leaders, and militia officers who owed their rank to enlisted men's votes. They were farmers and artisans and small traders. They were men who had found themselves in the Revolution. Unsure neophytes at first, elected for the most part because they had proven themselves in the resistance movement, they gradually learned to work with one another, to speak with their own political voice, and to organize continuing popular support. Others who were unlike them also sought office and frequently won it, especially in the larger towns. By roughly 1786, one could tell from the roll-call votes of almost every legislature who was on which side. By about the same time, one could tell from what happened at the polls who would control the next session. The development of this politics of openly competing parties was not an accident. It grew out of trends and changes that had run through the whole Revolution. The same transformations would lie behind the way the federal Constitution brought the era to its end.

· 6 ·
One Republic

The creation of one republic out of thirteen colonies forms the last great drama of the Revolution. Just as we can mark the Revolution's beginning at 1765, when the people of the British provinces made it impossible to enforce Parliament's Stamp Act, so can we mark its end at 1787 and 1788, when the people of the American states accepted their federal Constitution. Events, it seems, had come almost full circle. Instead of Parliament, with its House of Lords and its House of Commons, there would be Congress, with its Senate and its House of Representatives. Instead of a king, there would be a president. Indeed, for as long as George III survived and George Washington wanted the office, both king and president would bear the same name. Had anything really changed? Had a quarter century of turmoil, disruption, and upheaval simply led the American people back to where they had begun?

One of the greatest and longest-running debates in the writing of American history has turned on those questions. Throughout the nineteenth century, most people who thought about the Revolution at all regarded the Constitution as its fitting result. The Founding Fathers, or Framers, who met in convention at Philadelphia to write it were the very men who had made the Revolution. There was George Washington, in the chair. There were Benjamin Franklin,

Alexander Hamilton, James Madison, John Dickinson, Gouverneur Morris, Robert Morris, and William Livingston among the members. Of the top American leaders, only a few, such as Thomas Jefferson and John and Samuel Adams, were absent. All three of them did, in fact, support ratification, though Sam Adams had his doubts for a while. George Bancroft drew the obvious conclusion in his enormous, and enormously influential, *History of the United States*: the Revolution had been a struggle to secure American liberty, and the Constitution was liberty's greatest protection.

But not everyone was so sure in 1787 and 1788. Rhode Island sent no delegates to the Convention at all, and along with North Carolina, it refused to ratify. Opinion ran heavily against the Constitution in much of Virginia and New York, and it seemed as if these states, too, would reject the document. In Massachusetts, South Carolina, New Hampshire, people were seriously divided. The historical geographer Orin Libby published maps in 1894 that showed how widespread opposition had been. His work transformed our understanding of how the republic came to be. No longer could the Constitution be taken as the Revolution's foregone conclusion. Instead, it was a problem to be solved. Two decades later, the historian Charles A. Beard set out to follow Libby's lead. Beard's book *An Economic Interpretation of the Constitution of the United States* became, in Jack Greene's words, "one of the half dozen most influential books ever written in American history." Taking the Founding Fathers down from their pedestal, Beard asked what they had stood to gain if the Constitution took effect. He examined the kinds of property they held, and he found that they owned a great many paper securities whose value had depreciated to almost nothing. The backing of a strong government determined to raise taxes and to pay off debts would raise the value of those securities. The case seemed proven. For Beard, the Constitution marked not much more than a triumph for men who were on their way to wealth at other men's expense.

Beard's argument opened up whole new dimensions of the history of the 1780s. For Bancroft, and for his nineteenth-century colleague John Fiske, the decade had been a disaster, "the critical period of American history." The Articles of Confederation, under which the country was governed until 1788, represented total political foolishness. State studies written in Beard's shadow chipped away at Bancroft's and Fiske's understanding of the Confederation years, and by the 1930s Beard's theory was the one taught in most American college classrooms. In 1940, Merrill Jensen published an account of the Articles that was very different from Fiske's, arguing that they, not the Constitution, represented the democratic spirit of 1776. In his book *The New Nation*, Jensen went on to examine the record of the 1780s and found that it was one of achievement, not one of failure. Jensen's student Jackson Turner Main has expanded that point in many different directions, beginning with his sympathetic account, *The Antifederalists*, and culminating with his reconstructions, *The Sovereign States* and *Political Parties Before the Constitution.*

But in the 1950s, Beard's work received a terrible pounding from historians whose goal was to stress the matters on which Americans had agreed rather than those about which they had argued. Most notably, Forrest McDonald used Beard's own methods to demonstrate that leading opponents of the Constitution had stood to gain as much from it as its leading supporters. With Beard's view seemingly demolished, other historians tried to create an alternative. Clinton Rossiter's *1787: The Grand Convention* put the Founding Fathers back on their pedestal. Stanley Elkins and Eric McKitrick found them to be the "Young Men of the Revolution," driven not by self-interest but by their own youthful energy and the frustrations they had known as congressmen, diplomats, and ranking army officers. John P. Roche turned them into modern politicians, men who understood the need for reform and who carefully calculated the best strategy for achieving it.

Yet Beard's voice remained alive. In the mid-1960s, Staughton Lynd baldly described New York's Federalist leaders as a "governing class on the defensive" and traced the interplay in the Constitution's making among owners of merchant capital, great landed estates, and large slave forces. Gordon Wood's massive, prize-winning *Creation of the American Republic* pays honor to Beard from another direction. Examining the intense political debates of the late 1770s and the 1780s, Wood finds that the Framers did indeed repudiate the democratic politics of 1776. In so doing, they created a lasting "American Science of Politics," rather than a financial windfall for themselves. But the debt to Beard is still apparent: the republic as we know it was born in disagreement and struggle, not in consensus and continuity.

On one matter Beard was certainly wrong: far more was going on than simple pocketbook calculation. As Lynd notes, what was under way was the settlement of a revolution, and it settled as it did because some men and some groups wanted it that way. What, then, led to this settlement? Who were the people who drove events? How did they diagnose their society's ills, and what cure did they prescribe? Most important, what kind of America did they want, and how did they convince others, people unlike themselves, to accept their diagnosis, their prescription, and at least a part of their vision?

I

With hindsight, we might easily say that the colonies moving toward independence and the states traveling toward the Constitution were both following clearly marked roads. The milestones and the intersections seem perfectly visible, and each destination seems certain. In fact, the metaphor deceives as much as it helps. Both roads led people into territory that was not even explored, let alone well mapped. We cannot understand independence without understanding the anxiety, the turmoil, and the fear arising from the Stamp Act, the Townshend taxes, the Boston Tea Party, and the outbreak of war. Similarly, we cannot understand the Constitution without understanding the major points of conflict and crisis that lay between 1776 and 1788.

When the Continental Congress appointed a committee to draft a declaration of independence, it named two others of equal importance. One had the task of beginning the new nation's foreign policy and especially of seeking aid and recognition. Its great success came in 1777, when it found both in France. The other's responsibility was to establish a firm, enduring basis for the union of the independent states. The result was the Articles of Confederation. The committee presented its draft of the Articles to Congress in 1777, and the document was finally accepted by the separate states in 1781.

The Articles gave legal form to the structure that events had already thrown together. "The United States in Congress Assembled" was the official title of the central body. Though a state might send as many delegates as it pleased, it enjoyed only one vote. Congress had some of the qualities of a national government, but in other ways it was more like an alliance of sovereign republics. The Articles gave it alone the power to make war and peace, and it was in Congress's name that a peace was finally negotiated with Britain in 1783. To that extent, the states were one nation, dealing with other nations as equals. But Congress had no power to tax, and no power to enforce its will. It might levy requisitions on the states, but they could pay or not pay as they chose. It might insist that its own decisions and the treaties its envoys made overrode state law, but state, not federal courts, would decide whether that really was so. It took the votes of nine states to make major decisions of policy. It took the consent of the legislatures of all thirteen to change the Articles in any way. To prevent congressmen from becoming a separate caste, no person could be a member for more than three years in a row. A state legislature could recall a delegate whenever it might choose. Were these men representatives? Were they ambassadors? No one could really be sure.

One major reason why the states took so long to accept the Articles was the problem of Western lands. Some states, Virginia most of all, had inherited British grants that stretched from sea to sea. Others, like Pennsylvania, were limited by clearly established western boundaries. At the very end of the colonial period, Virginia and Pennsylvania had been in sharp dispute over the upper Ohio Valley. Still other states, such as Connecticut, had *both* fixed boundaries *and* remote claims in the West. States without a hold on the West were jealous of states that had one. States claimed ownership and even jurisdiction over land that lay within the boundaries of others. Speculators everywhere scrambled for advantage in this battle of ambiguities. In 1781, the main issue was finally resolved, when the states with sea-to-sea colonial charters surrendered their claims to Congress. The effect was twofold. A major reason for contention between the separate states had come to an end. Congress, agent for the people of all the states, became the owner of the vast domain that lay in the interior. Whatever its relationship to the seaboard states, Congress now was sovereign over the West, provided that the British, who had troops there, and the Indians, who had their own way of life there, agreed.

The British agreed in principle two years later, when their agents signed the Treaty of Paris that ended the war. The treaty conceded not just the independence of the thirteen original states but also American control over virtually the whole region south of the Great Lakes and east of the Mississippi. Only Florida, the southern parts of what are now Alabama and Mississippi, and the region around New Orleans were excluded. Gone was the Proclamation Line. Gone was control over the Mississippi Valley by Quebec. Gone was the British support that had enabled Indians like the Iroquois Confederacy of New York, the Hurons and Wyandottes to the West, and the Cherokees, the Creeks, and the Choctaws in the South to stave off settlers who wanted to invade their land.

The result was an explosion of westward migration. New Englanders spilled into western New York, and New Yorkers and Pennsylvanians pushed into Ohio. Virginians crossed the Blue Ridge into what we know as Kentucky, and Carolinians began crossing the Great Smokies into Tennessee. Problems rapidly emerged: how would these people be governed; what basis would they have for titles to their land; what would their relationship be to Congress and the original thirteen states?

In effect, the newly freed former colonies faced a colonial problem of their own. They rapidly resolved it by accepting the principle that new states might join the first thirteen and by establishing procedures to allow them to do so. Pressure from below as well as statesmanship from above was responsible. Vermont, which held on to its independence despite the fact that neither Congress nor its former masters in New York would recognize it, could not be ignored. Nor could the abortive attempt to establish a "State of Franklin" west of the Carolinas. Congress never had any real say in either the Green Mountains or the emergence of Kentucky and Tennessee. But in a series of "Northwest Ordinances" it established principles for the development of territory that it did control.

The first ordinance grew from a proposal by Thomas Jefferson to create ten new states. He wanted to call them Sylvania, Michigania, Cherronesus, Assenisipia, Metropotamia, Illinoia, Washington, Saratoga, Polypotamia, and Pelisipia. For once, Jefferson's pen had failed him, and the names were rapidly abandoned. The principle, however, remained. In its final form, the Northwest Ordinance of 1784 provided for the temporary government of Western "territories" whose settlers would have the right to call conventions, make their own constitutions, and eventually be ad-

mitted "into . . . the United States, on an equal footing with
the original states." Three years later, another Northwest
Ordinance changed some of the details and procedures and
forbade slavery north of the Ohio River. But the principle
that was established in 1784 governed the admission of new
states down to the entry of Hawaii and Alaska in the middle
of this century. A third ordinance, passed in 1785, established
the way that Congress and later the federal government
would dispose of the Western lands. It ordered the creation
of square townships, six miles on a side, each to be divided
into thirty-six lots of one square mile each. Half the townships would be sold whole, and the other half in lots. The
effect was threefold. It established the grid pattern of freehold farms along which much of the West would be developed. It gave Congress the hope of income independent
of whatever the separate states might appropriate. It established Congress's working ownership and sovereignty over a
region considerably larger than the New England and Middle
Atlantic states.

The Treaty of Paris placed other responsibilities on Congress. The British negotiators had been insistent that loyalists
be subjected to no further punishment and that penalties
already imposed be revoked. The American diplomats—
John Jay, Benjamin Franklin, and John Adams—knew that
neither they nor Congress could promise so much, for the
states alone made loyalist policy. The final treaty was a
compromise: it bound Congress to "earnestly recommend"
that the states confiscate no more Tory property and that
they return confiscated property if the loyalist owners had
not actually taken up arms. It was an empty formula. Con-
fiscations tapered off, but they were fewer because the passions of the war years wound down, not because of the treaty.
Returning property already seized was out of the question,
for both large-scale speculators and ordinary people had a
direct stake in preventing it. Congress may have been sovereign over its Western lands, but its treaty commitments meant

nothing if they conflicted with the policies of the original states.

Congress also ran into trouble on matters of revenue. Throughout the war years, it had to get by with its depreciating paper, with whatever the states might grant it, and with aid from the French and loans from the Dutch. It never could raise enough. The supply and pay of the army were always a disgrace, whether we look at the early campaigns, at the misery of Valley Forge and Morristown, or at the final encampment at Newburgh, New York, in 1783, before the army disbanded. When the army did break up, its men took with them pay for only one month in coin and for two months more in certificates. Small wonder that the entire contingents of the states of Pennsylvania and New Jersey broke into open mutiny in January 1781, that a band of soldiers marched on Congress in June 1783, and that hotheaded officers in the Newburgh encampment toyed with the notion of a *coup d'état*.

George Washington must be given a great deal of credit for the fact that the threats of military takeover faded. He repressed the enlisted men's mutinies sharply, and when he learned that his officers were gathering to discuss their discontents, he preempted the meeting and held it to a republican agenda. The states, in turn, began in mid-decade to take responsibility for paying what Congress owed their citizens. But an immense debt was still owed overseas, and Congress did not have enough revenue even to pay the interest, let alone the principal. Three times—in 1782, 1783, and 1786—Congress tried to solve the problem by asking the states to let it collect duties, or "imposts," on goods arriving in American ports. Three times, the proposal failed. Rhode Island said no in 1782, and New York refused on the two other occasions. Both were states where opposition to the movement for the Constitution would be strong.

New York, in particular, had everything to lose if the impost was granted. Its great harbor at the mouth of the

Hudson was the port of entry for northern New Jersey and western Connecticut, and the state collected duties on all goods that came in, whatever their final destination. That had happy consequences for the tax bills of its own citizens, but ill ones for its relations with its neighbors and with Congress. With no sure revenue to pay foreign debts, Congress faced a world of diplomacy and international finance that treated it with little more than contempt. The severe depression that fell on the North Atlantic market in the war's aftermath only made matters worse. In no way was it Congress's fault, and it began to lift well before the Constitution was written, but to people who felt its effects, the link between economic depression and the political order seemed unmistakable.

By 1785 or 1786, few people with political awareness would have denied that the Articles of Confederation needed serious change. By then, even fewer held any hope that change could come by the legal means that the Articles prescribed, originating in Congress and winning the acceptance of all thirteen legislatures. The repeated failures to secure an independent revenue were evidence enough. Many observers drew the parallel between a single state's ability to block any change and the "liberum veto," which allowed a single member of the Polish nobility to block any policy that displeased him. The infant United States did not have Poland's misfortune of sharing borders with Russia, Prussia, and Austria-Hungary. But the British still ruled north of the St. Lawrence, and despite the Treaty of Paris, they would occupy forts that were legally American until well into the next decade. The Spanish Empire, sprawling to the south and west, was weak, but who was to say that it would not regain its vigor? Neither power was friendly to the United States, and no one with any sense wanted to take a chance on sharing Poland's unhappy fate. Some other route to change would have to be found.

The first steps were taken in 1785, when commissioners from the states of Virginia and Maryland met at Mount Vernon, the home of George Washington. Their immediate subject was the river that flowed almost past their feet, for if navigation on the Potomac was to be developed in any way, Virginians and Marylanders would have to do it together. However, from the beginning, some had a larger purpose in mind, and the main result of the conference was a call for delegates from all the states to meet the next year at Annapolis, the capital of Maryland. Their task would be to discuss the commercial problems that the whole country faced.

Despite the halo of patriotism and prestige that hung over Mount Vernon and its owner, only five states responded to the call. But New York and Virginia were among them, and thus Alexander Hamilton and James Madison were among the delegates who gathered at Annapolis in September 1786. Over the next two years, Hamilton and Madison would form one of the most effective political partnerships in the history of the United States. Though they were later to separate, that in no way detracts from what they accomplished then. Each had been preparing himself for years for the task that he knew lay ahead. Each worked out a detailed analysis of what was wrong, and each had clear ideas about what was to be done. Neither was prepared to let wishful thinking or received wisdom interfere with his conclusions. Each was not only an incisive thinker and a masterful writer but also a skilled politician, adept at the art of timing moves and arranging alliances.

Their first step toward getting what they wanted was to convince the Annapolis meeting to step beyond its brief. The meeting assembled with the task of improving American commerce. It broke up with a call for a convention that would propose amendments to the Articles of Confederation. It would meet the next year in Philadelphia. If no more states sent delegates than had responded to the call for the Annapolis meeting, the project would be doomed. So the men behind the call persuaded Congress to second it, and then set out to make sure they would be present themselves. Already, suspicions were rising. Alexander Hamilton got himself elected to the New York state assembly so he would be in a position to go. The legislature agreed that he should be a delegate, but it also sent Robert Yates and John Lansing. Both were politically at odds with Hamilton, and both numbered among the many New Yorkers who had no faith either that a strong central government could work or that one was needed. Their task was to keep Hamilton in check.

The Convention assembled with twelve of the thirteen states represented. Rhode Island's absence was, in fact, a victory for the men who wanted change; it meant that one certain center of opposition would have no voice in Philadelphia at all. The makeup of the Convention marked another triumph. There were a few men present—Yates, Lansing, Luther Martin of Maryland—who had fundamental suspicions about what was going on, and there were some others who decided afterward that they did not like what the Convention had done. But in no way was their number proportionate to the people who would be doubtful when it came time to ratify. For the most part, the Convention's members agreed that thoroughgoing political change was needed if the country's immense problems were to be resolved. It was because they already agreed on so much that they could also agree to meet in secret, so they could argue out their differences among themselves and then show a single face to the world. In terms of democratic political practice, it was a long step backward, for one change the Revolution had brought was the end of just such secrecy among the rulers of the states. But from the point of view of the Convention's ability to get things done, that secrecy was an immense benefit.

When the Convention assembled in June, Madison was ready to seize the initiative. He had worked out "amendments" to the Articles which, in effect, eliminated the Articles themselves and started once again from the beginning. The first step in this Virginia Plan was to end the possibility that one state's veto could prevent any change at all, no matter how much the other states might want it. That was accomplished by taking an initial resolution that the new Constitution be submitted not to the state legislatures but rather "to an assembly or assemblies of Representatives, recommended by the state legislatures to be expressly chosen by the people, to consider & decide thereon." The original proposal said nothing about unanimity, and the final draft required the approval of only nine of the thirteen states. A nay-sayer or two might remain outside, but it would take at least five states to keep the "amendments" from going into effect.

The substantive changes that the Virginia Plan proposed were truly sweeping. In its original version, it would have established a central government considerably more powerful than the one that the United States Constitution eventually created. There would have been a two-house legislature, with the lower house elected by the people and the upper house chosen by the lower. A chief executive and judges for the courts would have been chosen by both. The states would have been reduced to little more than administrative units, for the central government was to have the power to veto acts of their legislatures and to interfere directly in cases where the "states are incompetent or in which the harmony of the United States may be interrupted." If necessary, the government would even have been able to use military force to make a state conform.

These proposals set the terms of debate for the whole summer. The Convention's task would be to propose sweeping changes, not to offer piecemeal amendments. Hamilton, in fact, wanted to go well beyond the Virginia Plan, and in a six-hour speech he called for a government centered on a monarch elected for life. None of the other delegates took him seriously. But many did listen carefully when William Paterson of New Jersey offered a plan which was much closer than Madison's to the existing state of affairs. In it, Congress would remain as it was under the Articles but would be given the right to raise its own revenue and to control interstate and foreign commerce. It would have the power as well to elect "a federal Executive" and to appoint a federal judiciary, and its acts and treaties would be "the supreme law of the respective states."

Madison's proposals and Paterson's New Jersey Plan defined the limits of debate for the rest of the summer. The central problem was not whether to give the government more power; almost everyone in the Convention agreed that that was necessary. It was in the New Jersey Plan that the phrase "supreme law" was first used to describe how treaties and federal law would stand in relation to the laws of the states. Neither Paterson nor Madison wanted to see a continuation of one state's ability to embarrass the republic overseas by frustrating treaty obligations. Rather, the question was what, or who, would be represented in the federal legislature. If Madison's plan won, the central government would be truly national, for it would owe its power to direct election by the people. But a victory for Paterson's proposals would mean that it would remain genuinely federal, deriving its authority through the states rather than from the people themselves. The states would continue to be sovereign corporate entities. The problem of whether Congress's members were ambassadors from the states or representatives of the people would remain unresolved. As Madison put it in response to Paterson's move, "the great difficulty lies in the affair of Representation; and if this could be adjusted, all others would be surmountable."

By 1787, the revolutionary generation had grown used to arguments about political representation. Now three separate dimensions of the problem intersected: population, wealth, and the corporate existence of the states. None was easily resolved. If simple numbers became the basis of representation, the smaller states effectively would be eliminated as political forces. Moreover, the reason that Virginia was by far the largest state and that South Carolina, North Carolina, and Maryland stood well up on the population table was the presence in each of many slaves. State law regarded those blacks as not much more than objects, liable to punishment but lacking almost every legal right that a free citizen enjoyed. For purposes of federal law, were they to be counted nonetheless as full human beings? To many Northern delegates, the notion seemed preposterous, for the law itself gave the slaves no political identity or will. The reality was that counting slaves among those to be represented would mean nothing more than recognizing the special interests of the owners of one particular form of wealth.

One state constitution after another had tried to find a way of giving special representation to wealth. But none of the schemes had proved to be successful, and the more insightful members of the Convention knew that there was not much point in further experiment. Madison, a sizable slaveholder himself, tried to skate over the issue by suggesting that for one house of the national legislature only free people be represented but that, in the other, representation be "according to the whole number counting the slaves as if free." But Gouverneur Morris pointed out that if the Convention accepted one special interest it would have to accept others. New England, with its fisheries, and the middle states, with their commerce, were just as central to America's economic life as the South, with its slaves. Morris was not an anti-slavery zealot, but he did find human bondage distasteful, and he understood how anomalous it would be if slavery were to enjoy representation. Both the great flaw in republican American society and the line of stress along which the political fabric would finally rip apart lay bare, for the whole Convention to see.

In 1787, unlike 1861, compromise was possible. The New Jersey Plan had already pointed the way with a proposal that three-fifths of the enslaved population be counted for purposes of requisitions on the states, should the federal government have to make them. This, in fact, drew on a policy that Congress had used, at James Madison's own suggestion, as early as 1783. In mid-July, Connecticut's three delegates used it to work out a way around the problem, proposing to make this three-fifths rule the basis of representation in the lower house. This would be joined to an upper house in which all the states would enjoy equal weight, regardless of size or wealth. The proposal met heavy resistance. On the first attempt to count three-fifths of the blacks, only four state delegations voted yes and six voted no. It may be that Gouverneur Morris spoke for many Northerners when he declared that he was "reduced to the dilemma of doing injustice to the Southern States or to human nature, and he must therefore do it to the former." Madison put the central issue, telling the Convention that "it seemed now to be pretty well understood that the real difference of interests lay, not between the large & small but between the N. & South^n States. The institution of slavery & its consequences formed the line of discrimination." But on July 16 the Convention accepted Connecticut's proposal. Both the tension between large and small states and the tension between North and South had simply disappeared. How did this come about?

There is no absolutely conclusive evidence, but the answer seems to be that during the second and third weeks of July not one but several agreements were worked out. Staughton Lynd has suggested that the real compromise was not over any particular issue, but rather with the great principle of 1776 that "all men are created equal." There can be no doubt that the Constitution gave a special protection to slavery that it gave to no other single interest. The first step came on July 12, when the Convention reconsidered the three-fifths formula and decided to accept it by six ayes, two nays, with two state delegations divided. The states that changed from nay to aye were Pennsylvania and Maryland. The ones that changed from nay to divided were Massachusetts, which had been against any representation for slavery at all, and South Carolina, which had hoped to see its many slaves count for representation as the equals of free men. Other steps came later, as the Convention included a clause to assist masters of runaways and another to forbid interfering with the slave trade for twenty years.

The slaveholders had won enormous gains, but they had to pay a price. It may be, as Lynd has argued, that they paid it not in the Convention but elsewhere. The day after the Convention adopted the three-fifths compromise, "the Continental Congress, meeting in New York City, adopted the Northwest Ordinance," with its clause forbidding slavery north of the Ohio River. As Lynd admits, there is no absolute proof that the two actions were tied together. But considerable circumstantial evidence does suggest that that was so. What is certain from the records of the Convention is that the tide of regional tension which had been running so high suddenly ebbed. It took only four days to move from the three-fifths compromise to the compromise on the structure of the Senate and the House.

With the matter of representation worked out, other questions proved to be less contentious. No one doubted that there should be an executive and a judiciary, but how to choose them caused some headaches. Madison's original idea, that the executive be chosen by the two houses of Congress together, was only a point of departure. By July, he was arguing that "if it be essential to the preservation of liberty that the Legisl: Execut: & Judiciary power be separate, it is essential . . . that they should be independent of each other," and that "the Executive could not be independent of the Legislure, if dependent on the pleasure of that branch." He made that point when it was still thought that the legislature would elect the executive, speaking against a proposal that the executive be eligible for reelection. But his logic pointed just as readily toward having it derive its power directly from the people, in the manner of the governorships of New York and Massachusetts. The actual method of electing the president, by electors chosen in the states, was devised by a small committee that was appointed late in the Convention's life

to deal with "postponed matters." As John Roche has suggested, the Electoral College was "merely a jerry-rigged
improvisation." The Convention itself expected that the
college would fail to deliver a majority "nineteen times in
twenty" and the House of Representatives would normally
be the place where the president would be chosen.

By mid-August, the Convention was well on the way to
completing its work. At the end of the month an eleven-man
committee was named to deal with all unfinished business,
and on September 8 a five-man committee was appointed to
give the document a final polish. It included Madison and
Hamilton, but the main task was done by Gouverneur Morris,
and the committee presented its report on September 12.
Finally, on September 17, after a last round of speeches, the
members signed the document and adjourned. As they were
on the point of dissolution, Benjamin Franklin drew the
attention of members nearby to an image of the sun that was
painted on the chair Washington had occupied. He had
often looked at it, he said, "without being able to tell whether
it was rising or setting: But now at length I have the happiness to know that it is a rising and not a setting Sun." With
that, the Convention offered the nation its work.

II

What the Convention had done was illegal by any standard
that held when it first assembled. Its first illegality was the
decision to bypass the whole procedure that the Articles
themselves specified for their own amendment. Its second
was the delegates' decision to abandon their assignment of
proposing amendments and draft a whole new document.
Linked to that was its assumption that the Convention had
the right to speak for the whole nation. "We the People of
the United States of America" begins the Constitution's
preamble. But, in fact, the delegates had gone to Philadelphia
to represent their separate states, and they had voted in the

Convention on the basis of state equality. As opposition to
ratifying the Constitution took shape, many a critic, including some people who ended up supporting ratification,
noticed these points. "I confess, as I enter the Building, I
stumble at the threshold," was how Samuel Adams put it.

Anticipating such objections, the Convention did its best
to bow in the direction of the dying confederation. On
September 10, Elbridge Gerry of Massachusetts had announced his objections "to proceeding to change the government without the approbation of Congress," and Alexander
Hamilton, of all people, concurred. He proposed that "the
plan should be sent to Congress in order that the same, if
approved by them, may be communicated to the State Legislatures, to the end that they may refer it to State Conventions." It was window dressing, for nothing could hide the
fact that the Convention had far exceeded its mandate. In
Hamilton's case, it was outright hypocrisy, since no one held
the confederation Congress in greater contempt. But it was
also smart politics, the first step toward turning the Convention's work from a proposal into the "supreme law of the
land."

Congress cooperated, resolving unanimously to send the
Constitution to the states. At least, the opposition would not
be able to claim that the Convention had wholly ignored
Congress. Then the men behind it set out to make the state
conventions ratify the document. Understanding the importance of momentum, they saw to it that the first states to
convene their conventions were ones that were certain to be
in favor. States that were highly commercial, that were weak
in the existing order, or that had been badly ravaged during
the war were likely to favor a strong new government, and
Delaware, New Jersey, and Georgia each fitted at least one
of those descriptions. The conventions of all three ratified
by unanimous votes, the first two before 1787 was out, and
the third on the second day of the new year. Pennsylvania
also ratified rapidly, by a margin of two convention votes in

favor for every one against. The victory reflected the strength that the state's "Republican" party enjoyed. It marked a repudiation of the radical democracy of 1776 as much as a vote for a stronger central government. Connecticut followed, by an overwhelming margin. It had everything to gain from a central government that would help it escape New York's economic and political shadow. Maryland and South Carolina took longer, not ratifying until the end of April and late May respectively. But in neither was the outcome in doubt. The margin in Maryland's convention was 63 to 11, and in South Carolina's, 149 to 73. With ratification readily accomplished in seven states, only two more were needed to make the new government a reality.

One of them, Massachusetts, had in fact already come into the fold, but ratification did not come easily to it. The margin of victory was narrow, with a final tally of 187 in favor and 168 against. During the months before the ratifying convention, newspapers carried essay after essay on both sides of the question. The debate went on not only in the Boston press but also in inland sheets like the *Worcester Magazine* and the *Connecticut Courant*, which had a large Massachusetts readership. Its convention divided on roughly the same line of stress that had run through Massachusetts life for a decade, but prominent men from the coastal towns joined inland farmers in having their doubts. Among those prominent men were Sam Adams and Governor John Hancock; between them, they probably had enough power to tilt the balance against ratification. That would have been disastrous for the Federalist movement. The men who wanted the Constitution had to avert the possibility of an alliance between westerners and such eastern waverers. The convention dragged interminably, examining the Constitution line by line. While the delegates debated, supporters of ratification put all the pressure they could on Adams and Hancock.

For Adams, the deciding element was the decision of Boston's artisans to support the Constitution. We will look later at what the artisans did and how they did it. In Hancock's case, it was vanity. He was offered the chance to propose amendments to the Constitution, and he began to hear hints that he was the logical choice for vice-president. Should Virginia not ratify and George Washington thus not be eligible, he might be the right man for the presidency itself. He and Adams both swung, and Massachusetts ratified.

Only one more state was needed, but whether it would be found was by no means certain. Rhode Island clearly would not ratify, and North Carolina elected a convention that was overwhelmingly hostile. Virginia was split, and when New Yorkers voted, they chose 46 delegates against the Constitution and only 19 in favor of it. Had either of those major states rejected the Constitution in the spring, the whole project might have been lost. But, in both, the conventions debated well into the summer. That gave the Constitution's supporters their chance to turn the question from whether there would be a republic to whether Virginia or New York would have a part in it.

They found their chance in New Hampshire. The state had all the makings of a stronghold of opposition. It was remote; its way of life was essentially noncommercial; it had no Great Men to throw their influence behind the Constitution; it had suffered little during the war; unlike Connecticut, Delaware, and New Jersey, it did not live in the economic shadow of a powerful neighbor. Not surprisingly, when its people elected their convention, they instructed it not to ratify. When the convention met in the dead of winter, it followed instructions. Had matters rested there, no United States might ever have existed. The convention did not, however, actually reject the Constitution. Instead, it adjourned until June, without taking a final decision. That gave the state's people a chance to reconvene their town meetings and decide whether they wanted their instructions to stand. Supporters of the Constitution set out to change New Hampshire's stance. They raised the issue in town meetings. Planning intensively for the day when the convention reassembled, they linked New Hampshire into a communications network that stretched south to New York and Virginia. Now the Constitution's friends in all three conventions would know what the others were doing. According to historian Forrest McDonald, the New Hampshire convention finally ratified on an afternoon when men in favor of the Constitution had gotten a number of their opponents drunk enough at lunch to miss the session. Whether or not that is so, New Hampshire's decision on June 21 established that the Constitution would go into effect.

That still left New York and Virginia. Each was vital, for reasons of wealth, of population, of strategic location, and of the political importance of its leaders. Each had powerful forces and well-known men publicly opposed to ratifying. Among these were Virginians Patrick Henry, Richard Henry Lee, and George Mason, and New York's governor, George Clinton. By the time their conventions met, opponents of the Constitution had finally learned the necessity of organization, and they had a well-coordinated structure of committees in operation. It was centered on Clinton and his political ally John Lamb. These men, too, had couriers ready to ride between Portsmouth, Poughkeepsie, and Richmond, where the three conventions sat; but in the end, they were outflanked.

One reason was the array of talent and prestige that the Constitution's supporters mobilized. Washington, Madison, George Wythe, Hamilton, Robert R. Livingston, and John Jay topped the list. A second reason was sheer hard politics. At one point in the Virginia convention, Madison so thoroughly demolished a claim by Patrick Henry that Jefferson, absent in France, opposed the Constitution that Henry was left looking like either a liar or a fool. In New York, there came a point when Hamilton openly threatened to separate New York City, which supported the Constitution, from the rest of the state, which did not.

Two other elements proved equally important. One was the quality of argument in the Constitution's favor. Whether major political decisions ever turn on purely intellectual conviction may be doubtful, but it is the case that the campaign in New York generated some of the most sophisticated political writing in American history. It emerged as *The Federalist,* a series of eighty-five essays that Madison, Hamilton, and Jay produced between October 1787 and August 1788. Addressed "To the People of the State of New York" and signed by "Publius," *The Federalist* was a masterpiece. Its title marked the capture of high ground by its authors. Logically, the term came closer to describing the Constitution's enemies than its friends; emotionally, "Federalist" was an extremely positive word in the language of the time. Yet, by making it their own, the Constitution's supporters forced its enemies onto the defensive. They thrust about, looking for a word of equal power to describe themselves. "Anti-Federal" was the label most of them ended with, but it could not help sounding simply negative. Others, such as "Democratic Federalist" or "Federal Republican" or "Impartial Examiner" or the now antiquated "Son of Liberty," simply did not work. The Federalists, as we now call them, had seized a symbol that had every possible political virtue.

The other element in their victory came with their handling of the issue of amendments to their document. Opponents of the Constitution had different reasons for wanting to see it changed. For some, it offered a way to reconvene the Convention and raise once again all the issues that the Federalists had thought were finally resolved. Others understood that ratification with conditions could amount to the same thing as no ratification at all; it was exactly the same trick that New York's legislature had used in 1786 to stem the drive for an independent revenue for Congress. There were others who were happy with a great deal of what the Constitution offered and who simply wanted some tinkering and additions. One of the most common objections was that, unlike most of the state constitutions, the federal document had no bill of rights.

The issue of amendments became most pressing in Virginia and New York. In both states, the Federalists averted the disaster of a ratification with conditions. What they secured instead was an unconditional ratification, combined with a strong statement of each convention's desire to see the Constitution modified. Virginia's instrument of ratification called for a lengthy bill of rights and for a series of changes in the document itself. New York's declared that the state's ratification was "in full confidence" that the amendments which it proposed would "receive an early and mature Consideration." It called on the state's "Representatives . . . to Exert all their Influence, and use all reasonable means to obtain" a long series of changes. In both cases, the formula came very close to the position of some Anti-Federalists, while retaining all that the Federalists needed. In both, other opponents remained unconvinced. But, in both, enough men with objections were mollified to make ratification possible. Eleven states were in, and Rhode Island and North Carolina found soon enough that they had no real choice about joining as well. The Anti-Federalists had lost, and opposition to the Constitution dissolved, but it was they who pointed strenuously to the need for a bill of rights as a protection for citizens against the government. That such a bill was swiftly adopted in the form of the first ten amendments to the Constitution is owing largely to them.

With the Constitution's acceptance, the political revolution was over. Where a seemingly solid but in fact deeply flawed British Empire had stood, there was now a republic, itself of imperial dimensions. As the subsequent century would show, it was a republic with an immense capacity for growth and development. However, as this narrative suggests, it was by no means certain even as late as the spring of 1788 that there would be any such republic at all. If the story of the Federalists' victory constitutes the Revolution's last great drama, understanding why it happened presents the Revolution's last great problem.

III

We can begin to understand if we compare the Constitution with what went before. The contrast with the Articles of Confederation is obvious, but Gordon Wood and J. R. Pole have shown that the real frame of reference lies in the states. The Framers wrote a document that bore a strong resemblance to the New York constitution of 1777 and to the Massachusetts constitution of 1780. Like them, it provided for an executive that would be much more than simply a means for carrying out the legislature's will. Like them, it established a legislature of two houses, roughly equal in power and neither dependent on the other. Like the Massachusetts constitution, it rested its claim to legitimacy on having been written by a special convention and then ratified in a manner that approached a popular decision. The Constitution was most emphatically a republican document. It established a political order that came as close as possible to having its basis in the consent of the people whom the government would rule.

But even by the standards of the day, it was not democratic. Consent is not the same as involvement, and the Constitution aimed to limit involvement, not to encourage it. The president would owe his power to the people. But the Electoral College and possibly the House of Representatives would stand between them. The senators would owe their office to the state governments, not to direct election. That and their six-year terms would give them considerable immunity from popular pressure. Because there would be only two from each state, it was a fair prediction that only a man of considerable prominence could hope to win a seat. Even the

House of Representatives was a far remove from the state assemblies. Initially, it would have only sixty-five members, making it not much more than a quarter the size of the assembly of Massachusetts. The House would represent constituencies as large as thirty thousand people, which was nearly the population of the whole state of Delaware. Like would-be senators, aspiring congressmen would have to have considerable local visibility.

Wherever these men met to do their business, it would be far from where most of the people they represented lived. Though the journals of the two houses would be published, there would be little of the close, almost day-to-day observation of what the legislators were doing that had become possible in some of the states. The two-year term of the representatives would be twice as long as the terms of most state assemblymen. Again and again, the framers of the state constitutions had insisted that the representative assemblies should closely reflect the people of the state itself. Again and again they had insisted that officeholders should never forget that they were only the people's servants, and that political practices should keep them from becoming a separate caste. But, under the Constitution, representatives, senators, and the president all would know that exceptional was just what they were. The methods of their election, the size of their constituencies, and the lengths of their terms all served to insulate them from what "the people" might want.

During the confederation years, "exceptional men" had had a rough time in political terms. What Jackson Turner Main has called the "democratization of the legislatures" meant that artisans, small traders, farmers, and men with mud on their boots had come to power. They had passed tax laws, Tory laws, currency laws, land laws, debt laws, and a host of other laws that worked against the material, the social, and the economic interests of the old colonial upper class. To a large extent, what they did also worked against the interests of modernizers, developers, and men of new money. The elder Charles Carroll ranted on about the evil policies of Maryland's wartime legislature, and Robert Livingston, Jr., lord of the manor that bore his name, did the same in New York. Though both had chosen the Revolution, each was a living symbol of what once had been. But Robert Morris and Alexander Hamilton, harbingers of the new capitalism, were equally appalled. The Pennsylvania assembly annulled the charter of Morris's Bank of North America because the bank seemed a threat to all that a republic should be. But, for Morris and his friends, the bank was necessary to create the kind of society they wanted.

The final straw was Shays' Rebellion. Though this rising of Massachusetts farmers was brief and easily suppressed, it exposed a line of stress that ran through all the states. Would independent America be organized around law, contract, and the needs of large-scale commerce? Or would it be organized around custom and the needs of local community? Put another way, could a republic survive if it had within it interests that were in fundamental conflict? Men of property and commerce in Massachusetts had taken every step to guarantee both that their republican government would be stable and that it would protect them and their needs. Now it seemed that even the most careful arrangements could achieve neither of those goals.

Here, then, was one social driving force behind Federalism. Men with land, men with fortunes, men with visions of development and wealth, men with far-flung connections, men with memories of the surety with which their fathers had ruled, all these were developing the distaste for state-level democracy on which Federalism fed. In Pennsylvania, they had been working together for a decade and they called themselves Republicans. In Massachusetts, they were the men of commerce in the port towns. They had won a great victory in 1780, and they understood the relentless logic of the Atlantic market, but by 1787 neither their victory nor their logic seemed to count. In New York, they were the urban merchants and professionals and the upstate landlords who came together in response to the legislature's mid-1780s radicalism. In South Carolina, they were men used to power who bemoaned the loss of the "harmony we were famous for." In Maryland, they were the planters who had written the arch-conservative constitution of 1776.

But not all of Federalism's support can be explained in those terms. For men who had experienced the Revolution at the center of affairs and in the highest offices, Congress and the states alike were simply the components of a nightmare. To men who had had to raise military supplies, it seemed that the policy of the states had been "to starve the army at pleasure." To diplomats who had served the new nation abroad, the way the states frustrated the treaty of 1783 was a disgrace. To men who had been colonels and generals in the Continental Army, it seemed that their own heroism and dedication simply had been taken for granted. The popular outcry against "aristocracy" when former officers tried to organize themselves into the Society of the Cincinnati was evidence enough. To men who had spent the war in Congress, struggling endlessly to win cooperation from states that would not give it, it was in the states that the fault lay.

Let the case of Alexander McDougall of New York illustrate the point. McDougall had been a popular street leader before independence. John Lamb, his comrade of those days, was at the center of organized Anti-Federalism in 1788. McDougall's broadside of 1769, "To the Betrayed Inhabitants of the City and Colony of New-York," brought him an extended and highly publicized imprisonment at the hands of the colonial assembly. His defiance when the assembly called him before it led one member to threaten him with the "long, hard penalty" of being crushed to death with rocks. In 1773, when the tea crisis was impending, he baited the cautious lawyer and council member William Smith by proposing that "we prevent the landing [of the tea] and kill [the] Govr. and all the Council."

But during the war McDougall's fortunes soared and his opinions cooled. He reached the rank of major general in the Continental Army, and disgruntled fellow officers picked him several times to argue their case before Congress. He spent some time in Congress, and when the war ended, he accepted the presidency of the Bank of New York, a project dear to Alexander Hamilton's heart. His daughter married John Lawrence, a merchant and politician who was one of Hamilton's close associates. McDougall died in 1786, but it is easy to predict where he would have stood in the debates of 1787 and 1788. He was at the same time a veteran of the popular revolutionary movement, a committed republican, a man with a nationalist perspective, and a man fully in tune with the capitalist order that was rapidly taking shape.

What was the appeal of the Constitution to men whose lives ran parallel to McDougall's? For some, it may have been the expectation that they would find themselves elected to Congress or the Senate. For others, it may have been the relief of having a government that would not change its laws from year to year and that would not let the class interest of lesser people be translated into public policy. The powers that the Constitution gave to Congress were appealing. Its mandate to regulate foreign and interstate commerce meant an end to state tariffs. Its powers to establish a uniform bankruptcy law, to coin and regulate money, to "fix the standard of Weights and Measures," to regulate patents and copyrights, and to establish a network of post offices and post roads all pleased the entrepreneurial mind. So did its guarantee that "full faith and credit" would be "given in each state" to laws and court decisions of other states and that the citizens of any state would enjoy equal "privileges and immunities" in all the others. With the Constitution in effect, states would be unable to "emit Bills of Credit; make anything but Gold or Silver Coin a Tender in Payment of Debts," or "pass any . . . Law impairing the Obligation of Contracts." Clearly, the Constitution established political conditions that were extremely favorable to the way that the American economy would develop in the next century.

The Constitution was thus a social document as well as a political one. Like the state constitutions, it was the product of a specific coalition, and like them it reflected the interests and the problems of the different groups that made that coalition up. To say as much is not to denigrate the Framers' achievement. The fact that the structure they established has endured for two centuries is evidence enough that they understood the needs of their own society and planned well for the future course of American development. The Constitution's acceptance, and the rapid end of opposition to it, are evidence that even in its own time the document satisfied people other than former generals who felt themselves slighted, great landlords annoyed at finally having to pay taxes, and merchants who saw prosperity and radical democracy as natural enemies.

IV

By themselves, all the discontents in the world could not have established the new government. The task of defining what was wrong, of working out a remedy, and of justifying that remedy to the world was carried out by a remarkable group of writers and thinkers. Political intellectuals debated the problem of republican government throughout the 1780s. They had inherited an "Atlantic republican tradition" of political thought that stretched back to seventeenth-century England and Renaissance Italy. But by the time ratification was completed they overturned practically every idea within it. They developed instead a framework of understanding which served two functions, both of immense importance. One was to mediate between the direct interests of people who stood to gain from the Constitution and the overriding ideological imperative that the final settlement be republican.

James Madison expressed their understanding perfectly when he wrote of the need for "a republican remedy for the diseases most incident to republican government." The other function was to make possible a reconciliation between the interests of the few and the experience of the many. There were writers in the Federalist camp who turned out nothing more than special pleading. But the best of them tried to understand their whole revolutionized society.

From the beginning, the writers who joined in the Federalist movement possessed the self-confidence that characterized Paine and Jefferson but that was so lacking in Daniel Dulany and the early John Dickinson. No longer awkward provincials, these people knew that they were carrying out the most advanced political analysis the world had yet seen. Among the most noteworthy of them were Jefferson, James Wilson, Noah Webster, John Adams, and Benjamin Rush. Jefferson incorporated sharp criticisms of the settlement in his own state in his *Notes on the State of Virginia*. Wilson, Webster, and Rush carried on a running criticism of Pennsylvania-style radical democracy. Adams's *Defence of the Constitutions of Government of the United States of America* was a monumental compilation of the whole history of republican experience and thought. Surrounding these were many others who turned out pamphlets, newspaper essays, and books. Among the contributors to the debate must be counted the major voices of Anti-Federalism, such as Richard Henry Lee of Virginia and Abraham Yates of New York. They, too, wrote at length; the recently compiled *Complete Anti-Federalist* takes five full volumes to survey what they turned out. The major Federalist thinkers made their breakthroughs in an atmosphere of argument, not in one of calm reflection.

Of all the voices, those of Hamilton and Madison resounded loudest. They were classic examples of the "Young Men of the Revolution" whom Stanley Elkins and Eric McKitrick have found at Federalism's core. Hamilton was a rank outsider whom good fortune brought to New York City and to King's (Columbia) College in the early 1770s. While still a student, he was writing anti-British pamphlets, and he was barely out of King's when he became first a captain of artillery and then Washington's aide-de-camp. His experience of telling generals what to do and his marriage to Philip Schuyler's daughter established his social point of view. Madison's career, if less spectacular, was also marked by early success. Born into Virginia's planter class, he studied at the College of New Jersey, now Princeton. He was only twenty-four when he became chairman of his county's revolutionary committee. Between 1775 and 1783, he served in various Virginia conventions, on Virginia's Council of State, and for three and a half years in the Continental Congress. When he was in Congress, its problems with the states were at their worst.

Despite their similarities, the two men came to Federalism by different routes, for Hamilton's analysis was shaped by his immersion in New York's world of commerce, and Madison's by his experience as an upper-class, white Virginian. Neither was friendly to slavery, but Hamilton freed the blacks his marriage had brought him and joined the New York Manumission Society, whereas Madison remained a slaveholding planter. Their work represented the way that Federalism brought together emergent capitalism and enlightened planter republicanism.

Hamilton's route to Federalism led, as we have seen, from his frustrations on Washington's staff during the war through his experience of the problems of the New York elite during the 1780s. From a very early time, he looked to Congress to find a remedy for what was wrong in the states. In his "Continentalist" essays of 1781 and 1782 and his "Letters from Phocion" of 1784, he argued the importance of Congress's having its own revenue and of the peace treaty's terms being honored. His public writings consistently took the high ground of principle and constitutionalism, but from the start he understood that Congress could gain political strength only from a strong commercial economy. Hamilton sympathized with much of the emerging ideology of the free market, especially with its critique of the way that corporatism sought to use political power in order to achieve social welfare. But he also had sharp things to say about the gospel according to Adam Smith, for he understood that without public support and protection an independent American economy could never take shape. That theme emerged most powerfully in the *Report on Manufactures* that he wrote in 1791, when he was Secretary of the Treasury, but it is also present in much of his earlier writing.

In the mid-1780s, Hamilton's prime concern was to restore New York City's commercial life. During the war he had been as willing as anyone to take harsh measures against the Tories, but now he wanted a rapid end to their persecution. His correspondence in 1783 shows why. Tory and neutral merchants, fearful of the victorious Revolution, were lining up to leave with the British. They were taking their capital and their skills and their business connections with them, and these losses outweighed any amount of republican zeal. "Many merchants of the second class, characters of no political consequence, each of whom may carry away eight or ten thousand guineas have I am told lately applied for shipping to convey them away. Our state will feel for twenty years, at least, the effects of this popular phrenzy" was how he put it to Robert R. Livingston.

We have already seen how Hamilton turned his close attention to state politics, rallying merchants and landlords and "those who are concerned for the *security of property* . . . to endeavour to put men in the Legislature whose principles are not of the *levelling kind*." His other passion, besides putting the upper class back in power, was for predictability and order in the making and the enforcement of the law. He understood one of the Revolution's central lessons, which was that American liberty was "the *right* to a *share* in the government." But, in general, Hamilton was at pains to defend the liberty to be left alone, rather than the liberty to take part. An artisan's interest was not to have a real voice in the making of the laws. It was "that there be plenty of money in the community, and a brisk commerce to give it circulation and activity." The "true sense" of liberty was "the enjoyment of the common privileges of subjects under the same government."

The driving force behind both the writings and the actions of this man was his need to realize a program that was made up of many different elements but that was held together by a dominant vision. The elements were a market that was free from the government's interference but still protected by the government's power, the quiet reintegration of former Tories, predictable taxation and secure credit, rule by the best, and a citizenry that stayed out of politics except when it was time to vote. The vision was of a strong central government under which all these specific goals could be achieved. A centralized, energetic republic and a prosperous capitalist economy were the two causes to which he devoted his career. The enormous contribution that he made to the Federalist argument represents his effort to bring those causes together.

If Hamilton was the Constitution's prophet, crying out for the need for change through the 1780s in his essays and his endless correspondence, Madison was its evangelist. His great task after the Convention adjourned was to explain why the changes the Constitution made were the ones America needed. Both men did, of course, assume something of both roles. It was Hamilton who instigated *The Federalist*, who invited Madison and John Jay to join in writing the series, and who wrote two-thirds of the total text. Conversely, Madison spent an extended period just before the Convention working out his own analysis, partly in his unpublished "The Vices of the Political System of the United States" and partly in his correspondence with the absent Jefferson.

Madison shared most of Hamilton's concerns, but he had a way of putting the same points with a different inflection. In Hamilton's vision, the overriding element was commercial prosperity and development; in Madison's, it was making sure that the republic did not prove a failure. The Virginian began the serious development of his ideas later, writing "The Vices of the Political System" immediately before the Convention. He accepted the argument that the problem lay in the states more than in Congress, and he built on two central themes that had emerged in what was becoming Federalist writing. One, developed especially by the Pennsylvania jurist James Wilson, was the dissolution of the traditional distinction between a subject people and a sovereign ruler. In place of that distinction, Wilson was beginning to locate sovereignty in the people themselves. The notion was fully implicit in the making of the state constitutions, but the older view died hard. That view saw a constitution as a *contract* between people and their chosen rulers, rather than as a special act which stated the terms on which people would rule themselves. It was central to much of the Anti-Federalist argument against the Constitution.

The other theme pitted "the people against the legislatures." As Gordon Wood has suggested, when Federalists developed this thought they came close to hypocrisy, for one of their major goals was to get ordinary people out of the legislatures. Their argument ran that despite every effort to make the state legislatures servants of their people, they had become the masters, and capricious, uncontrollable masters at that. Thomas Jefferson put it most succinctly in his *Notes on the State of Virginia* when, referring to the size of the state's House of Delegates, he observed that "173 despots would surely be as oppressive as one." The ideas that Madison developed drew on both these lines of thought.

As Douglass Adair and several other scholars have noted, Madison also drew on the ideas of the Scottish historian and philosopher David Hume. Writing in the middle of the eighteenth century, Hume addressed one of the oldest problems in political theory: how large and complex could a republic become before its own contradictions drove it to destruction. The very word "republic" suggested an answer: it had to be small and simple. Derived from the Latin for "public thing," the word implied that a society stood a chance of ruling itself only if its size was limited and if it had no conflicting interests within it. Let it grow larger, let more interests develop, and conflict could not be avoided. Let conflict erupt and tyranny was foreordained. All history seemed to say so, and so did all republican thinkers from Machiavelli to Montesquieu.

Hume thought otherwise. He speculated in 1752 that not only was a republic possible in a large and complex society but that size and complexity themselves might be the keys to the endlessly vexing problem of how a republic could survive. The great difficulty was that once people began to think *for* themselves, they also thought *of* themselves, and that selfishness and republicanism could not avoid conflict. Eighteenth-century people called it faction, putting one's own interests before the interests of the community. But, wrote Hume, though "it is not easy, for the distant parts of a large state, to combine in any plan of free government," there was nonetheless "more facility, when once it is formed, of preserving it steady and uniform, without tumult or faction." In Hume, it was simply a suggestion that some "large state, such as France or Great Britain" might be "modelled into a Commonwealth." For Madison, it resolved the whole problem of what the future of other large states, such as Massachusetts, New York, and Virginia, would be.

Madison developed his argument in *The Federalist*, and especially in papers Number 10 and Number 51. For him, the basic reality was that the states were already too large and complex. Each had several interests within it, and it was the clash of those interests that posed the problem. If an interest, or faction, included only a minority of the people, there was no difficulty: "relief is supplied by the republican principle, which enables the majority to defeat its sinister views." But "when a majority is included in a faction, the form of popular government . . . enables it to sacrifice . . . both the public good and the rights of other citizens." How could those rights be secured without losing "the spirit and the form of popular government"? It would be easy enough to remove "the causes of faction . . . by destroying the liberty which is essential to its existence." It might be possible to do it "by giving to every citizen the same opinions, the same passions and the same interests." But the first remedy was "worse than the disease" and the second was "as impracticable as it would be unwise."

Instead, Madison offered other solutions. The first was to use a large political system "to refine and enlarge the public views by passing them through the medium of a chosen body of citizens, whose wisdom may best discern the true interest of their country." The larger the republic, the greater the probability that such men rather than fools or demagogues would come to the fore. Size alone would sort out the best, a task at which property requirements and complex electoral arrangements had so clearly failed. The second solution was more innovative. A single "public good" could not be obtained even in as small a state as Rhode Island, let alone Pennsylvania. There were bound to be parties: it was "sown in the nature of man." The danger was not parties; it was that in a small society one party could much more easily become the majority and then "the more easily will they concert and execute their plans of oppression." But in a really large republic the danger diminished, for "among the great variety of interests, parties and sects . . . a coalition of the majority of the whole society could seldom take place on any other principles than those of justice and the general good." America's future would be as a society in which interest confronted interest in an unending struggle for self-preservation and for gain. Its "public good" would take the form of people's surety that they would not be crushed and that they would enjoy stable conditions in which to continue the struggle. Surety and stability would emerge as different interests, all self-seeking, balanced one another off and canceled one another out.

Madison understood that faction could have many causes, but he agreed with Hamilton that at the root of the problem lay class. "The most common and durable source of factions," he wrote, "has been the various and unequal distribution of property." Pressed hard enough, he would have had to admit that the "majority factions" he criticized were most likely to be made up of debtors and people without property. His analysis also had much in common with Adam Smith's *The Wealth of Nations*, for his argument that the conflict of many factions would bring political stability was very close to Smith's position that competition in a free market offered the best way to abundance and low prices. Whether or not Smith was correct about the benefits that free-market capitalism would bring, he did foresee the course of Western economic development. The United States was to be in the forefront of that development, and Madison's greatest achievement may well have been to recognize the political sociology of a system in which capital would be safe. As Gordon Wood has put it, the Constitution marked a "repudiation of 1776" in its rejection of radical democracy. To that extent, it marked not only the end of the Revolution but also a reaction against it. Yet, politically "conservative" though the Constitution was, it was also fully in tune with the needs of what were then the most progressive economic forces in the world. The structure it created would serve those forces well.

It would serve the needs of many people, however, besides landowners, planters, and emergent capitalists. The Constitution reflected not just the needs of one or a few social groups but also the experience that the Revolution had given to Americans of many kinds. Had it been a truly unpopular document, or one that contradicted how most ordinary Americans understood their world, the ritual of ratification would never have given it the widespread acceptance that it so quickly won. To understand how the political settlement of the Revolution meshed with and reflected the social experience of the revolutionaries, we must return to the revolutionaries themselves.

· 7 ·

"Should I Not Have Liberty"

The day was July 4, 1788, and the place was Philadelphia. It was a dozen years since the city's people had stood to hear the Declaration of Independence as it was read out. Even then, in the midst of war and danger, they had celebrated, for a way of life that they wanted to leave behind had come to an end. Now Philadelphians knew that ten states, including all-important Virginia, had ratified the new Constitution. For days they had been preparing to rejoice again, this time not for the fall of an empire but for the rise of a republic. How they marked that day amounted to a summing up both of the way they had made their Revolution and of the differences the Revolution had made for them.

The city greeted the dawn with a peal from the bells of Christ Church and with a salvo of cannon from the ship *Rising Sun*. Ten other ships stood down the length of the harbor, each fully dressed with banners and pennants. By eight o'clock, people were beginning to assemble their "Grand Federal Procession." Grand it certainly was. The *Pennsylvania Gazette* needed three and a half pages of dense type to describe it. Eighty-six units, some large and some small, made up the march. The first few presented a capsule history of the era. After "Independence" came the "French Alliance" and the "Treaty of Peace," represented by a rider bearing an olive branch. Another rider honored "Washington, the Friend of

His Country." A gentleman on horseback "attended by a trumpet" proclaimed a "New Era." Then came the "Convention of the States" and the Constitution itself, borne by the justices of the Pennsylvania supreme court. Ten gentlemen accompanied it, "walking arm in arm, emblematical of the Union."

The centerpieces of the parade were two elaborate floats. The first, called the "New Roof, or Grand Federal Edifice," was an elegant structure drawn by ten horses. It had thirteen Corinthian columns, ten of them completed and three left unfinished. Ten gentlemen "as representatives of the citizens at large" were sitting on the float, and behind it marched the city's architects, house carpenters, sawmakers, and file makers. The "Federal Ship Union," which came behind, had twenty guns and a crew of twenty-five men. Pilots, boat builders, sailmakers, ship carpenters, ropemakers, and finally "merchants and traders" followed it through the streets.

Then came the rest of the city's tradesmen. Some groups of artisans had floats of their own, and most bore banners and emblems. Six men were making shoes in a cobbler's shop on wheels. A team of blacksmiths was beating swords into sickles and plow irons. Wheelwrights were making another plow and a wagon wheel. Printers were striking off copies of a federal ode, written especially for the day. Bakers distributed bread that they made as they went along. The tradesmen's banners bore their mottoes. "Both Buildings and Rulers Are the Work of Our Hands," said the bricklayers. "By Unity We Support Society," announced the chairmakers. "Time Rules All Things" was the slogan of the clock and watchmakers. "Let Us Encourage Our Own Manufactures," said the whip and cane makers. "With the Industry of the Beaver We Support Our Rights" was the motto of the hatters. "The Death of Anarchy and Confusion Shall Feed the Poor and Hungry," said the victualers. "The Potter Hath Power over His Clay," announced the potters. "By Hammer and Hand, All Arts Do Stand," proudly declared the smiths.

On the parade went: saddlers, stonecutters, and sugar refiners; gunsmiths, goldsmiths, and engravers; tanners, upholsterers, and brushmakers, coopers and carvers; ribbon makers and stocking makers; brewers and tobacconists. At the very end came city and state officials, physicians, clergymen, and the students and professors of the College of Philadelphia. When the procession finally completed its journey, the jurist James Wilson mounted the "Federal Edifice" and delivered an "Oration, Suited to the Day."

Philadelphians had much to celebrate on that Fourth of July, including independence, George Washington, victory in the war, the return of peace, and the Constitution. But, most of all, they were rejoicing in themselves. From the first church bells and cannon, everything they did was heavy with symbolism, and we can read the day's events as an enormous collective statement about the city, its people, and the place of both in the world. The day's early beginning proclaimed that Philadelphians took seriously the maxims of their most famous townsman, Benjamin Franklin. The church bells announced that they were religious. The roar of the cannon and the contingents of cavalry, artillery, and foot soldiers scattered through the parade bespoke their history of warfare. The merchant ships with their flags and the many invocations of prosperity showed that they were a commercial people. They were all of these, and they were patriotic and republican. They were not just Pennsylvanians now but also citizens of the United States.

Most of all, the parade demonstrated Philadelphians' pride that they were equal productive members of a society of free men. The march had an internal structure that gave it coherence and meaning. The marchers themselves understood that a gentleman on horseback and an artisan in his leather apron were not the same. But gentlemen did not enjoy precedence: the first places in the parade went to symbols of the history all Pennsylvanians had helped make. Nor did the gentry take pride of place immediately after the Federal Edifice and the

Federal Ship. That went to the house building and shipbuilding tradesmen whose skilled hands had created the two floats. The way that all the city's tradesmen marched in groups, the slogans on their banners, the moving workshops in which some of them were laboring, and the bread, the shoes, and the plowshares they were producing all proclaimed their message. These men had helped to make the Revolution and the republic; the goods they produced were essential to their community's well-being; their rights, both as citizens and as producers, were equal to anyone's. The mechanic need not defer to the merchant; the ship carpenter could look the shipowner in the eye. The republic was theirs.

The parade also proclaimed that Philadelphians now valued coalition, not conflict. Only nine years earlier, the city's militia had besieged "Fort Wilson," and there must have been many men in the parade who remembered their part in that rising. But now James Wilson himself marched among them, and when he addressed the throng that afternoon, people stood silent to listen. It was not deference; Wilson's audience reserved the right to judge what he had to say. But equality of rights was one thing and equality of condition another. However strongly Philadelphians valued the first, they did not seek the second, not, at least, on July 4, 1788.

In effect, these people were acting out the understanding of American society that Madison had presented in Number 10 of *The Federalist*. There was no single "public"; instead, there were many separate groups, each asserting itself and its worth, none attempting to crush or control the others, at least on the day of the parade. The procession's enormous length and its many divisions reflected the complexity of American society; its précis of republican history showed what the people of that society had done in the past they shared. The pride of the marchers lay in what they could do together, not in what any one of them might have by himself. These people wanted a republic organized around productivity and usefulness, not around simple greed.

There were people missing from the parade, silences in the midst of all the noise made by speakers, marching feet, "bands of musick," and, we may be sure, by slogans that men chanted. Where were the Penns, the family that had founded Pennsylvania and that had been its feudal overlords until only twelve years before? Where were the Quakers, who had dominated colonial life? Where were such once-great figures as Joseph Galloway? Where were the radicals of 1776, who had turned Pennsylvania into a simple, austere democracy? All had had their chance to rule, but now their voices were still. The Penns were gone, leaving only their name. Royalism had given way to republicanism. The Quakers were just another church. Though the state constitution of 1776 would survive for two more years, it was doomed.

Other voices were heard only in whispers. Somewhere in the parade, an "Indian Chief" was smoking a "Calumet of Peace" with a "Citizen," but he was no more a real Indian than the "Mohawks" who had dumped the tea at Boston. There were women at work on the float of the Manufacturing Society, but they were there just as employees. They did not stand in any way for their sex. There must have been some blacks in this vast throng of workingmen. But the *Gazette*'s description makes no mention of any, and certainly of none as a group. The new republican ideology of equal rights had no room yet for people who were not white or not male. Yet, in time, both blacks and women would invoke it, and even in 1788 the bases of their claim that it applied to them had been laid.

To understand the Revolution's large meaning, we must understand both the voices and the silences of that day in July. John Adams once observed that the real revolution was over before a shot was fired, for its essence lay in the changes of heart and mind that turned Britons who lived overseas into Americans who lived in their own country. But that was only half the change. The contrast between the marching

mechanics of 1788 and the rioters of 1779 is just as overwhelming as the one between the rebels of 1776 and the loyal
colonists of 1760. The artisans present the clearest example of
how the Revolution changed ordinary people, not just in
Philadelphia, but in New York, Boston, and smaller towns as
well. But we can see something similar happening among
farmers, and elements of it among both blacks and women.
Let us trace the way these people lived through their American Revolutions.

I

The artisans' path to 1788 wandered through a twisted
landscape of coalition and conflict. The fathers and the grandfathers of the men who marched to celebrate the Constitution
were never a downtrodden, oppressed class. In Philadelphia,
they were the most vibrant, vital element in society as early
as mid-century. The "Junto" of ambitious, self-improving
men that formed around Benjamin Franklin presents evidence enough: from it emerged such truly remarkable figures
as David Rittenhouse, whose "orrery" displayed the complexity of the solar system in mechanical form, and the painter
Charles Willson Peale. The hunger for knowledge that these
men felt was by no means restricted to Philadelphians; it
gnawed at Paul Revere in Boston and at John Lamb in New
York as well; and they were not alone.

Some men of this sort had scrambled for knowledge and
perhaps for office in the hope that they would rise in the
world. The path that led Abraham Yates of Albany from a
cobbler's bench to a law office, the Albany Common Council,
and the post of county sheriff shows how such a man could
change his life even in the colonial era. But Yates confronted
uncrossable barriers when he tried in 1761 to go on to the provincial assembly. His experience showed the limits beyond
which no colonial artisan could go. Most artisans understood

those limits; that is why George Robert Twelves Hewes of
Boston never expected to be anything other than a cobbler.
For men like him, the way to take part in the late colonial
world had not been through earnest self-improvement. It had
been through their volunteer fire companies, their Pope's Day
crowds, and, for some of them, their trade associations. Such
associations were not necessarily "radical" in their politics.
The "White Oaks" of late colonial Philadelphia were an
organized, self-conscious group of shipwrights. In Boston and
New York, such men had a major hand in the explosions of
1765. But the White Oaks were close to Benjamin Franklin
and through him to Joseph Galloway, still Franklin's asso-
ciate. The stance they took was one of the reasons Philadelphia remained quiet that year.

But in all three major cities the end of the 1760s saw independent artisan consciousness on the rise. We have seen how
artisans and merchants split over whether to end non-
importation in 1770. That dispute inaugurated a decade and
a half during which these people were much more likely to
argue than to agree. From the start, the argument was posed
in terms of class. New York merchants claimed the right to
make the decision regarding non-importation on their own.
But a mechanic replied that nothing could be "more flagrantly
wrong than the assertion of some of our mercantile dons, that
the Mechanics have no right to give their Sentiments." A
Philadelphia broadside put it in even stronger terms:

And will you suffer the Credit and Liberties of the Province of Pennsylvania to be sacrificed to the Interests of a
few Merchants in Philadelphia? Shall the GRAND
QUESTION, whether America shall be *free* or *Not*, be
determined by a few Men, whose Support and Importance must always be in Proportion to the Distresses of
our Country? In determining Questions of such great
Consequence, the Consent of the Majority of the Tradesmen, Farmers and other Freemen . . . should have been

obtained. .... The Tradesmen who have suffered by the
... Agreement are but few, when compared to the Number of those who have received great Benefit from it.

The piece was signed "A Tradesman." Using such a pseudo-
nym was an old device, and many a Great Man had employed
it. But there is no reason to assume that this author was a
lawyer or a trader in disguise. Whatever he was, he was
presenting a powerful blend of principle, patriotism, and
self-interest.

The issue soon spilled into day-to-day politics. By the
autumn of 1770, "Brother Chip" was arguing that it was
necessary for artisans to nominate their own candidates, including men drawn from their ranks. That applied to even
the highest elected offices. "If we have not the Liberty of
nominating such persons whom we approve," he said, "our
Freedom of Voting is at an end." By then, even the steadfast
White Oaks were deserting Joseph Galloway and the "old
ticket" to become revolutionaries. We know that from no less
a source than Galloway himself.

Artisan involvement, artisan self-consciousness, and artisan
self-organization were central to the making of the independence crisis. We can watch the New York diarist William
Smith learning in the autumn of 1773 "by hints that the
Mechanics convene at Beer Houses" in order "to concert
Measures." It was from such half-secret meetings that the
city's "Body of Mechanics" and "General Committee of
Mechanics" took shape over the next year. They bought a
meeting place and named it Mechanics Hall. There they
found themselves gathering as often as once a week, and their
leaders were always ready to run off handbills and fliers calling them to meetings and to action. It was a mechanic initiative that led to the election of the city's first revolutionary
committee, and artisans sat on it and on both of its successors.
When word got around in 1776 that the printer Samuel
Loudon was putting out a reply to *Common Sense*, the Body

of Mechanics ordered him to suppress it. Then the chairman of the mechanics' committee, together with a tavernkeeper, a carpenter, and a pewterer, led a crowd that seized and burned the printed sheets. These were the same artisans who only a few months later demanded a constitutional right to renew popular committees whenever the people might want to.

New England artisans took a different path, but it led them to the same awareness of themselves as actors at the center of the political stage. The dominant theme of Boston's most radical writers and speakers was always community rather than class. There were times when radical Boston leaders did not hesitate to crush anyone who differed from themselves. The fate of Ebenezer MacIntosh, strutting in front of the crowd in 1765 and languishing in a debtor's jail in 1770, is exemplary. But we have seen how the grievances of rope-workers helped set in motion the events that led to the Boston Massacre. Artisans and skilled workers were equally important to the success of the Tea Party. There may have been gentlemen among the "Mohawks" who set out "to save the country" when Sam Adams signaled that it was time. But the swiftness with which the tea was hauled out of the ship and dumped is evidence enough that among the party there were men used to finding their way around in dark holds, used to rigging a block and tackle, and used to raising heavy cargoes with nothing more than the power of their muscles.

One of those men was the diminutive shoemaker George Robert Twelves Hewes. By 1773, Hewes had learned some things that he had not known eleven years before, when he had stood trembling at John Hancock's door. He had lived through a decade of turmoil, and he was a different man for it. The leaders of the Tea Party singled him out, giving him the responsibility for seeing that the ship's hatches were opened. In the course of the action, Hewes stood up to "one Captain O'Connor," who was filling his own pockets with tea instead of throwing it overboard. Barely a month later, Hewes stood up again, this time to a bullying customs man named

George Malcolm. Hewes came upon Malcolm as he was threatening a young boy with a beating for the crime of getting in the way. Four years before, in February 1770, Bostonians had seen another young townsman die because of a customs man's wrath, and now Hewes intervened. Malcolm cursed him for an "impertinent rascal" and then beat him with a heavy cudgel, giving the shoemaker serious injuries. But that evening, when an enormous crowd gathered to tar and feather him and threaten him with worse, the customs man found he had gone too far. The next time Malcolm and Hewes passed on the street, the official treated the cobbler with respect.

In 1778, Hewes found himself once again confronting official arrogance. Now it came from the lieutenant of an American privateer whose crew Hewes meant to join. But standing up for himself had become a habit with Hewes. When the officer demanded that Hewes doff his hat as a sign of respect, the cobbler walked off the ship and joined the crew of another. For Hewes, that was what being a citizen meant.

Others learned the lesson in different ways. Blacksmiths in the inland town of Worcester, Massachusetts, resolved in 1774 that they would not "do or perform, any blacksmith's work or business . . . for any person or persons whom we esteem enemies to this country." They recommended "to all denominations of artificers that they call meetings of their respective craftsmen . . . and enter into associations and agreements" to do the same. The smiths were acting for the common cause, but they were also thinking for themselves. *They* and no one else would decide whom they esteemed "enemies to this country."

We have seen how central the involvement of artisans was to the emergence of both the organized Sons of Liberty and the popular committees. We have seen how Sons, committeemen, and crowds all acted within the pattern of beliefs about politics and economics summed up in the word "corporatism." We have also seen how that pattern came under increasing pressure, in both practice and theory, and how Philadelphia's leather workers went over to the side of free trade during the conflicts of 1779. They explained their position at some length, and what they said is worth close attention:

> The committee . . . hint that their fixing the prices of our commodities first, was in a great measure to give us "the preference of setting the first example as a rule for other trades, for though only one was mentioned, all were intentionally and inclusively regulated." And we would gladly have made that honour our own, by a compliance, did not we see . . . that any partial regulation of any number of articles would answer no end but that of destroying the tradesmen whose prices are limited, and . . . leaving the country in absolute want of those articles.

Other mechanics might have argued when the leather workers declared that trade should be "as free as air, uninterrupted as the tide." But they would have endorsed the fact that the tanners and curriers and shoemakers were thinking and acting for themselves. They would have respected the leather workers' refusal to be the only men to sacrifice themselves to the will of others.

By the mid-1780s, artisans were laying claim to a central place in the politics of the states. They wanted men of their own kind in office. If merchants and men of finance obtained special privileges, they wanted similar privileges for themselves. Both issues found expression in New York. Though New York City's artisans were scattered in 1776 by the British invasion of their city, some of their number spent the war as assemblymen and state senators. These men held their places by appointment, "representing" constituencies that the enemy had occupied. But, as the British prepared to depart in 1783, artisans prepared for the city's first republican election. Robert R. Livingston told John Jay that three parties were contending: former loyalists "who still hope for power . . .

violent Whigs, who are for expelling all tories," and men of moderation. The "violent Whigs" won, and among the new assemblymen were the artisans John Lamb, John Stagg, and Hugh Hughes. Mechanics were on the winning ticket at the next election, in June 1784, and on the one after that, in June 1785. They never formed a united party, for some voted regularly with outspoken radicals and others just as frequently with men of conservative views. But they were in the assembly.

That bothered Alexander Hamilton. He tried in a heavy-handed way to convince them that "there is a certain proportion or level in all the departments of industry. It is folly to think to raise any of them," and men who worked with their hands should know enough to stick to their tools. It bothered Aaron Burr as well, and when New York's mechanics petitioned the legislature to incorporate their General Society in 1785, he led the opposition. According to a hostile witness, Burr's judgment was that incorporating the mechanics would "give them too much *political importance*, and that they ought to be '*kept down*' or '*under.*' " The legislature granted the petition, but the high judges on the state's Council of Revision exercised their veto. They reasoned that allowing incorporation would transform New York from "a community of free citizens pursuing the public interest" to "a community of corporations, influenced by partial views." Their argument passed lightly over the way that other New Yorkers already had a Chamber of Commerce and a Bank of New York to serve their "partial views" and that both the chamber and the bank enjoyed all the privileges incorporation could confer.

Thus, by 1786, artisans not just in New York but all over the country found themselves caught in a tangle of contradictions. Their experience of Revolution had convinced them that they had as much right as anyone to a voice in the governance of their world. Their experience of dispute with other Americans, of runaway inflation, and, in the war's aftermath, of depression had convinced them that only by asserting themselves could they get what they wanted. The frustration of their attempts to gain privileges like incorporation had taught them that greater men would still rebuff them if they could. From the interplay among these emerged the artisans' enthusiasm for the Constitution.

The first sign came in January 1788, when Paul Revere presided as four hundred Boston mechanics announced their endorsement of the Constitution and organized a tradesmen's committee to support it. Without doubt, Revere and the others at the center were in communication with leading Federalists. Without doubt, one purpose of the meeting was to put direct pressure on Samuel Adams, who was wavering in the state-ratifying convention. But the artisans were acting for themselves. When Massachusetts ratified the following month, Bostonians celebrated with the first of many processions in honor of the Constitution. A committee of artisans organized it. Members of over forty different trades turned out, including 73 blacksmiths, 136 carpenters, 30 mast makers, 40 bakers, and 50 cobblers. One newspaper called it "an exhibition to which America has never witnessed an equal." Merchants and farmers did join the march, but it was at the artisans' invitation.

The example proved contagious. Charleston, Baltimore, New York City, and smaller places followed it, as their respective states ratified. Philadelphia's great procession on July 4 was only the most notable. Except in Boston, the Federalist leaders rather than artisan committees organized the parades. But it was artisans who began them and who made them what they were: enormous celebrations of the Revolution that lay behind, of the new political order that was being founded, of a future men thought they could control, and of the proud, productive, and patriotic self.

The historian Sean Wilentz has noted that in some ways these parades drew on old British traditions. But they were utterly new to America, and the fact that artisans now marched in them rather than remain part of the crowd is a measure of how much city life had been transformed. So is the fact that when Boston tradesmen elected their committee in January it was for the sake of organizing a parade rather than of trying to control the market, as such a committee might once have done. Wilentz and others have pointed out that the 1788 coalition of artisans and Federalists would be very short-lived. Artisan parades would be frequent events in the decades that followed. But they rapidly became a way by which artisans could resist what the rulers of the United States were up to, rather than a means for showing agreement with it.

The year 1788 was thus a special moment. In symbolic terms, it marked the end of revolutionary upheaval and the beginning of republican citizenship. It marked the end of the long tradition of submerging the self in the "public good" and the acceptance instead of the understanding that men had a right to decide what their own happiness was and to pursue it. It marked a point when men like Hamilton, driven by a vision of capitalist development and national glory, could look in the same direction as blacksmiths and shoemakers whose vision was of a society built on equal rights and self-respect. The republic would endure. It would protect the acquisition and the development of property on a scale of which no man dreamed in 1788. It would also protect its citizens' enduring belief that the republic itself is, or should be, their own. But this moment when blacksmiths and bankers faced the same way, agreed on what needed to be done, and marched as equals in the same parades would not last.

II

There were contingents of farmers in the great parades of 1788 as well. But, for most country people, the story was somewhat different. In effect, the Revolution concluded where it began, in the cities, with the resolution of city problems. The farther one journeyed from the urban centers in 1788, the less support for the Constitution one was likely to find. Only Rhode Island, intensely commercial and intensely Anti-Federal at the same time, seems an exception to this rule.

During the Revolution, small farmers had proven as capable as anyone of deciding what was wrong in their lives and of organizing themselves so they could do something about it. The enthusiasm of rural New Englanders as they gathered to support the Grand Cause in 1774 is evidence enough. Country people also learned how important it was that men of their own kind represent them in the new state legislatures. They learned about political organization. By 1785 or 1786, farmer representatives formed the core of the Constitutionalist Party in Pennsylvania and of the radical group centered on Governor George Clinton of New York, to cite only two cases. All the material for a farmer equivalent of the artisan parades seems to have been in place. Yet somehow it did not take shape.

One reason may have been the experience of defeat. For some, it came because of loyalism. From the Carolinas to New York, unhappy small farmers either took the king's side or tried to remain neutral. To do either was to make a serious mistake. Neutrality brought suspicion, extra taxes, and investigation by such political police as New York's "Commissioners for Detecting and Defeating Conspiracies." Outright loyalism brought involvement on the losing side in a vicious civil war. It brought retribution by the winners, including exile, the loss of political rights, and the confiscation of what one had. People who had lived through such a storm and who were still in the United States had little reason to think that by organizing themselves again and acting in concert they could help control the world they lived in. Their whole experience had taught them otherwise.

Patriot farmers learned that it was perfectly possible for them not to fare any better. The last gasp of the original spirit of the Revolution, with all its belief in community and cooperation, came from the Massachusetts farmers who gathered behind Daniel Shays in 1786. The resolutions and addresses of their county committees in the year or two before the rebellion said exactly what all sorts of people had been saying in 1776. But the failure of their rebellion taught the Massachusetts farmers that the old ways no longer worked. For many the lesson was painful, as they found themselves forced to grovel and beg forgiveness from rulers who claimed to be the people's servants.

However much urban mechanics may have accepted what James Madison and Adam Smith were saying, it seems entirely probable that many country people still did not. The historians James Henretta and Michael Merrill have argued that, well into the nineteenth century, small farmers in the interior were still organizing their lives around the lineal family, not the isolated individual, and around exchange for the sake of community, not trade for the sake of gain. Even the constant buying and selling of land for which backcountry Americans were becoming famous makes more sense if we view them in these terms rather than as simple speculators. Through the 1770s and the 1780s, Benedict Alford and Rebecca Owen Alford were trading Vermont land incessantly, sometimes in his name and sometimes in hers. But by then Benedict was the father of fifteen children, nine the product of his first marriage and six more of his marriage to Rebecca. Their greatest concern was to see that the sons would have farms and the daughters dowries. What they wanted from the land was a way of life, not a means of profit.

Nonetheless, the Revolution brought change to their world. One of its major consequences was to cut short the tendencies toward a neo-feudal society that had been gathering strength in the late colonial era. By the war's end, such families as the Penns, the Fairfaxes, the Calverts, the De Lanceys, the Philipses, and the Johnsons were gone. Their estates were confiscated and sold; their power extinguished. The legislators who passed the confiscation laws did not intend, for the most part, to make a social revolution; they wanted to punish people for choosing the wrong side. Though some confiscated estates, like Philipse Manor in New York, were broken up and put into the hands of former tenants, others, like the De Lancey holdings of New York City, were simply transferred to speculators. Nor did landlordship and tenancy end. In New York alone, probably half the great estates survived, and as the West began to open up, small men seeking land would find time after time that they had to deal with great men who already owned it. Landlords continued to coerce their tenants to vote as they wanted; the Livingstons did so with great effect as they began their climb back to power in 1785. Some still expected and received obsequious groveling as well.

Nonetheless, the countryside was different. No more would landholders dream of building stable communities where their word would be law to "amiable and innocent tenants." No more would they claim the actual ownership of court-houses and jails, or special seats in the assemblies. Land dealing would be a business, not a way of life. The land itself would be a commodity to buy and sell. Landlords were becoming rural capitalists, full of the spirit of innovation. It was no accident that the Hudson Valley landholder Robert R. Livingston was the financial sponsor of the world's first successful steamboat, in 1807, or that its inventor, Robert Fulton, named it *Clermont*, after Livingston's estate.

James Fenimore Cooper caught the change perfectly in his novels. In *Satanstoe* and *The Chainbearer*, both set before the Revolution, Cooper creates landlords who expect awe and receive it, as a matter of hereditary right. One character, speaking in a heavy Dutch accent, describes himself. He is "a colonel and a memper [of the provincial assembly]; my fa'ter was a colonel and a memper; and my grand fa'ter woult have peen a colonel and a memper, but dere vast no colonels and no mempers in his time." But in *The Pioneers* Cooper chronicles a different world. The novel presents a fictional version of the attempt that Cooper's own father made in the 1790s to build an estate in central New York. Judge Temple is the squire of Templeton, just as Judge William Cooper was of Cooperstown when his son was growing up. But he is a half-comic figure, not a man to command deference. The people of his town acknowledge that he owns the land they live on, but they do not bow before him. Temple is a judge, but that is no guarantee that his son or son-in-law will follow him onto the bench. The shadow of feudalism had seemed to be lengthening in the 1760s, as owners of land looked for ways to breathe new life into old forms. But by the 1790s it was simply gone. The laws themselves declared that, for Americans, feudal land tenure of any sort was a thing of the past.

As neo-feudalism died, New England's ethos of community weakened. The failure of Shays' Rebellion showed clearly that the old ways of the village simply could not cope with the new ways of the world. By the early 1790s, a town like Concord, Massachusetts, was so much a place of business that a description of it "read much like a present-day Chamber of Commerce pamphlet." The change saved Concord in one sense: it transformed it from a place locked in decay and trouble to one alive with prosperity and aware of possibility. It ended the town's timid cultural isolation and opened it to all the sophistication of the world. Within half a century, Concord would find that, instead of perching on the edge of that world, it would briefly be one of its capitals, thanks to Henry David Thoreau, Ralph Waldo Emerson, Margaret Fuller, the Alcotts, and Nathaniel Hawthorne. In the words of its historian, Concord became "a new town for a new republic." But the old New England dream of living in "a corporate body free from power-seeking, from conflict, from hard bargaining among separate interests, from exploitation of the weak" was gone. Only the town's name remained, still signifying the vision its people once had held.

A third great change also took place, as country people surged westward, faster than any colonist could have imagined. Even Thomas Jefferson, whose horizons stretched far, predicted that white America's conquest of its continent might take a thousand years. The explosive social energy that the Revolution helped generate completed the task in less than one hundred. Well before independence, colonial speculators had their eyes on the Oswego and Genesee country south of Lake Ontario, on the Ohio Valley, and on the western Appalachians. After the Revolution people bent on building farms and towns turned not only their eyes to the West but their feet as well. Places like Pittsburgh and Columbus began to be transformed from outposts of war and trade to centers of settlement. Travelers began to write about the wonders that were available in western New York, Kentucky, and Tennessee.

Let one small example show what was happening. In 1774, a mapmaker named Claude Joseph Sauthier drew an elaborately detailed plan of the province of New York. He showed dense settlements along the Hudson River between New York City and Albany. But he showed almost nothing save some empty speculative tracts beyond a line that was no more than thirty miles west of the Hudson. The only exception was a thin band of towns and farms that stretched along the Mohawk Valley, pointing west toward Lake Ontario. What lay beyond was not empty, of course, but to a man like Sauthier, Indians did not count. Both the white settlements that the map did show and the Indian villages that it did not were devastated by civil war between 1775 and 1782.

However, only ten years later, all was different. A traveler who passed between Albany and Niagara in 1792 described how "every house and barn" was rebuilt, "the pastures crowded with cattle, sheep & the lap of Ceres full." Sauthier's map had noted an outpost called Fort Schuyler not far east of Oneida Lake, sitting in an otherwise unpopulated tract known as Cosby's "Mannor." In 1784. Hugh White, a Connecticut migrant, settled there and established Whitestown. Eight years later, the place seemed "enchanted ground" where "an extensive weli built" settlement was surrounded by "highly cultivated fields." Historian Mary Ryan's account of how that community grew in the nineteenth century shows the many changes that took place as Whitestown mushroomed into the city of Utica. In 1792, though true urbanization lay well in the future, the ways of the New England village were already being left behind. Had Hugh White left Connecticut in 1764 instead of twenty years later, he might have taken the path that led Benedict and Rebecca Alford to the Green Mountains. There he and his fellows would have tried to make their village similar to what they had left behind. Instead, White helped to create "a patchwork of detached farms and dwelling units rather than a dense nucleated New England village." Whitestown's fate was not to be a "closed, corporate Christian utopian community," such as Dedham, Massachusetts, once had been; rather, it and many a settlement like it would be a "cradle of the middle class." By no means did the future of all American farmers lie in the ranks of that class. A Populist of the 1890s or a dust-bowl Okie of the 1930s would have laughed at any such notion. But the Northern farmers of the revolutionary era lived through changes in which that class had one of its beginnings.

III

Rebecca Owen Alford has little voice of her own in the genealogical records that tell us something of her, but the women of the era found that their lives were very different by the time the Revolution was over. She personally experienced one significant and unusual change, for as early as 1775 she was buying and selling land in her own name. For most married women of the eighteenth century, the possibility of independent economic action simply did not exist. Both their persons and their property were by law submerged in those of their husbands, and only by an elaborate procedure in which male trustees acted for them might they get around that status. A woman of independent wealth might find such a procedure worthwhile, but most did not bother. Nor, in most places, would the law be changed to allow a woman control over what was hers, until well into the next century. The legal doctrine that she was a *feme covert*, or "covered woman," still held.

But some women of the Revolution did find that they had voices and energies. Some used those energies to kick at the constraints all around them. The most famous instance comes from a prominent woman, Abigail Smith Adams, wife of John, who called on her husband to "remember the ladies" when he and his fellow statesmen were writing their republican constitutions. Her warning that she and her sisters were "determined to foment a rebellion" was bravado, not a real threat, and John brushed it off with condescension. But Abigail already had a great deal of experience at running "his" business affairs while he played politician, and she would gain a good deal more in the years of diplomacy and high office that lay ahead. She loved John deeply, as their endless correspondence shows, but she was also an angry woman who thought for herself. Her letters to other women, such as the historian Mercy Otis Warren, make that plain.

Abigail Smith Adams was a woman who became used to great prominence and to hobnobbing with important people. Women very unlike her felt the same frustrations and experienced similar changes in their relations with the men in their lives. Some, in fact, went considerably further than she.

War and the disruptions it brought were nothing new to eighteenth-century American women. If they lived on the frontier, danger had long been part of their lives. If they lived closer to the seaboard, they had had many chances to watch their husbands and sons and uncles and cousins and lovers march off, knowing that many would not come back. But the struggle for independence made war an immediate reality for everyone at some point. British occupation, militia call-ups, the marching of armies back and forth became facts of life, facts that frequently pulled the lives of women and men in different directions. Many women shared Abigail Smith

Adams's experience of taking control of affairs, and this experience made a difference to how they saw the world. Mary Beth Norton shows in her study of women's revolutionary experience how roles changed. No longer ignorant of the world beyond the household, unable to turn to someone else, women learned "to rely increasingly on their own judgment and ability, for they had no alternative."

Even their language changed. Norton describes women who stopped telling their absent husbands about "your farming business" and began to speak of "our farming business." She writes as well of men who learned to live with the change, telling their wives about business matters instead of keeping them ignorant, and treating them with respect instead of condescension. Norton's subjects tend to be prominent, the sort of people who kept diaries, carried on extended correspondence, and thought both worth preserving. But a very ordinary New Jersey wife, Mary Hay Burn, provides a striking example of where a woman's experience of running her own life could lead. In the autumn of 1776, she and her children were living in New Hackensack, and she found herself faced with terrible problems. Her husband, John, was off with Washington's army, and a man named Dirrick Hoogland had "warranted me to go out of my house, and has forewarned me to repair it, for he says he will pull off the roof and fetch it all home. What I shall do I know not." But she did know that what was happening was wrong. She wanted John or one of his officers to intervene, "since you are listed for to go and fight for liberty. Why should I not have liberty," she asked, "whilst you strive for liberty?" Mary May Burn was claiming much more than a share in someone's farming business. Confronted by injustice, stricken with fright, she was still asserting that American liberty meant nothing if it did not mean something for her.

Individual consciousness and concerted political action are not the same. In a way, it was appropriate that no organized groups of women marched in the Philadelphia parade. The

parade celebrated the collective awareness and the cohesion
that the artisans of the revolutionary generation had gained.
The granddaughters of that generation, women such as Elizabeth Cady Stanton, would be the ones to face the task of creating a durable and serious movement among their own sex. But
the women of the Revolution did take steps in that direction.

Some men actually encouraged it. As early as the 1760s,
radical propagandists were urging women to support the cause
by giving up tea and finery. These people often looked down
on the women they were addressing, and there were times
when male writers made bitter fun of the whole notion of
women in politics. Nonetheless, women were being told that
they could do something that counted in the world. The late
1760s saw "Daughters of Liberty" gathering to spin thread
and weave cloth for the sake of replacing British manufactures. Their gatherings became as ritualized as any crowd
action, and, as Norton puts it, "the entire community became
involved." Their movement, if such it was, was short-lived,
and to at least some extent it was under male guidance. In the
summer of 1780, however, a movement more genuinely
women's own took fleeting shape. It began in Philadelphia
with a broadside called "The Sentiments of an American
Woman." The work of Esther DeBerdt Reed, an English
migrant who had married a prominent Pennsylvanian, the
broadside asserted women's right to be actively patriotic. It
called on women to sacrifice their luxuries and donate the
money they saved and thus help remedy the wretched conditions that American troops were enduring.

Women responded, first in Philadelphia and then elsewhere. They went door-to-door making collections; they
formed committees to deal with the money; ultimately, they
raised a considerable sum. In one sense, their role was traditional, for they were offering men their support. But in another it was not, for they were acting in concert without the
slightest male control. Moreover, when the money was collected, they insisted that *they* would decide how it would be

used. The women simply wanted to give the soldiers hard cash to spend as they pleased, but General Washington himself intervened, insisting that it be put toward shirts instead. Both imagery and autonomy were at stake, for Washington was pushing them toward a more traditional role and was asserting authority over them. The general won, but for a brief moment women of the Revolution had organized themselves and had acted on their own.

The war's end saw loyalist women and patriot women living very differently. Many Tory widows appear in the records of Britain's commissioners for compensation. For them, it seemed that nothing had changed. They confessed their inability to deal with important affairs; they pleaded their ignorance about what their husbands had owned and done; they threw themselves on the commissioners' mercy. But the patriot women had developed a "reverence of self." They were asserting the right of their daughters to education and were founding schools to provide it. They were reading newspapers and discussing public events. Some were beginning to think that it was not their duty simply to bear child after child.

What was developing was an awareness of contradictions, not complete change. Traditional images and roles remained powerful. But now they conflicted with both the experience of upheaval and the ideology of equality. Linda Kerber's study *Women of the Republic* has shown how "republican motherhood" offered one way of resolving the problem, at least for the time being. The first task of a republican mother was to train her sons for active citizenship. She needed education, strength, and awareness of the world about her, and those needs "justified women's absorption and participation in the civic culture." Invented by women, the role defined them as partakers in public life. If they were to succeed in molding republican citizens, they needed to imbibe a fair amount of republicanism themselves.

At times it went further, at least in imagery. Throughout

the era, artists portrayed American liberty in female form.
The image was derived from earlier images of Britannia, and
invariably it showed a woman who was young, with loose,
flowing garments covering a body that was strong and assertive
rather than weak and trembling. She carried a shield and a
spear, on whose tip a cap of liberty rested. Some representa-
tions show her at the point of defilement by wicked, leering
men, but her own posture is one of outraged resistance. In
others, she leads men into combat. One woodcut that won
considerable popularity carries the point further, and perhaps
comes closer to reality. It shows not a demigoddess with the
costume, cap, and insignia that convention required but
rather a crudely drawn real woman. She wears a dress of her
time, not a classical robe, but she also wears a man's tricorn
hat and carries a powder horn and a musket. Female imagery
remains dominant, but she has taken on some of the identify-
ing marks of the other sex. The representation expresses perfectly both the dilemmas and the opportunities that the Revolution brought.

One other image is even more tantalizing. Painted in 1792
under a commission from the Library Company in Philadelphia, it shows the goddess of liberty in the costume and with
the iconography that had become familiar. But her feet rest
on a broken chain, and she is offering the arts and the sciences
to a woman and two men who sit in front of her. They are
black, and in the background are more blacks in an "attitude
expressive of Ease & Joy." The Library Company had told the
artist what it wanted. It is as if its members foresaw how intertwined the future struggles of American blacks and American
women were to be.

IV

For a sizable number of blacks, the promise suggested by
that painted broken chain came true. For many more, it did
not. But for black America the Revolution did make a differ-

ence. It was not simply that some whites took the Revolution's rhetoric of liberty seriously enough to do something about the real slaves in their midst. Nor was it just that others, whose parents had lived unthinkingly on slave labor, now realized the magnitude of their dilemma. Both did happen. Massachusetts and Vermont ended slavery completely by 1780. Other Northern states began the task of abolishing it, albeit sometimes with painful slowness. Manumission societies took shape. People across the whole political spectrum from High Tory to Ultra-Democrat discussed the evils of slavery, both in public and in private. A wave of manumissions started slaveholding Maryland and Delaware down the path that led to their refusal to join the Confederacy in 1861. Even farther south, planters felt the currents of the time. As Richard Dunn has noted, "The number of free blacks in the Chesapeake rose from a few thousand in 1776 to 60,000 by 1810."

What is much more important is that blacks felt and responded to those currents. The story of Lord Dunmore's "Ethiopian Regiment," raised by offering the king's freedom to slaves who would leave their rebel masters, is well known. So is the way that black refugees left by the thousands with the departing British Army in 1783. But only in very recent years have historians begun to appreciate that the choice was more than one of flee with the British or remain enslaved, perhaps hoping for manumission. The Revolution had different effects on blacks in different places, just as it did on whites. Blacks themselves began to find their own voices and to shape the ways of living and the institutions that would make them a people.

What might the course of the Revolution's events have been for someone like Sam, the South Carolina slave introduced in Chapter 1? The man who claimed Sam as his property was a noted revolutionary, serving in the highest ranks of the army and helping to frame the Constitution. Indeed, Charles Cotesworth Pinckney's whole family were ardent republicans. Historians have selected his mother, Eliza, as a perfect repre-

sentative of the ideal of republican motherhood. Sam was a
skilled carpenter and he was privileged to hire out his own
time, sometimes. When he was working on his own, he may
have come in contact with the white artisan republicanism
that was developing in Charleston. Beliefs that were clearly
derived from it appeared among freed blacks when Carolina
slavery ended three-quarters of a century later. Blacks had
picked them up, made them their own, and passed them down
somehow. Sam may have overheard men like Pinckney in political conversation, and he may have decided to turn their fine
rhetoric to his own use. Blacks to the north, in the Chesapeake
region, dia barrage "the courts with freedom suits" after independence. T e masters may have spoken of liberty, may even
have promised it, but it was the slaves who took steps to win it.

Most probably, Sam's experience was somewhat different.
Unlike Virginians, few South Carolina planters ever had any
real qualms about slavery. Black Carolinians, instead of seeing
a fair number of their fellows win freedom, whether by manumission, running away, or lawsuit, briefly found that the
Revolution gave them considerable autonomy within slavery.
During the war years, the masters simply were not there.
Slaves on the rice and indigo plantations had to cope for themselves and sometimes even ran the estates. Whether in Carolina or in Virginia, blacks who could not escape slavery began
to generate a much more intense community in the quarters.
As Rhys Isaac notes, it took place while white Virginians were
losing their "public" way of life and becoming an individualistic, private people.

The emergence of black community had at least three distinct dimensions. One was cultural and might be symbolized
by the development of Gullah among Carolina and Georgia
slaves. Gullah, an English-based Creole language, blended
patterns and words derived both from Africa and from the
masters in a speech the slaves alone could understand. Its development had nothing to do with the Revolution, beyond
the fact that it was taking place at about the same time. But

it did give the slaves who spoke it a means of communication that was all their own. A second dimension lay in the beginnings of the black American family. This, too, had nothing directly to do with the Revolution. But all recent scholarship on the subject has stressed two qualities that marked black family life as it took shape. One was the considerable difference between the patterns and the customs that made it up and those that whites observed, which is a significant sign that blacks were in control of their own moral and personal lives. The other is the way that those patterns and customs helped the people who lived within them to cope with the immense pressures that slavery placed upon them. Enslaved blacks were in no position to display the openly political self-consciousness of white artisans, or even to experiment with it, as white farmers and some white women did. But, in ways that hardly any whites could have understood, they were shaping their own identity.

Among the growing number of free blacks farther north, something else, of equally great importance, was happening: the creation of organized black Christianity. Gary Nash has noted recently how difficult it was for these people to forge their own freedom. In the Revolution's aftermath, as in so much later American history, the freedom that the law gave was in no way the freedom to live in decency and dignity. On the contrary, it usually meant enforced squalor, poor employment, exclusion from public life, and inferior education. It also meant the unending possibility of having to endure mindless victimization by whites who thought that torture was fun. Robert Gross tells of the agony of a Concord black named Brister Freeman who accepted the offer of "a little job to do" in a slaughterhouse. He found himself facing a ferocious bull, and as he fought for his life, he had to listen to gales of laughter from whites looking on. It marked him for life.

In religion, blacks found the chance to define a privileged place that was really theirs. It was not until 1816 that the African Methodist Episcopal Church took formal shape, but for half a century before, blacks had been creating their own form of evangelical Christianity. Partly, they were responding to the initial promise of brotherhood and sisterhood that white Baptists and Methodists offered. Partly, they were reacting against the way that Baptists and Methodists began to reject blacks not long after. In part, perhaps, they were using Christianity to keep alive what was left of their own African heritage. But, in any case, as they developed their churches, they were creating a set of institutions of which many whites were suspicious, to which some were hostile, but which could not be destroyed. It was, after all, the Protestant gospel of salvation that black ministers were preaching.

The importance of their churches for black Americans' later struggles needs no elaboration. Merely to mention Martin Luther King, Jr., makes the point. The church would not be the only source of black resistance, but unlike either Gullah or black family life, it would provide a direct link to the Revolution. It was, after all, in evangelical enthusiasm that some of the first cracks in the old colonial order of human inequality began to appear. And among the people who even then pushed furthest the Revolution's message that all people were indeed created equal, evangelicals had a prominent place.

V

What, then, was the American Revolution? Was it simply the decision of the thirteen colonies to declare their independence? Did it arise from the strains of war, as Britain struggled unsuccessfully to retain its hold? Did the Revolution lie in the replacement of monarchy by a republican government? Did it take place in Americans' consciousness, their mentality, their ideology, or in the real world of their social and political relationships? Was it the work of a united people? Did it pit different kinds of Americans against one another? Or was *the* Revolution no single one of these but rather a grand transformation that bound together many separate changes?

Without the great political events of the 1760s, of 1776, and of 1787, we would not speak of any revolution at all. Here the bare story seems simple enough. Beginning in 1763, Britain challenged the traditional autonomy of the colonies with its imperial reforms and with its new taxes. The colonies responded, nullifying first those policies and then their tie to Britain itself. Then they created a republic where an empire had been. Destroying British rule was an achievement of immense significance. Like the Dutch revolt against Spain almost two centuries earlier, it showed that even a power which commanded the world could be defeated by people who were determined to stand their own ground. If there is any link between this movement by white settler-colonists and anti-colonial struggles in the modern-day Third World, that is it. Creating the Republic was also of the highest importance. The dream of republicanism had a long history by 1787, and other people had tried to make it come true. But the undoubted success of the American attempt helped to wipe out many bad memories of republican failures. It would encourage people to try again even after the bright hopes of revolutionary France were dashed by Napoleon and by the eventual restoration of the Bourbon monarchy.

The Revolution wrought changes in the language of human freedom. Hesitant provincial writing gave way to prose that was sure and self-confident. Entrapment in beliefs that had been handed down yielded to clear-eyed creative analysis. What began as a defense of traditional ways became an assertion of human liberty and equality. Thanks to Tom Paine and to others like him, an erudite discourse that had been the preserve of the upper class turned into a raucous debate in which all sorts of people found their voice. A political theory founded on stasis among unchanging "orders" of men was replaced by one that accepted change among people of many kinds. Gordon Wood is correct when he describes it all as "worthy of a prominent place in the history of Western thought."

Power and thought both turn on human relationships, and it is there that we find the Revolution's heart. The most visible immediate change came in what we might call political society, the pattern of beliefs and customs that mediates between men who govern and the people they rule. The year 1776 saw the collapse of virtually all old political relations. It inaugurated a search—energetic, frantic, and hopeful—for new relations to take their place. The search was necessary because people who once had been content to stand to the side now insisted on coming to the center. People began to say that a private was as good as a colonel, a baker as good as a merchant, a plowman as good as a landlord, and that was no small change. Some began to think and say the same about blacks and women, and that was considerably more.

"Lesser" white males, privates, artisans, and farmers, were, of course, already half-participants in the world of colonial politics. For them to become full citizens was a real jump, but not an impossibly long one. Most of those same men believed that they had a direct interest in keeping women and blacks "in their place." But change did begin. Like artisans and farmers of the revolutionary era, women and blacks would have to go through a long, painful struggle to win their freedom. Together with later generations of white workingmen, they would find that even once grasped, the goal was evasive, and that keeping it could take just as much effort as winning it. Both the ideals and the history of the Revolution gave that quest a legitimacy it had never before enjoyed. Workers on strike against conditions in early New England mills, the women's rights convention at Seneca Falls, New York, in 1848, Populists in Oklahoma and Texas in the 1890s, and the Black Panther Party of the late 1960s all would claim the Revolution's heritage as their own.

That heritage was to be one of national strength as well as one of personal and political freedom. It was from people's involvement in the nation's life that that strength came. Madison's whole point in the tenth *Federalist* was that an enduring republic would be possible only if it suited the needs of the kinds of people Americans had become. It did suit them, and that was what enabled the federal government to endure as the United States conquered a continent, waged a civil war, transformed itself to industrial ways, and won, for a time, mastery of the world.

Now we live with problems that no one who was involved in the making of the republic could possibly have foreseen. Our once-unquestionable world dominion is receding. What was our industrial heartland is becoming a post-industrial wasteland. Hispanic and Asian immigrants who follow the well-trodden paths to the republic's cities find dazzling wealth and choking poverty side by side. In the space of only minutes, the power of our weapons could become the means of our own and the world's destruction. But the founders of the republic were human beings, not demigods. Like the people of any era, some were extraordinary and most were very plain. Some were producers and givers, and others were consumers and takers. Some enjoyed wide vision, and some had narrow sight. These people made their Revolution in a world very different from ours, but what they did still has lessons for us. One is that if our own problems are to be faced and resolved as creatively as theirs were, it is up to us to do it. Another is that we must respect the equal right of other people to do the same for themselves. Equal rights, after all, were what it was all about.

Bibliographical Essay

A full bibliography of the Revolution would be at least as long as this book, and it is not my intention to present one here. Instead, this essay points out some of the high points in the study of the subject, suggests some approaches to the work of earlier historians, and discusses in some detail the studies produced in our own time.

George Bancroft looms above all other nineteenth-century historians of the Revolution. His *History of the United States from the Discovery of the Continent*—"The Author's Last Revision," 6 vols. (New York: D. Appleton, 1890) is a sweeping, vividly written account of the rise of American liberty and found a wide readership. Like Bancroft, John Fiske wrote for a popular audience. In *The Critical Period of American History, 1783–1789* (Boston: Houghton Mifflin, 1888), he agreed with Bancroft's assertion that the federal Constitution marked liberty's final triumph. But, from the beginning, other voices were also heard. The New York Anti-Federalist Abraham Yates wrote a history of the movement for the Constitution which was framed in very different terms, and the modern historian Staughton Lynd edited and published it in the *William and Mary Quarterly*, 3rd ser. [hereafter WMQ], 20 (1963), 223–25.

The doubts that Yates first expressed lay behind the writing of the early-twentieth-century "Progressive" historians, all of whom quarreled with the notion that the Revolution was a simple, direct struggle for liberty. The work of Carl Becker, Charles A. Beard, J. Franklin Jameson, and Arthur Schlesinger, Sr., sums up their approach. Becker's *History of Political Parties in the Province of New York, 1760–1776* (Madison: University of Wisconsin Press, 1909) proposed that the Revolution "was the result of two general movements: the contest for home-rule and independence, and the democratization of American politics and society." His *The Declaration of Independence: A Study in the History of Political Ideas* (New York: Alfred A. Knopf, 1922) was for decades the major study of the Declaration. Beard's *An Economic Interpretation of the Constitution of the United States* (New York: Macmillan, 1913) argued that the Constitution marked the triumph not of abstract principles but rather of self-seeking speculators. It built on evidence first presented in Orin G. Libby, *The Geographical Distribution of the Vote of the Thirteen States on the Federal Constitution, 1787–8* (Madison: University of Wisconsin, 1894). Jameson's short book, *The American Revolution Considered as a Social Movement* (Princeton University Press, 1926), developed in broad terms the assertion that the Revolution had social roots and consequences; and Schlesinger's *The Colonial Merchants and the American Revolution, 1763–1776* (New York, 1918; reprinted New York: Atheneum, 1968) traced the experience of one group that was central to the Revolution's making. The Wisconsin historian Merrill Jensen kept their tradition alive in a scholarly career that stretched from *The Articles of Confederation* (Madison: University of Wisconsin Press, 1940) to *The American Revolution Within America* (New York University Press, 1974).

The other major approach of early-twentieth-century historians centered on Yale and the figure of Charles McLean Andrews. His *Colonial Background of the American Revolution: Four Essays in American Colonial History* (New Haven: Yale University Press, 1924) summarized a position that he and his many graduate students adopted, maintaining that British imperial administrators were honest, fair-minded men concerned with running an empire, not with establishing tyranny. Lawrence Henry Gipson, in particular, developed that position. *The British Empire Before the American Revolution* (New York: Alfred A. Knopf, 1939–70) is a multi-volume achievement in the spirit of Bancroft; and *The Coming of the Revolution, 1763–1775* (New York: Harper & Row, 1962) distills his argument.

In the mid-twentieth century, a different approach appeared, critical of both "Progressive" and "Imperial" historians. Two books were central. Robert E. Brown's *Middle-Class Democracy and the Revolution in Massachusetts* (Ithaca: Cornell University Press, 1955) challenged the notion that the Revolution had internal causes, and marked the beginning of a long attack by Brown on Carl Becker's professional reputation. Forrest McDonald's *We the People: The Economic Origins of the Constitution* (Chicago: University of Chicago Press, 1958) used Charles Beard's own methods to demolish Beard's argument. The work of both scholars was essentially critical, but the era brought positive achievements as well. Edmund S. Morgan and Helen M. Morgan argued in *The Stamp Act Crisis: Prologue to Revolution* (Chapel Hill: University of North Carolina Press, 1953) that political principles counted, and showed how the colonials responded to the first stage of the imperial crisis. Jack P. Greene's *The Quest for Power: The Lower Houses of Assembly in the Southern Royal Colonies, 1689–1776* (Chapel Hill: University of North Carolina Press, 1963) explored the political matrix from which a large proportion of the revolutionary leadership emerged.

The work of these historians must stand for that of many others who addressed similar questions. Jack P. Greene discussed at length the historiography of the Revolution to 1968 in the introductory essay of his *The Reinterpretation of the American Revolution, 1763–1789* (New York: Harper &

Row, 1968), which also includes the work of a wide range of writers. Among the essays reprinted are Stanley Elkins and Eric McKitrick's portrayal of the Founding Fathers as "Young Men of the Revolution" and John P. Roche's account of them as a "Reform Caucus in Action. Edmund S. Morgan, ed., *The American Revolution: Two Centuries of Interpretation* (Englewood Cliffs, N.J.: Prentice-Hall, 1965), and Esmond Wright, ed., *Causes and Consequences of the American Revolution* (Chicago: Quadrangle, 1966), likewise survey earlier writing. They can be read in conjunction with the pre-World War II essays in Richard B. Morris, ed., *The Era of the American Revolution* (New York: Columbia University Press, 1939).

Since Greene surveyed the literature in 1968, an immense amount of writing has appeared. One way to approach it is through review essays, which consider major writing and discuss achievements, problems, and possibilities. A number of these have concerned themselves with the historiography of early New England. They include Richard R. Beeman, "The New Social History and the Search for 'Community' in Colonial America," *American Quarterly* [hereafter AQ] *29* (1977), 422–43; Richard S. Dunn, "The Social History of Early New England," AQ *24* (1972), 661–84; Rhys Isaac, "Order and Growth, Authority and Meaning in Colonial New England," *American Historical Review* [hereafter *AHR*] *76* (1971), 728–37; James A. Henretta, "The Morphology of New England Society in the Colonial Period," *Journal of Interdisciplinary History 2* (1971–72), 379–98; and John M. Murrin, "Review Essay," *History and Theory 11* (1972), 226–75. Douglas Greenberg surveys writing on the middle colonies in "The Middle Colonies in Recent American Historiography," WMQ *36* (1979), 396–427. New studies of the South are considered in Edward Countryman, "Stability and Class, Theory and History: The South in the Eighteenth Century," *Journal of American Studies* [hereafter JAS] *17* (1983), 243–50. A number of review essays consider writing on the process and achievements of the Revolution. Among them are Edward Countryman, "The Problem of the Early American Crowd," JAS 7 (1973), 77–90; Pauline Maier, "Why Revolution? Why Democracy?" *Journal of Interdisciplinary History* 6 (1975–76), 711–32; Richard B. Morris, " 'We the People of the United States': The Bicentennial of a People's Revolution," AHR 82 (1977), 1–19; Robert E. Shalhope, "Toward a Republican Synthesis: The Emergence of an Understanding of Republicanism in American Historiography," WMQ 29 (1972), 49–80, and "Republicanism and Early American Historiography," WMQ 39 (1982), 334–56; James H. Hutson, "Country, Court and the Constitution: Antifederalism and the Historians," WMQ 38 (1981), 337–68; and Michael Zuckerman, "The Irrelevant Revolution: 1776 and Since," AQ 30 (1978), 224–42. The collection edited by Jack P. Greene and J. R. Pole, *Colonial British America: Essays in the New History of the Early Modern Era* (Baltimore: Johns Hopkins University Press, 1984), contains very thorough essays on practically every aspect of recent writing about early America.

During the bicentennial decade, many other anthologies appeared on the Revolution. In some cases, they present short statements of arguments that appear more fully elsewhere; in others, the essays stand by themselves. Among the more noteworthy are Erich Angermann et al., eds., *New Wine in Old Skins: A Comparative View of Socio-Political Structures and Values Affecting the American Revolution* (Stuttgart: Klett, 1976); Bernard Bailyn and John B. Hench, eds., *The Press & the American Revolution* (Boston: Northeastern University Press, 1981); Richard Maxwell Brown and Don E. Fehrenbacher, eds., *Tradition, Conflict and Modernization: Perspectives on the American Revolution* (New York: Academic Press, 1977); W. Robert Higgins, ed., *The Revolutionary War in the South: Power, Conflict and Leadership: Essays in Honor of John Richard Alden* (Durham, N.C.: Duke University Press, 1979); Ronald Hoffman and Ira

Berlin, eds., *Slavery and Freedom in the Age of the American Revolution* (Charlottesville: University Press of Virginia, 1983); Ronald Hoffman and Peter J. Albert, eds., *Sovereign States in an Age of Uncertainty* (Charlottesville: University Press of Virginia, 1982); Richard M. Jellison, ed., *Society, Freedom and Conscience: The American Revolution in Virginia, Massachusetts and New York* (New York: W. W. Norton, 1976); Stanley Nider Katz, ed., *Colonial America* (Boston: Little, Brown, 1971); Stephen G. Kurtz and James H. Hutson, eds., *Essays on the American Revolution* (Chapel Hill: University of North Carolina Press, 1973); *The Development of a Revolutionary Mentality* (Washington, D.C.: Library of Congress, 1972); James Kirby Martin, ed., *The Human Dimensions of Nation Making: Essays on Colonial and Revolutionary America* (Madison: State Historical Society of Wisconsin, 1976); J. G. A. Pocock, ed., *Three British Revolutions: 1641, 1688, 1776* (Princeton University Press, 1980); and Alfred F. Young, ed., *The American Revolution: Explorations in the History of American Radicalism* (De Kalb: Northern Illinois University Press, 1976).

Recent historians have paid relatively little attention to the link between Britain and the colonies, but some significant studies have appeared. Colin Bonwick's *English Radicals and the American Revolution* (Chapel Hill: University of North Carolina Press, 1977) is one of several discussions of the opposition within Britain to British government policies. John Brewer, *Party Ideology and Popular Politics at the Accession of George III* (New York: Cambridge University Press, 1976), is the most recent statement in a debate launched long ago by Sir Lewis Namier. John Brooke's *King George III* (New York: McGraw-Hill, 1972) is a fair-minded biography. J. M. Bumsted discusses the beginning of the idea of independence in " 'Things in the Womb of Time': Ideas of American Independence, 1633 to 1763," *WMQ 31* (1974), 533–64. Paul G. E. Clemens, *The Atlantic Economy and Colonial Maryland's Eastern Shore: From Tobacco to Grain*

(Ithaca: Cornell University Press, 1980), and Ralph Davis, *The Rise of the Atlantic Economies* (Ithaca: Cornell University Press, 1973), both consider the pre-revolutionary Atlantic trading network. The same subject is discussed in Jacob M. Price, *France and the Chesapeake: A History of the French Tobacco Monopoly, 1674–1791* (Ann Arbor: University of Michigan Press, 1973). R. C. Simmons, *The American Colonies from Settlement to Independence* (New York: David McKay, 1976), is a well-received survey.

A number of scholars have explored the political aspects of the transatlantic tie. Among the resulting studies are James A. Henretta, *"Salutary Neglect": Colonial Administration Under the Duke of Newcastle* (Princeton University Press, 1972); Michael Kammen, *A Rope of Sand: The Colonial Agents, British Politics, and the American Revolution* (Ithaca: Cornell University Press, 1967), and *Empire and Interest: The American Colonies and the Politics of Mercantilism* (Philadelphia: J. B. Lippincott, 1970); Stanley Nider Katz, *Newcastle's New York: Anglo-American Politics, 1732–1753* (Cambridge: Harvard University Press, 1968); Alison Gilbert Olson, *Anglo-American Politics, 1660–1775: The Relationship Between Parties in England and Colonial America* (New York: Oxford University Press, 1973), and "The London Mercantile Lobby and the Coming of the American Revolution," *Journal of American History* [hereafter JAH] *69* (1982), 21–41. Among recent studies of specific aspects of British policy are John L. Bullion, *A Great and Necessary Measure: George Grenville and the Genesis of the Stamp Act, 1763–1765* (Columbia: University of Missouri Press, 1983); Robert J. Chaffin, "The Townshend Acts of 1767," WMQ *27* (1970), 90–121; John Derry, *English Politics and the American Revolution* (New York: St. Martin's Press, 1976); Joseph Albert Ernst, *Money and Politics in America: A Study in the Currency Act of 1764 and the Political Economy of Revolution* (Chapel Hill: University of North Carolina Press, 1973); Philip Lawson, "George Grenville and America: The Years of Opposition,

1765–1770," WMQ *37* (1980), 561–76; and P. D. G. Thomas, *British Politics and the Stamp Act Crisis: The First Phase of the American Revolution, 1763–1767* (Oxford: Clarendon Press, 1975). The imperial problem is considered in wide terms in Ian R. Christie and Benjamin W. Labaree, *Empire or Independence, 1760–1776: A British-American Dialogue on the Coming of the American Revolution* (New York: W. W. Norton, 1976), and in Robert W. Tucker and David C. Hendrickson, *The Fall of the First British Empire: Origin of the War of American Independence* (Baltimore: Johns Hopkins University Press, 1982). In addition, two anthologies deal specifically with imperial relations: Peter Marshall and Glynn Williams, eds., *The British Empire Before the American Revolution* (London: Frank Cass, 1980), and Alison Gilbert Olson and Richard Maxwell Brown, eds., *Anglo-American Political Relations, 1765–1775* (New Brunswick: Rutgers University Press, 1970). These studies provide a context for the ideas advanced in Thomas C. Barrow, "The American Revolution as a Colonial War for Independence," WMQ *25* (1968), 452–64, and in Richard B. Morris, *The Emerging Nations and the American Revolution* (New York: Harper & Row, 1970).

The study of early American social development has been extremely rich during recent years, both in terms of synthesis and overviews and in terms of narrowly focused monographs. Jack P. Greene, "The Social Origins of the American Revolution: An Evaluation and an Interpretation," *Political Science Quarterly 88* (1973), 1–22, and Kenneth A. Lockridge, "Social Change and the Meaning of the American Revolution," *Journal of Social History 6* (1972–73), 397–439, both consider the problem in wide terms. So do the essays by T. H. Breen collected as *Puritans and Adventurers: Change and Persistence in Early America* (New York: Oxford University Press, 1980). A number of studies have dealt with the demography of the revolutionary era. They include James A. Henretta, *The Evolution of American Society,*

1700–1815: An Interdisciplinary Analysis (Lexington, Mass.: D. C. Heath, 1973); Peter Charles Hoffer, *Revolution and Regeneration: Life Cycle and the Historical Vision of the Generation of 1776* (Athens: University of Georgia Press, 1982); Gary B. Nash, *Red, White and Black: The Peoples of Early America* (Englewood Cliffs, N.J.: Prentice-Hall, 1974); and Robert V. Wells, Jr., *The Population of the British Colonies in America Before 1776: A Survey of Census Data* (Princeton University Press, 1975). Since 1973, a multi-volume series has been providing up-to-date histories of the thirteen colonies, beginning with Hugh T. Leffler and William S. Powell, *Colonial North Carolina: A History* (New York: Charles Scribner's Sons, 1973). There are volumes on New Jersey (by John E. Pomfret), New York (by Michael Kammen), Rhode Island (by Sydney V. James), Pennsylvania (by Joseph E. Illick), Georgia (by Kenneth Coleman), Massachusetts (by Benjamin Labaree), Delaware (by John A. Munroe), Connecticut (by Robert J. Taylor), New Hampshire (by Jere R. Daniell), Maryland (by Aubrey C. Land), and South Carolina (by Robert M. Weir). Since 1979, the series has been published by KTO Press, Millwood, N.Y.

A number of studies have considered economic and social development in specific regions, provinces, and communities. Among the studies on New England are Kenneth A. Lockridge, "Land, Population and the Evolution of New England Society, 1630–1790," *Past & Present*, No. 39 (April 1968), 62–81, and *A New England Town: The First One Hundred Years: Dedham, Massachusetts, 1636–1736* (New York: W. W. Norton, 1970); Michael Zuckerman, *Peaceable Kingdoms: New England Towns in the Eighteenth Century* (New York: Alfred A. Knopf, 1970); and Edward M. Cook, Jr., *The Fathers of the Towns: Leadership and Community Structure in Eighteenth-Century New England* (Baltimore: Johns Hopkins University Press, 1976), together with his "Social Behavior and Changing Values in Dedham, Massachusetts, 1700 to 1775," WMQ 27 (1970), 546–80. Among studies of rural

Massachusetts are Richard L. Bushman, "Massachusetts Farmers and the Revolution," in Jellison, *Society, Freedom and Conscience*; Philip J. Greven, Jr., *Four Generations: Population, Land and Family in Colonial Andover, Massachusetts* (Ithaca: Cornell University Press, 1970); Robert A. Gross, *The Minutemen and Their World* (New York: Hill and Wang, 1976); Gregory H. Nobles, *Divisions Throughout the Whole: Politics and Society in Hampshire County, Massachusetts, 1740–1775* (New York: Cambridge University Press, 1983); Bettye Hobbs Pruitt, "Self-Sufficiency and the Agricultural Economy of Eighteenth Century Massachusetts," WMQ *41* (1984), 333–64; and William Pencak, *War, Politics and Revolution in Provincial Massachusetts* (Boston: Northeastern University Press, 1981). New Hampshire is considered in Jere R. Daniell, *Experiment in Republicanism: New Hampshire Politics and the American Revolution, 1741–1794* (Cambridge: Harvard University Press, 1970), and in Lynn Warren Turner, *The Ninth State: New Hampshire's Formative Years* (Chapel Hill: University of North Carolina Press, 1983). Among studies of Connecticut are Richard Buel, Jr., *Dear Liberty: Connecticut's Mobilization for the Revolutionary War* (Middletown: Wesleyan University Press, 1980); Richard L. Bushman, *From Puritan to Yankee: Character and the Social Order in Connecticut, 1690–1765* (Cambridge: Harvard University Press, 1967); Christopher Collier, *Roger Sherman's Connecticut: Yankee Politics and the American Revolution* (Middletown: Wesleyan University Press, 1971); and Bruce C. Daniels, *The Connecticut Town: Growth and Development, 1635–1790* (Middletown: Wesleyan University Press, 1979).

Modern debate on colonial urban development was launched by James A. Henretta's article "Economic Development and Social Structure in Colonial Boston," WMQ *22* (1965), 75–92. Gary B. Nash develops Henretta's argument and its implications in *The Urban Crucible: Social Change, Political Consciousness, and the Origins of the American*

Revolution (Cambridge: Harvard University Press, 1979). G. B. Warden criticizes Henretta's conclusions in "Inequality and Instability in Eighteenth-Century Boston: A Reappraisal," *Journal of Interdisciplinary History 6* (1975–76), 585–620. John K. Alexander discusses urban poverty before and after independence in *Render Them Submissive: Responses to Poverty in Philadelphia, 1760–1800* (Amherst: University of Massachusetts Press, 1980), as do Alan Kulikoff, "The Progress of Inequality in Revolutionary Boston," *WMQ 28* (1971), 375–412, and Raymond A. Mohl, "Poverty in Early America, A Reappraisal: The Case of Eighteenth-Century New York City," *New York History 50* (1969), 5–27.

A number of studies have considered the development of the interior of the middle colonies. Among studies of New York are Patricia U. Bonomi, *A Factious People: Politics and Society in Colonial New York* (New York: Columbia University Press, 1971); Edward Countryman, *A People in Revolution: The American Revolution and Political Society in New York, 1760–1790* (Baltimore: Johns Hopkins University Press, 1981); Sung Bok Kim, *Landlord and Tenant in Colonial New York: Manorial Society, 1664–1775* (Chapel Hill: University of North Carolina Press, 1978); and Jessica Kross, *The Evolution of an American Town: Newtown, New York, 1642–1775* (Philadelphia: Temple University Press, 1983). Studies of New Jersey include Larry R. Gerlach, *Prelude to Independence: New Jersey in the Coming of the American Revolution* (New Brunswick: Rutgers University Press, 1976); Dennis P. Ryan, "Landholding, Opportunities and Mobility in Revolutionary New Jersey," *WMQ 36* (1979), 571–92; and Donald Wallace White, *A Village at War: Chatham, New Jersey, and the American Revolution* (Rutherford, N.J.: Fairleigh-Dickinson University Press, 1979). Pennsylvania society is the subject of James T. Lemon, *The Best Poor Man's Country: A Geographical Study of Early Southeastern Pennsylvania* (Baltimore: Johns Hopkins University Press, 1972), and of Stephanie Grauman Wolf, *Urban Village:*

Population, Community, and Family Structure in German-town, Pennsylvania, 1683–1800 (Princeton University Press, 1977).

A number of recent books and essays have dealt with the South in the revolutionary era. Two anthologies on the subject are Jeffrey J. Crow and Larry E. Tise, eds., *The Southern Experience in the American Revolution* (Chapel Hill: University of North Carolina Press, 1978), and Ernest McNeill Eller, ed., *Chesapeake Bay in the American Revolution* (Centreville, Md.: Tidewater Publishers, 1981). Among essays that provide overviews are Alan Kulikoff, "The Colonial Chesapeake: Seedbed of Antebellum Southern Culture?" *Journal of Southern History 45* (1979), 513–40, and Carville Earle and Ronald Hoffman, "Staple Crops and Urban Development in the Eighteenth-Century South," *Perspectives in American History 10* (1976), 7–80. Development in Maryland is considered in Ronald Hoffman, *A Spirit of Dissension: Economics, Politics and the Revolution in Maryland* (Baltimore: Johns Hopkins University Press, 1974), and in Gregory A. Stiverson, *Poverty in a Land of Plenty: Tenancy in Eighteenth-Century Maryland* (Baltimore: Johns Hopkins University Press, 1978). Virginia society is studied in Richard R. Beeman, *The Evolution of the Southern Backcountry: A Case Study at Lunenburg County, Virginia, 1746–1832* (Philadelphia: University of Pennsylvania Press, 1984); Marc Egnal, "The Origins of the Revolution in Virginia: A Reinterpretation," WMQ *37* (1980), 401–28; Rhys Isaac, *The Transformation of Virginia, 1740–1790* (Chapel Hill: University of North Carolina Press, 1982); Edmund S. Morgan, *American Slavery, American Freedom: The Ordeal of Colonial Virginia* (New York: W. W. Norton, 1975), and Jan Lewis, *The Pursuit of Happiness: Family and Values in Jefferson's Virginia* (Cambridge University Press, 1983), among many others. The most recent synoptic account of North Carolina is A. Roger Ekirch, *"Poor Carolina": Politics and Society in Colonial North Carolina, 1729–1776*

258 · BIBLIOGRAPHICAL ESSAY

(Chapel Hill: University of North Carolina Press, 1981); and the most recent study of South Carolina is Jerome J. Nadelhaft, *The Disorders of War: The Revolution in South Carolina* (Orono, Maine: University of Maine Press, 1981). Also important for South Carolina is Robert M. Weir, " 'The Harmony We Were Famous For': An Interpretation of Pre-Revolutionary South Carolina Politics," WMQ *26* (1969), 473–501. South Carolina slavery is studied with great sophistication in Peter H. Wood, *Black Majority: Negroes in Colonial South Carolina from 1600 Through the Stono Rebellion* (New York: Alfred A. Knopf, 1975), which should be read in conjunction with Betty Wood, *Slavery in Colonial Georgia, 1730–1775* (Athens: University of Georgia Press, 1984). Florida, not one of the thirteen colonies that rebelled, is considered in J. Leitch Wright, Jr., *Florida in the American Revolution* (Gainesville: University Presses of Florida, 1975); and the frontier is discussed in Jack M. Sosin, *The Revolutionary Frontier, 1765–1783* (New York: Holt, Rinehart and Winston, 1967). John Hope Franklin discusses the large problem of regionalism in "The North, the South and the American Revolution," JAH *62* (1975–76), 5–23. Almost all these studies stand in debt to Jackson Turner Main, *The Social Structure of Revolutionary America* (Princeton University Press, 1965). All of them can be read in conjunction with the maps contained in Lester J. Cappon et al., eds., *Atlas of Early American History: The Revolutionary Era, 1760–1790* (Princeton University Press, 1976). Large interpretive frameworks for understanding rural development are also offered in James A. Henretta, "Families and Farms: *Mentalité* in Pre-Industrial America," WMQ *35* (1978), 3–32; in Michael Merrill, "Cash Is Good to Eat: Self-Sufficiency and Exchange in the Rural Economy of the United States," *Radical History Review*, No. 4 (1977), 42–71; and in Rowland Berthoff and John M. Murrin, "Freedom, Communalism and the Yeoman Freeholder: The American

Revolution Considered as a Social Accident," in Kurtz and Hutson, eds., *Essays on the Revolution.*

Economic as opposed to social development has been the subject of a considerable amount of recent work. Marc Egnal offers a short overview in "The Economic Development of the Thirteen Continental Colonies, 1720–1775," WMQ *32* (1975), 191–222. Edwin J. Perkins presents a book-length discussion of the same subject in *The Economy of Colonial America* (New York: Columbia University Press, 1980). Jacob M. Price has written on the subject in a number of places, most recently in *Capital and Credit in British Overseas Trade: The View from the Chesapeake, 1700–1776* (Cambridge: Harvard University Press, 1980). Also important are James F. Shepherd and Gary M. Walton, *Shipping, Maritime Trade and the Economic Development of Colonial North America* (Cambridge: Harvard University Press, 1972) and *The Economic Rise of Early America* (Cambridge University Press, 1979). The difference between recent and earlier writing on the early American economy is considered in Gary M. Walton, "The New Economic History and the Burdens of the Navigation Acts," *Economic History Review*, 2nd ser., *24* (1971), 533–42. All students of the subject stand in debt to the monumental achievement of Alice Hanson Jones in *American Colonial Wealth: Documents and Methods* (New York: Arno Press, 1977) and *Wealth of a Nation to Be: The American Colonies on the Eve of the Revolution* (New York: Columbia University Press, 1980). Marc Egnal and Joseph Ernst offer suggestions about the links between economics and politics in "An Economic Interpretation of the American Revolution," WMQ *29* (1972), 3–32.

Recent study of the Revolution, as opposed to colonial development, has concentrated on two broad problems: the political culture of the era and the social and political experience of the revolutionary generation. It is, of course, silly to slot any author or writing into one position or the other and confidently assert that one "knows" what he or it has to say. But it is the case that most scholars who have dealt with political culture have concentrated on ideas and language that the revolutionary generation shared, and that most scholars who have dealt with experience have been interested in what set different kinds of Americans apart.

The study of the language of the Revolution had its beginning in 1948, with Edmund S. Morgan's essay "Colonial Ideas of Parliamentary Power, 1764–1766," WMQ *3* (1948), 311–41. In the decade that followed, Clinton Rossiter expanded on Morgan's point in *Seedtime of the Republic* (New York: Harcourt, Brace and World, 1953); and Caroline Robbins developed their English background in *The Eighteenth Century Commonwealthman: Studies in the Transmission, Development and Circumstance of English Liberal Thought from the Restoration of Charles II until the War with the Thirteen Colonies* (Cambridge: Harvard University Press, 1959). H. Trevor Colbourn demonstrated in *The Lamp of Experience* (Chapel Hill: University of North Carolina Press, 1965) how the intellectuals of the revolutionary era read history and drew lessons from it. At the same time, Douglass Adair and Cecilia Kenyon were publishing a number of important essays on the political ideas of the years following independence. Adair's eventually appeared together as *Fame and the Founding Fathers* (New York: W. W. Norton, 1974). The central statement in this mode of understanding is Bernard Bailyn's *The Ideological Origins of the American Revolution* (Cambridge: Harvard University Press, 1967), which appeared originally as the book-length introduction to his *Pamphlets of the American Revolution* (Cambridge: Harvard University Press, 1965). Bailyn's *The Origins of American Politics* (New York: Alfred A. Knopf, 1968) supplements the argument made in *The Ideological Origins*.

Since then, a number of scholars have expanded on and argued with Bailyn's central contentions. Gordon S. Wood's

"Rhetoric and Reality in the American Revolution," WMQ 23 (1966), and his enormous *The Creation of the American Republic, 1776–1787* (Chapel Hill: University of North Carolina Press, 1969) are both important statements. J. R. Pole writes within much the same framework in *Political Representation in England and the Origins of the American Republic* (New York: St. Martin's Press, 1966), in *The Pursuit of Equality in American History* (Berkeley: University of California Press, 1978), and in *The Gift of Government: Political Responsibility from the English Restoration to American Independence* (Athens: University of Georgia Press, 1983). The French scholar Elise Marienstras takes a different approach in *Les Mythes Fondateurs de la Nation Américaine: Essai sur le Discours Idéologique aux Etats-Unis a l'Epoque de l'Indépendance (1763–1800)* (Paris: François Maspero, 1977). Two German writers have also joined the discussion, and their works are available in English translation. The first is Gerald Stourzh, *Alexander Hamilton and the Idea of Republican Government* (Stanford University Press, 1970), and the second is Willi Paul Adams, *The First American Constitutions: Republican Ideology and the Making of the State Constitutions in the Revolutionary Era* (Chapel Hill: University of North Carolina Press, 1980). State constitutions are also considered in Ronald M. Peters, Jr., *The Massachusetts Constitution of 1780: A Social Compact* (Amherst: University of Massachusetts Press, 1978), and in Peter S. Onuf, "State Making in Revolutionary America: Independent Vermont as a Case Study," JAH 67 (1980–81), 797–815.

Several historians have tried to place the problem of American republicanism in a larger context. One is Jack P. Greene, who launched a debate with Bailyn in "Political Mimesis: Consideration of the Historical and Cultural Roots of Legislative Behavior in the British Colonies in the Eighteenth Century," AHR 75 (1969–70), 337–67. J. G. A. Pocock placed the subject within a larger explanation of the development of early modern thought, in a number of studies, most notably *The Machiavellian Moment: Florentine Political Thought and the Atlantic Republican Tradition* (Princeton University Press, 1975). Garry Wills looked to the influence of eighteenth-century Scottish thinkers in *Inventing America: Jefferson's Declaration of Independence* (New York: Doubleday, 1978) and in *Explaining America: The Federalist* (New York: Doubleday, 1981).

For Bailyn, political language, centered on the abstract notions of "liberty" and "power," was enough in itself to explain the Revolution. For Wood and Pocock, the key terms were "virtue" and "corruption," and for both, ideas took on importance as they interacted with social reality. "Corruption," for instance, was eighteenth-century shorthand for what we now call "capitalist" or "modern" society. By the mid-1970s, a number of intellectual historians were turning to the link between political ideas and political economy. The lead was taken by Staughton Lynd in "Beard, Jefferson, and the Tree of Liberty," in his *Class Conflict: Slavery and the United States Constitution: Ten Essays* (Indianapolis: Bobbs-Merrill, 1967), and by William Appleman Williams in *The Contours of American History* (New York: New Viewpoint, 1973). Edwin G. Burrows and Michael Wallace showed the link between national liberation and the decline of patriarchal control, in "The American Revolution: The Ideology and Psychology of National Liberation," *Perspectives in American History 6* (1972), 167–306, and Jay Fliegelman has done something similar in *Prodigals and Pilgrims: The American Revolution Against Patriarchal Authority, 1750–1800* (New York: Cambridge University Press, 1982). J. E. Crowley set off in a different direction in *This Sheba, Self: The Conceptualization of Economic Life in Eighteenth-Century America* (Baltimore: Johns Hopkins University Press, 1974). At the same time, Joyce Appleby was writing "Liberalism and the American Revolution," *New England Quarterly 49* (1976), 3–26, and "The Social Origins of American Revolutionary Ideology," JAH *64* (1977–78), 935–58. More recently, she has produced *Capitalism and a New Social Order: The Republican Vision of the 1790s* (New York University Press, 1984). Also noteworthy are Drew McCoy, *The Elusive Republic* (Chapel Hill: University of North Carolina Press, 1980), and Nathan O. Hatch, *The Sacred Cause of Liberty: Republican Thought and the Millennium in Revolutionary New England* (New Haven: Yale University Press, 1977), together with Lance Banning, "Republican Ideology and the Triumph of the Constitution, 1789 to 1793," WMQ *31* (1974), 167–88.

The relationship between the Revolution and American law has been the subject of considerable recent study. John Philip Reid has discussed it in three books: *In a Defiant Stance: The Condition of Law in Massachusetts Bay, the Irish Comparison and the Coming of the American Revolution* (University Park: Pennsylvania State University Press, 1977), *In a Rebellious Spirit: The Argument of Facts, the Liberty Riot and the Coming of the American Revolution* (University Park: Pennsylvania State University Press, 1979), and *In Defiance of the Law: The Standing-Army Controversy, the Two Constitutions, and the Coming of the American Revolution* (Chapel Hill: University of North Carolina Press, 1981). William E. Nelson has explored *Americanization of the Common Law: The Impact of Legal Change on Massachusetts Society, 1760–1830* (Cambridge: Harvard University Press, 1975), and Morton J. Horwitz has developed a similar argument in *The Transformation of American Law, 1780–1860* (Cambridge: Harvard University Press, 1977).

Republicanism was the central concept in the culture of the revolutionary era, and it found expression in other ways beside formal political discourse. Kenneth Silverman's *A Cultural History of the American Revolution* (New York: Thomas Y. Crowell, 1976) explores developments in painting, music, literature, and the theater. Michael Kammen's *A Season of Youth: The American Revolution and the His-*

torical Imagination (New York: Alfred A. Knopf, 1979) deals with similar material. The era produced several remarkable artists who have been the subject of recent biographies and critical assessments. See Irma B. Jaffe, *John Trumbull: Patriot-Artist of the American Revolution* (Boston: New York Graphic Society, 1975); Robert C. Alberts, *Benjamin West: A Biography* (Boston: Houghton Mifflin, 1978); and Jules David Prown, *John Singleton Copley*, 2 vols. (Cambridge: Harvard University Press, 1966). Also informative are the catalogues of the many exhibitions that were mounted at the time of the Bicentennial. One of the best is Charles F. Montgomery and Patricia E. Kane, eds., *American Art: 1750–1800, Towards Independence* (Boston: New York Graphic Society, 1976), produced for an exhibition mounted by Yale University and the Victoria and Albert Museum, London. It includes Frank H. Sommer's essay "The Metamorphoses of Britannia," from which some of my comments in Chapter 7 on the visual representation of women are drawn.

Three other studies that speak in different ways to cultural development should also be noted. They are Jack P. Greene, "Search for Identity: An Interpretation of the Meaning of Selected Patterns of Social Response in Eighteenth-Century America," *Journal of Social History 3* (1969–70), 189–221; Nathan O. Hatch, "The Christian Movement and the Demand for a Theology of the People," JAH 67 (1980–81), 545–67; and Stephen A. Marini, *Radical Sects of Revolutionary New England* (Cambridge: Harvard University Press, 1982).

Recent study of experience, as opposed to consciousness and symbolic expression, has taken a number of directions. Some scholars have concentrated on familiar problems and major events, such as the independence crisis and the making and ratification of the Constitution. Among studies of the former are Benjamin Labaree, *The Boston Tea Party* (New York: Oxford University Press, 1964); David Ammerman, *In the Common Cause: American Response to the Coercive*

Acts of 1774 (Charlottesville: University Press of Virginia, 1974); Carl Bridenbaugh, *The Spirit of '76: The Growth of American Patriotism Before Independence* (New York: Oxford University Press, 1975); Thomas Flemming, *1776: Year of Illusion* (New York: W. W. Norton, 1975); and Jack N. Rakove, "The Decision for American Independence: A Reconstruction," *Perspectives in American History 10* (1976), 217–78. Among recent work on the latter, in addition to Wood, *Creation of the Republic*, and Pole, *Political Representation*, are Stephen R. Boyd, *The Politics of Opposition: Anti-federalists and the Acceptance of the Constitution* (Millwood, N.Y.: KTO Press, 1979), and Linda Grant DePauw, *The Eleventh Pillar: New York State and the Federal Constitution* (Ithaca: Cornell University Press, 1966).

Others have looked in different ways at the changing quality of political experience. For some, this has meant the study of the way in which ordinary people participated in the events of the Revolution, including crowds, revolutionary committees, political parties, and the military. For others, the emphasis is on the changing experience of different groups, such as artisans, farmers, blacks, and women. Still others have created a remarkable collection of biographies of lesser leaders. Some studies have brought all these themes together.

Crowd action was a major topic of discussion in the late 1960s and the 1970s. Drawing on the work of European scholars such as George Rudé, E. P. Thompson, E. J. Hobsbawn, and Albert Soboul, a number set out to place early American crowds in their eighteenth-century context and show how they became instruments of revolution. A debate was launched by Staughton Lynd in the essays now collected as *Class Conflict, Slavery and the Constitution* and by Jesse Lemisch in "The American Revolution Seen from the Bottom Up," in Barton J. Bernstein, ed., *Towards a New Past: Dissenting Essays in American History* (New York: Random House, 1968), together with Gordon S. Wood in "A Note on

Mobs in the American Revolution," WMQ *23* (1966), 635–42. Pauline Maier made the first major statement in *From Resistance to Revolution: Colonial Radicals and the Development of American Opposition to Britain, 1765–1776* (New York: Alfred A. Knopf, 1972). When Dirk Hoerder published *Crowd Action in Revolutionary Massachusetts, 1765–1780* (New York: Academic Press, 1977), an extended literature had developed of which Hoerder gives a full bibliography to that time (n. 19, pp. 5–7). The central debate has turned on whether crowds were means by which cohesive communities defended their established interests, which is the position of Maier and a number of other scholars, or whether they were the source of internal conflict. The state and community studies by Nash, Countryman, Ekirch, Bonomi, and Kim have all contributed to the debate. One major question has been the distinction between urban and rural crowds. The conflicting positions in the debate on country crowds are elaborated in Richard Maxwell Brown, "Back Country Rebellions and the Homestead Ethic in America, 1740–1799," in his anthology *Tradition, Conflict and Modernization*, and by Thomas L. Purvis, "Origins and Patterns of Agrarian Unrest in New Jersey, 1735 to 1754," WMQ *39* (1982), 600–27. Other significant pieces include James P. Whittenburg, "Planters, Merchants and Lawyers: Social Change and the Origins of the North Carolina Regulation," WMQ *34* (1977), 215–38; A. Roger Ekirch, "North Carolina Regulators on Liberty and Corruption, 1766–1771," *Perspectives in American History 11* (1977–78), 199–258; and Edward Countryman, " 'Out of the Bounds of the Law': Northern Land Rioters in the Eighteenth Century," in Young, *The American Revolution*.

Meanwhile historians have also been studying the popular committees of the independence crisis. Gordon Wood began the discussion in *The Creation of the American Republic*, and he was followed rapidly by Richard D. Brown in *Revolutionary Politics in Massachusetts: The Boston Committee of*

Correspondence and the Towns, 1772–1774 (Cambridge: Harvard University Press, 1970). Richard Alan Ryerson provided an immensely detailed case study in *The Revolution Is Now Begun: The Radical Committees of Philadelphia, 1765–1776* (Philadelphia: University of Pennsylvania Press, 1978), and committees in New York constituted a central theme in Countryman's *A People in Revolution.*

A number of studies have focused on the development of political partisanship after independence. The two most important are Jackson Turner Main, *Political Parties Before the Constitution* (Chapel Hill: University of North Carolina Press, 1983), and H. James Henderson, *Political Parties in the Continental Congress* (New York: McGraw-Hill, 1974). Main's book should be read in conjunction with his *The Sovereign States, 1775–1783* (New York: New Viewpoint, 1973). Henderson's book should be balanced by Jack N. Rakove, *The Beginnings of National Politics: An Interpretive History of the Continental Congress* (New York: Alfred A. Knopf, 1979). Robert J. Dinkin contrasts the pre-independence and post-independence eras in two books: *Voting in Provincial America: A Study of Elections in the Thirteen Colonies, 1689–1776* (Westport, Conn.: Greenwood Press, 1977) and *Voting in Revolutionary America: A Study of Elections in the Original Thirteen States, 1776* (Westport: Greenwood Press, 1982). Two books have explored the politics of taxation in the era: Dale W. Forsythe, *Taxation and Political Change in the Young Nation, 1781–1833* (New York: Columbia University Press, 1977), and Robert A. Becker, *Revolution, Reform and the Politics of American Taxation, 1763–1783* (Baton Rouge: Louisiana State University Press, 1980).

A number of historians have examined the development of state-level partisan culture, showing how consensus and shifting factionalism gave way to more organized patterns, particularly in Massachusetts, New York, and Pennsylvania. The difference the Revolution made in Massachusetts can be seen by contrasting the findings of Robert Zemsky on the colonial era in *Merchants, Farmers and River Gods: An Essay on Eighteenth-Century American Politics* (Boston: Gambit, 1971) with those of Ronald P. Formisano on the early nineteenth century in *The Transformation of Political Culture: Massachusetts Parties, 1790s–1840s* (New York: Oxford University Press, 1983). What happened between Zemsky's period and Formisano's is treated in different ways in Stephen E. Patterson, *Political Parties in Revolutionary Massachusetts* (Madison: University of Wisconsin Press, 1973), and in Van Beck Hall, *Politics Without Parties: Massachusetts, 1780–1791* (Pittsburgh: University of Pittsburgh Press, 1972). Despite Linda Grant DePauw's assertion in *The Eleventh Pillar* that New York was consensual and nonpartisan at the time of the ratification struggle, it is clear that the state was deeply divided. See Alfred F. Young, *The Democratic–Republicans of New York: The Origins, 1763–1797* (Chapel Hill: University of North Carolina Press, 1967), and Countryman, *A People in Revolution*, chapters 7–10. There is an enormous debate on the struggle in Pennsylvania between "Constitutionalists" and "Republicans." The most recent and most sophisticated statement is Richard Alan Ryerson, "Republican Theory and Partisan Reality in Revolutionary Pennsylvania: Toward a New View of the Constitutionalist Party," in Hoffman and Albert, eds., *Sovereign States in an Age of Uncertainty*. The emergence of partisanship further south is the subject of Norman K. Risjord and Gordon Den Boer, "The Evolution of Political Parties in Virginia, 1782–1800," *JAH* 60 (1973–74), 961–84, and is touched upon in such state studies as Hoffman, *A Spirit of Dissension*; Isaac, *The Transformation of Virginia*; and Nadelhaft, *The Disorders of War*.

Staughton Lynd and Alfred F. Young launched the contemporary study of working people in the revolutionary era with their paired works, published with a jointly written introduction as "After Carl Becker: The Mechanics and

New York City Politics, 1774–1801," *Labor History 5* (1964), 215–76. Among books and essays that have appeared since then are Roger Champagne, "Liberty Boys and Mechanics of New York City, 1764–1774," *Labor History 8* (1967), 115–35; Philip S. Foner, *Labor and the American Revolution* (Westport: Greenwood Press, 1977); James H. Hutson, "An Investigation of the Inarticulate: Philadelphia's White Oaks," WMQ *28* (1971), 3–25; Jesse Lemisch, "Jack Tar in the Streets: Merchant Seamen in the Politics of Revolutionary America," WMQ *25* (1968), 371–407; Charles S. Olton, *Artisans for Independence: Philadelphia Mechanics and the American Revolution* (Syracuse: Syracuse University Press, 1975); Sharon V. Salinder, "Artisans, Journeymen and the Transformation of Labor in Late Eighteenth Century Philadelphia," WMQ *40* (1983), 62–84, and "Colonial Labor in Transition: The Decline of Indentured Servitude in Late Eighteenth Century Philadelphia," *Labor History 22* (1981), 165–91; and Billy G. Smith, "The Material Lives of Laboring Philadelphians. 1750 to 1800," WMQ 38 (1981), 163–202. See also Sean Wilentz, *Chants Democratic: New York City and the Rise of the American Working Class, 1788–1850* (New York: Oxford University Press, 1984). Richard Walsh, *Charleston's Sons of Liberty: A Study of the Artisans, 1763–1789* (Columbia: University of South Carolina Press, 1959), is an older work. Working people and their problems form a recurrent theme in Nash's *The Urban Crucible* and in Hoerder's *Crowd Action in Massachusetts.*

Working people provided most of the recruits for the revolutionary army and navy. The most stimulating recent study of the war experience is John Shy's *A People Numerous and Armed: Reflections on the Military Struggle for American Independence* (New York: Oxford University Press, 1976). Firsthand recollections of serving in the ranks are gathered in John C. Dann, *The Revolution Remembered: Eyewitness Accounts of the War for Independence* (Chicago: University of Chicago Press, 1980), and in Jesse Lemisch,

"Listening to the 'Inarticulate': William Widger's Dream and the Loyalties of American Revolutionary Seamen in British Prisons," *Journal of Social History 3* (1969–70), 1–29. The fullest account of the war is still Piers Mackesy, *The War for America, 1775–1783* (London: Longmans, 1964). Also significant are Sung Bok Kim, "Impact of Class Relations and Warfare in the American Revolution: The New York Experience," JAH *69* (1982), 326–46; Richard H. Kohn, *Eagle and Sword: The Federalists and the Creation of the Military Establishment in America, 1783–1802* (New York: Free Press, 1975); Don Higginbotham, *The War of American Independence: Military Attitudes, Policies and Practice, 1763–1789* (New York: Macmillan, 1971); Howard H. Peckham, *The Toll of Independence: Engagements and Battle Casualties of the Revolution* (Chicago: University of Chicago Press, 1974); Hugh F. Rankin, *The North Carolina Continentals* (Chapel Hill: University of North Carolina Press, 1971); and Charles Royster, *"A Revolutionary People at War": The Continental Army and American Character, 1775–1783* (Chapel Hill: University of North Carolina Press, 1979). E. Wayne Carp, *To Starve the Army at Pleasure: Continental Army Administration and American Political Culture, 1775–1783* (Chapel Hill: University of North Carolina Press, 1984), is the most recent addition to this literature.

Although we know a great deal about the social structure of revolutionary rural America, we have very few direct studies of the experience and consciousness of ordinary farmers. What we do have concentrates almost exclusively on the North, expecially New England. The most sophisticated statement is Richard L. Bushman, "Massachusetts Farmers and the Revolution," in Jellison, ed., *Society, Freedom and Conscience*. The same group is the subject of David Szatmary's *Shays' Rebellion: The Making of an Agrarian Insurrection* (Amherst: University of Massachusetts Press, 1980) and of Barbara Karsky's "Agrarian Radicalism in the Late

Revolutionary Period (1780–1795)," in Angermann et al., eds., *New Wine in Old Skins*. The best description of the day-to-day life of Northern farmers is Karsky's "Le Paysan américaine et la terre a la fin du XVIII*e* siècle," *Annales: Economies, Societés, Civilisations* (Nov./Dec. 1983), 1369–91. The early chapters in Mary Ryan's *Cradle of the Middle Class: The Family in Oneida County, New York, 1790–1865* (New York: Cambridge University Press, 1981) trace the experience of one group of post-revolution New England migrants, and her work can be compared with Jonathan Prude, *The Coming of Industrial Order: Town and Factory Life in Rural Massachusetts, 1810–1860* (New York: Cambridge University Press, 1983), and Gross, *The Minutemen and Their World*.

Three recent books have considered what the Revolution meant for Native Americans. They are Barbara Graymont, *The Iroquois in the American Revolution* (Syracuse: Syracuse University Press, 1972); James H. O'Donnell, *Southern Indians and the American Revolution* (Knoxville: University of Tennessee Press, 1973); and the superb study by Anthony Wallace, *The Death and Rebirth of the Seneca* (New York: Alfred A. Knopf, 1970). Two excellent books have explored the differences that the Revolution made for women: Mary Beth Norton, *Liberty's Daughters: The Revolutionary Experience of American Women, 1750–1800* (Boston: Little, Brown, 1980), and Linda K. Kerber, *Women of the Republic: Intellect and Ideology in Revolutionary America* (Chapel Hill: University of North Carolina Press, 1980).

The effect of the Revolution on slavery is an old subject. It receives its fullest modern treatment in David Brion Davis, *The Problem of Slavery in the Age of Revolution, 1770–1823* (Ithaca: Cornell University Press, 1975), which can be supplemented with Duncan MacLeod, *Slavery, Race and the American Revolution* (Cambridge, England: Cambridge University Press, 1974). A number of scholars are now turning to the experience of blacks, as opposed to the institution and concept of slavery. The collection edited by Hoffman and Berlin, *Slavery and Freedom in the Age of the American Revolution*, points the way for the work that is to come.

Blacks who fled with the departing British constituted one sizable group of loyalists, and they are considered in James W. St. G. Walker, *The Black Loyalists: The Search for a Promised Land in Nova Scotia and Sierra Leone, 1783–1870* (New York: Holmes and Meier, 1976). Many other scholars have also written on loyalism. Their work includes studies of individuals, such as Carol Berkin's *Jonathan Sewell: Odyssy of an American Loyalist* (New York: Columbia University Press, 1974), Bernard Bailyn's *The Ordeal of Thomas Hutchinson* (Cambridge: Harvard University Press, 1975), William Pencak's *America's Burke: The Mind of Thomas Hutchinson* (Washington: University Press of America, 1982), and Anne Y. Zimmer's *Jonathan Boucher: Loyalist in Exile* (Detroit: Wayne State University Press, 1978). Janie Potter explores the loyalist mind in *The Liberty We Seek: Loyalist Ideology in Colonial New York and Massachusetts* (Cambridge: Harvard University Press, 1983). Robert McCluer Calhoon gives a synthesis in *The Loyalists in Revolutionary America, 1760–1781* (New York: Harcourt Brace Jovanovich, 1973), which is complemented by Mary Beth Norton, *The British-Americans: The Loyalist Exiles in England, 1774–1789* (Boston: Little, Brown, 1972). Ordinary loyalists figure prominently in Robert A. East and Jacob Judd, eds., *The Loyalist Americans: A Focus on Greater New York* (Tarrytown, New York: Sleepy Hollow Restorations, 1975).

During the mid-twentieth century, the major leaders of the Revolution were well served both by comprehensive collections of their papers and by multi-volume biographies. Among the papers collected and published are those of Benjamin Franklin, ed. Leonard W. Labaree et al. (New Haven: Yale University Press, 1959———); Alexander Hamilton, ed. Harold C. Syrett et al. (New York: Columbia University Press, 1961———); Henry Laurens, ed. Philip Hamer et al.

(Columbia: University of South Carolina Press, 1968——);
John Adams, ed. Lyman H. Butterfield et al. (Cambridge:
Harvard University Press, 1962——); Thomas Jefferson, ed.
Julian T. Boyd et al. (Princeton University Press, 1950——);
and James Madison, ed. William T. Hutchinson et al. (Chi-
cago: University of Chicago Press, 1962——). These collec-
tions are indispensable research tools, and carefully read, they
tell about much else besides the life of the main subject.
Among the major modern biographies are Irving Brant's of
James Madison (Indianapolis: Bobbs-Merrill, 1941——),
with a one-volume synopsis; Dumas Malone's of Thomas
Jefferson (Boston: Little, Brown, 1962——); Douglas Southall
Freeman's of George Washington (New York: Charles Scrib-
ner's Sons, 1948–57), with a one-volume abridgment by
Richard Harwell (Scribner's, 1968); and Page Smith's of
John Adams (New York: Doubleday, 1962–63).

The major gain in biographical work has been in the study
of less prominent men, and sometimes of very obscure men.
Many books, theses, and essays have been produced; the
following indicate the kind of work that is under way. Pauline
Maier's account of *The Old Revolutionaries: Political Lives
in the Age of Samuel Adams* (New York: Alfred A. Knopf,
1980) provides capsule studies of lesser-known radical leaders,
such as Adams himself, Thomas Young, and Isaac Sears. Roger
Champagne's *Alexander McDougall and the American Revolution in New York* (Schenectady: Union College Press,
1975), Stefan Bielinski's *Abraham Yates, Jr., and the New
Political Order in Revolutionary New York* (Albany: New
York State American Revolution Bicentennial Commission,
1975), and Ruth Bogin's *Abraham Clark and the Quest for
Equality in the Revolutionary Era* (Rutherford, N.J.: Fair-
leigh Dickinson University Press, 1982) are excellent examples of illuminating studies of obscure leaders. Eric Foner's
Tom Paine and Revolutionary America (New York: Oxford
University Press, 1976) is invaluable both for Paine himself
and for the people among whom he lived. Perhaps most

stimulating of all is Alfred Young's "George Robert Twelves Hewes (1742–1840): A Boston Shoemaker and the Memory of the American Revolution," WMQ *38* (1981), 561–623, which comes as close as any published account to showing what the Revolution meant for the everyday man. My account of Sam, the South Carolina slave, is teased from evidence in Herbert Gutman, *The Black Family in Slavery and Freedom, 1750–1925* (New York: Pantheon, 1976), and in the essay that Gutman, Mary Beth Norton, and Ira Berlin jointly contributed to Hoffman and Berlin, eds., *Slavery and Freedom*. I know of Rebecca Alford from the happy accident of having been given records on her and her (and my) family by two genealogist uncles, C. Edmund Alford and Scott Alford. We still do not know all there is to know about the Revolution. This book has tried to summarize what historians now think. But it will be successful only if readers argue with it, and if some decide to go to the sources and encounter the Revolution for themselves.

Index

Adair, Douglas, 209
Adams, Abigail Smith, 234–5
Adams, John, 4–5, 20, 71, 77, 138–9, 176, 182, 205, 218, 234
Adams, Samuel, 71, 91, 98, 100, 176, 193–5, 222, 226
Albany, N.Y., 25–8
Alcotts, 231
Alford, Alexander, 39
Alford, Benedict, 22, 24–5, 39–40, 229, 231
Alford, Rebecca Owen, 20, 22–5, 36, 38–40, 229, 231
Allen, Ethan, 108, 135–6, 145
Allen, Heman, 135
Annapolis, convention at, 185
Anti-Federalism (ists), 197–8, 202, 205, 209, 228
Antifederalists, The, 177
Arnold, Benedict, 108, 142
Articles of Confederation, 139, 177, 179–80, 184–7, 192, 199
artisans, 7, 10, 21, 36–7, 39, 56, 78, 98–100, 103, 122, 131, 154–5, 157, 164, 169, 171–2, 174, 194–5, 200, 208, 215–16, 219–27, 240–1, 244; and Revolution, 219, 225, 236; and parades, 226–8
assemblies, 17, 26, 32, 42, 47, 51–2, 58, 64, 66–7, 82, 86, 94, 106, 117–19, 126–8, 131, 134, 136, 145, 200–2; *see also* legislatures
authors, 58–69, 71–3, 92, 105, 205–7

Bacon, Nathaniel, 31, 119
Bailyn, Bernard, 60
Bancroft, George, 145, 176–7
Bank of North America, 170, 201
Barré, Isaac, 97
Beard, Charles A., 176–8
Beard, James, 161
Becker, Carl, 123
Beekman, James, 20, 28–30, 40
Benson, Egbert, 151–3
Berkshire Constitutionalists, 133
Bernard, Francis, 94, 102
blacks, 11–12, 16, 32, 34–7, 74, 148–9,

162, 218–19, 238–42, 244; *see also* slavery
Bland, Richard, 72
Bloody Act, 80
Boston, 3, 9–10, 20–2, 28–9, 102; help for, 3–4, 106, 116, 118, 120; and tea, 3, 39, 42, 70, 90–1, 105–6, 179, 222; soldiers and sailors in, 21, 43, 50, 77, 79, 90, 92, 94–7, 108; resistance in, 88–91; economy in, 93, 95; and "Pope's Day," 101; and artisans, 219–20, 222; and Constitution, 226–7
Boston Gazette, The, 21, 102
Boston Massacre, 90, 96, 222
Bowdoin, James, 157, 159
Braddock, Edward, 44
Breed's (Bunker) Hill, 108
Breen, Timothy, 36
Bridenbaugh, Carl, 164
Britain, 43–4, 55, 105, 109, 140; colonies (ists) and, 3, 5–6, 10–11, 14, 16–18, 33, 39, 41–56, 58, 64–71, 75, 87–122, 138, 243; and trade, 4, 10–11, 42, 46–7, 52, 55, 58–9, 67, 71, 106, 109, 118; Indians and, 14–15, 180; and France, 14, 41, 43–4, 51, 56; *see* England, Parliament, *and* soldiers
Burgoyne, John, 140, 163
Burn, Mary Hay, 235
Burr, Aaron, 225
Bute, Lord, 88, 110

Calverts, 229
Cannon, James, 127
Carroll, Charles, 129, 150–1, 153, 201; father of, 150–1
Chapel Street, *see* theater
Charleston, 9, 36–7, 160–1, 163–4
Chew, Richard, 150
Clinton, George, 146–7, 151, 153, 171, 196, 228
Clinton, Sir Henry, 140–1, 160–1
Colden, Cadwallader, 89, 92, 94, 103, 110
colonies (ists), 5, 44–5, 56, 92–3; leaders of, 5, 10, 24, 30–2, 39, 57–8, 64, 78–9,

colonies (ists) (*Cont.*)
85–6, 104, 119; *see also* Britain *and* provinces
committees, 7, 21, 106, 138, 146, 148–9, 151–5, 167, 174, 179, 192, 196, 227; and Continental Association, 4–5, 106; of correspondence, 5, 106, 113–15; popular, 6, 114–15, 132, 139, 144–7, 153, 222–3; revolutionary, 58, 131, 138–9, 142, 144–6; county, 116, 229; Philadelphia and, 117–19; Virginia and, 119–20; of privates, 127
Common Sense, 111–12, 127, 221
Commons, John, 121–2
Complete Anti-Federalist, 205
Concord, changes in, 231; *see also* Lexington
Congress, Continental, First, 3–6, 92, 106–7
Congress, Continental, Second, 108–9, 122–4, 127, 179–82, 193; problems and powers of, 179–84, 187–8
Connecticut, 64, 159, 180, 194
Connecticut Courant, 194
Constitution, federal, 139, 174–9, 187, 203, 212–13, 216, 226; and slavery, 165, 188–91; ratification of, and opposition to, 175–7, 183, 193–8, 204, 209, 214, 226; amendments to, 197–8; provisions of, 199–200, 203
Constitutionalists, 154, 156, 169–71, 228
constitutions, state, 125–37, 156, 168, 189, 198–200, 204, 209, 218
Continental Army, 139–43
Cooper, James Fenimore, 230–1
Cooper, William, 231
Copley, John Singleton, 20, 100
Cornwallis, Lord, 140–1, 163
corporatism, 29, 78, 94, 143–4, 146–8, 154, 207, 223
Cortlandt Manor, 86
courts, 13, 19, 32, 43, 59, 80, 82, 86, 113–15, 118, 120, 129, 133–4, 138, 149, 151, 156, 158, 79; vice-admiralty, 43, 46, 48, 59–60
Creation of the American Republic, 178
Cromwell, Oliver, 102
crowds, action by, 6, 74–9, 87, 97, 100–1, 104, 107, 144, 167
culture, 5, 16–17, 23, 30–2, 92–3
Cunningham, William, 162
Cushing, William, 158–9

Dartmouth, 90–1
Darwin, Charles, 60
Declaration of Independence, 12, 71, 110–11, 122–4, 162

Declaratory Act, 50–2
Deep South, and independence, 160–7
Defence of the Constitutions of Government, etc., 205
De Lancey, Oliver, 28
De Lanceys, 99, 131, 152, 229–30
Delaware, 136, 159, 193, 239
Dickinson, John, 66–9, 71–3, 118, 121–2, 126, 176, 205
Discourses on the First Ten Books of Livy, 62
Drayton, William Henry, 161
Duer, William, 131–2
Dulany, Daniel, 41–2, 65–6, 68, 71–3, 110, 205
Dunmore, Lord, 119, 162, 239
Dunn, Richard, 239

East India Company, 42, 53–4, 87, 90
Economic Interpretation of the Constitution, etc., 176
economy, 5, 10–11, 19–20, 25, 29–30, 37, 46–7, 54–5, 58, 71, 93, 95–6, 98–9, 145, 147, 154, 156, 159, 168, 184, 204, 207–8, 212, 223; *see also* corporatism
Edwards, Jonathan, 23
Einstein, Albert, 60
Elkins, Stanley, 177, 205
Emerson, Ralph Waldo, 231
England, 62–3; *see also* Britain
Ethan Allen's Bible, 136
Extracts from the Proceedings of the Court of Vice Admiralty, 60

Fairfax, Lord, and family, 13, 229
Fanning, Edmund, 82
farmers, 14, 19, 81, 107–8, 113–14, 116, 129, 165–6, 170–2, 174, 200–1, 244; at Helderberg, 121–2; and war, 141–2; and loyalism, 148, 228; of Massachusetts, 156–9, 228–9; and slavery, 164; and Constitution, 194, 226; and Revolution, 227–9, 233; and politics, 228, 241
Federalist, The, 197, 208, 210–11, 217, 245
Federalists (ism), 173, 178, 194, 197–9, 201–2, 205–6, 208–9, 226–7
Fiske, John, 177
Foner, Eric, 148
Founding Fathers, 175–8, 199, 204
France, aid from, 109, 124, 140, 142, 179, 183; *see also* Britain
Franklin, Benjamin, 44, 126, 175, 182, 192, 216, 219–20
freedom, British, 17–18, 62–4, 77, 109
Freeman, Brister, 241
Freud, Sigmund, 60

Fuller, Margaret, 231
Fulton, Robert, 230

Gage, Thomas, 3, 105, 107, 113–15
Galloway, Joseph, 4, 71, 106, 121, 126, 218, 220–1
Gates, Horatio, 140, 142
George III, 5, 54, 70, 72, 107, 124, 175
Georgia, and Constitution, 193
Gerry, Elbridge, 193
Golden Hill, Battle of, 90, 95–6
Gordon, Thomas, 63
Grant, Anna, 14
Granville, Lord, 81–2
Grasse, Admiral de, 141
Great Awakening, 23–4, 103
Green Mountain Boys, 75, 80, 83, 86, 135
Greene, Jack, 176
Greene, Nathanael, 140–2
Grenville, George, 41–7, 50–1, 54–5, 58, 88, 101, 107, 110
Gross, Robert, 241
Gullah, 240–2

Hall, John, 129
Hamilton, Alexander, 71–2, 173, 176, 185–7, 192–3, 196–7, 201, 203, 205–9, 212, 225, 227
Hammond, Regin, 129
Hancock, John, 10, 20, 58, 94, 159, 194–5, 222
Harrington, James, 63
Hat Act, 45, 55, 70
Hawthorne, Nathaniel, 231
Henretta, James, 229
Henry, Patrick, 64, 196
Hewes, George Robert Twelves, 20–2, 26, 38–40, 91, 99, 220, 222–3
Hillsborough, Lord, 54, 110
History of the United States, 176
Hobbes, Thomas, 147
Hoffman, Ronald, 130, 150
Hopkins, Stephen, 58–60, 71
Howard, Martin, 71
Howe, William, 163
Hudson Valley, 14, 16, 24–8, 86; and land problems, 19, 27, 75, 79–80, 83, 87, 122, 135
Hughes, Hugh, 225
Hume, David, 210
Humphreys, Whitehead, 155
Hutchinson, Thomas, 21, 78, 88–91, 93–4, 97, 102–3, 110; sons, 90–1

independence, 108–9, 122–5, 127, 137–9, 178–9; see also Declaration
Indians, 14–15, 44, 50, 75, 83, 116–17, 218, 232; and land, 15, 74, 180–1

Intolerable Acts, 105, 113, 118–19
Iron Act, 45, 55, 70
Isaac, Rhys, 30, 120, 166, 240
Italy, and republicanism, 61–2

Jackson, Andrew, 165
James, Thomas, 89, 92, 103
Jay, John, 131–3, 151–3, 182, 196–7, 208, 224
Jefferson, Thomas, 20, 35, 69–73, 77, 110, 122, 167, 176, 181, 196, 205, 208–9, 231; and slavery, 12, 35, 71; and Declaration, 71, 110–11, 122–3, 162
Jensen, Merrill, 177
Johnson, Guy, 116
Johnson, John, 116–17, 119
Johnson, William, 13–14, 26–7, 32, 116; heirs of, 116, 152, 229
Joyce, George, 102
"Joyce, Jr.," 102, 144

Kerber, Linda, 237
King, Martin Luther, Jr., 242

Lafayette, Marquis de, 142
Lamb, John, 10, 98, 196, 202, 219, 225
land, 12–15, 19, 24, 74–5, 80–7, 172, 180–2, 230–1; see also Green Mountain Boys, Hudson Valley, and Indians
Lansing, John, 186
Laurens, Henry, 10, 59–60, 71–3
Lawrence, John, 203
Lee, Charles, 142
Lee, Richard Henry, 4, 20, 30, 32–5, 37–8, 40, 122, 196, 205
legislatures, state, 128–30, 132–4, 136, 147, 152–3, 156–60, 164–6, 170–4, 179–80, 184, 187, 193, 201, 207, 209, 224–5, 228–30
Leigh, Egerton, 59–60
Lewis, Jan, 31
Lexington, 107–8, 139, 141–2, 145
Libby, Oren, 176
Lincoln, Abraham, 165
Lincoln, Benjamin, 158
Livingston, Robert Jr., 26–7, 122, 201
Livingston, Robert R., 131–3, 151–3, 196, 207, 224, 230
Livingston, William, 176
Livingston Manor, 25, 27–8, 86
Livingstons, 13, 24–8, 99, 131, 230
Locke, John, 85, 123, 147
Longfellow, Henry Wadsworth, 100
Loudon, Samuel, 221–2
Louis XVI, as ally, 142
Louisbourg, capture of, 44

Loyal Nine, 98, 101–3
loyalists, 19, 123, 126, 129, 132, 139, 148–9, 151–3, 160–3, 172–3, 183, 224, 228
Lynd, Staughton, 178, 190–1

Macauley, Catharine, 63
McCulloh, Henry, 81–2
McDonald, Forrest, 177, 196
McDougall, Alexander, 99, 202–3
Machiavelli, Niccolò, 61–2, 210
MacIntosh, Ebenezer, 101–3, 222
Mackesy, Piers, 141
McKitrick, Eric, 177, 205
Madison, James, 176, 185–92, 196–7, 205–6, 208–12, 217, 229, 245
Maier, Pauline, 98, 110
Main, Jackson Turner, 174, 177, 200
Malcolm, George, 223
Marine Anti-Britannic Society, 163
Marion, Francis, 162
Marshall, Christopher, 127
Martin, Luther, 186
Marx, Karl, 60
Maryland, 64, 85, 194, 201, 239; and Revolution, 121, 128–9; constitution of, 125–6, 128–30; after independence, 149–50, 152, 159–60
Mason, George, 196
Massachusetts, 3, 64, 169, 201, 239; and Revolution, 106–8, 113–16, 121–2; constitution of, 125–6, 133–5, 156, 199; after independence, 149, 156–9; and Constitution, 176, 194–5, 226
Massachusetts Government Act, 113, 115
Matlack, Timothy, 127, 154–5
Mayhew, Jonathan, 21
merchants, 4, 10, 20, 22, 25, 29–30, 35–7, 42, 53–7, 59, 65, 77–8, 90, 98–9, 126, 130, 143, 146–8, 153, 157, 163–4, 171, 202, 207, 215, 220, 224, 226, 244
Merrill, Michael, 229
Mifflin, Thomas, 4
migration, westward, 181
militia, 127–9, 145, 149–51, 154–5, 174
Milton, John, 63
Mohawk Valley, 13–14, 26, 116–17, 119, 121
Molasses Act, 46–7, 53
money, after independence, 139, 143, 150, 156–7, 159, 172, 183–4
monopolizers, 143–4, 146
Montagu, Lord Charles, 81
Montesquieu, 63, 210
Morison, Samuel Eliot, 134
Morris, Gouverneur, 131, 176, 189–90, 192

Morris, Robert, 126, 153–5, 170, 176, 201
Mount Vernon, meeting at, 184–5

Nadelhaft, Jerome, 161–2, 166
Nash, Gary, 241
Navigation Acts, 11, 70
Navigation System, 46, 51–2
Netherlands, 43, 183
New Hampshire, 136, 159, 176, 195–6
New Jersey, 64, 75, 83, 85–7, 159, 193; Plan, 188–9
New Nation, The, 177
New York, 28, 36, 64, 85, 121, 183–4, 232; constitution of, 125–6, 130–3, 146, 151, 171, 199; after independence, 149, 151–3, 159; and political parties, 169, 171, 173–4; and Constitution, 176, 183, 195–8
New York City, 9–11, 28–30, 89–91, 93, 95–6, 121, 132–3, 196; British troops in, 30, 43, 51, 66–7, 90, 92, 94–6, 131, 151, 171–2, 224; Sons of Liberty of, 97–9, 103, 131
New York Journal, 103
Nicol, Rensselaer, 26
North, Lord, 54, 107, 110
North Carolina, 82, 85, 161, 176, 195, 198; Regulators in, 75, 79–83, 121
Northwest Ordinances, 181–2, 191
Norton, Mary Beth, 235–6
Notes on the State of Virginia, 205, 209

Oliver, Andrew, 10, 20, 88–9, 91, 93–4, 101
Oothoudt, Henry, 171
Otis, James, 46, 69, 71

Paine, Tom, 58, 98, 111–13, 122, 127, 136, 154, 170, 205, 243
Parliament, 65–6, 70, 80, 107; and taxation and legislation, 11, 41–2, 45–52, 54, 64–70, 114
"Parsons' Cause," 33–4
Paterson, William, 187–8
Paxton Boys, 75, 80, 83
peace, problems following, 163–7
Peale, Charles Willson, 154–5, 219
Penn, John, 118
Penn family, 85, 218, 229
Pennsylvania, 19, 64, 85, 180, 193–4, 201; constitution of, 19, 125–8, 136, 139, 145, 147, 149, 153, 218; after independence, 153–4, 159; and political parties, 156, 168–70, 174
People the Best Governors, 133–4
Philadelphia, 75, 83, 116–19, 121, 153–6, 219–20, 236; convention at, 185–93; parade in, 214–18, 226

Philipse, Frederick, 14
Philipse Manor, 230
Philipses, 24, 152, 229
Pickens, Andrew, 162
Pinckney, Charles C., 35, 38, 239–40
Pinckney, Eliza, 239–40
Pitt, William, 51
planters, 31–7, 45, 48, 64, 81–2, 87, 120–1, 128–9, 149–50, 160, 163–7, 202, 206, 239–40
Pocock, J. G. A., 60
Pole, J. R., 158, 199
Political Parties Before the Constitution, 177
politics, 5–6, 10–11, 17–19, 21, 23, 26–7, 31–3, 35, 38, 40, 57, 61, 63, 104, 113, 115, 119–20, 135, 143–4, 149, 156, 167–74, 207–8, 221, 223–5, 228, 241, 243–4; *see also* committees
Prendergast, William, 80
Price, Richard, 63
Proclamation Line, 15, 50, 180
provinces, 9–11, 14–16, 19; *see also* colonies
Puritans, 84–5, 95, 102, 144

Quartering Act, 51, 66–7
Quebec Act, 50
Quincy, Josiah, 77

Randolph, Peyton, 120
rebellion, rural, 79–87; *see also* violence *and* crowds
Reed, Esther DeBerdt, 236
Reed, Joseph, 155
Regulators, *see* North *and* South Carolina
religion, 6, 16, 19, 23, 31–5, 60, 74, 135–6, 163, 166–7, 241–2
Rensselaerwyck, 25–8, 86
Report on Manufactures, 207
republicanism, 61–2, 75, 167, 206, 210, 218, 237, 240, 243
Republicans, 153–6, 169–71, 194, 201
Resolves, 64
Restraining Act, 51, 70
Revenue Act, *see* Sugar Act
Revere, Paul, 10, 20, 99–100, 219, 226; ride of, 100, 107
Revolution, 7–8, 15–16, 18, 140–5, 175, 199, 212–13, 245; steps toward, 5–7, 15–16, 41–3, 49, 54, 73, 75, 87–8, 102, 106, 114–15, 119–21; changes brought by, 6, 18, 20, 25, 38–9, 57, 218–19, 229–40, 243–4; effect of, on individuals, 20, 25, 35, 38–40; and internal conflict, 75–6, 138–9; lessons, heritage, and explanation of, 207–8, 242–5; *see also* independence

Rhode Island, 58, 64, 159, 186; and Constitution, 176, 183, 195, 198, 228
Richardson, Ebenezer, 96
rioting, *see* violence
Rittenhouse, David, 154, 219
Robbins, Caroline, 60
Roberdeau, Daniel, 154
Robespierre, Maximilien, 100
Robinson, John, 33
Roche, John P., 177, 192
Rossiter, Clinton, 177
Royster, Charles B., 141
Ruggles, Timothy, 148
Rush, Benjamin, 98, 154–5, 169–70, 205
Ryan, Mary, 232–3
Ryerson, Richard Alan, 117–19, 144

sailors, British, *see* soldiers
Sam, 20, 35–40, 239–40
Sauthier, Claude Joseph, 232
Schuyler, Philip, 27–8, 151, 153
Schuylers, 26, 131
Seabury, Samuel, 71
Sears, Isaac, 10, 99
senates, state, *see* legislatures
Seven Years' War, 14, 20, 24, 28, 30, 41, 43
1787: The Grand Convention, 177
Shays, Daniel, farmers and, 229
Shays' Rebellion, 80, 139, 201, 231
Shelburne, Lord, 54
Shy, John, 141
Skene, Philip, 152
slavery (slaves), 11–16, 19, 34–7, 39, 57–8, 74, 81, 129, 148, 162–5, 167, 182, 206; Constitution and, 165, 188–91; abolition of, 239–40; language of, 240–1; *see also* blacks
Smith, Adam, 147, 154, 207, 212, 229
Smith, William, 131, 202, 221
Sneider, Christopher, 96
soldiers and sailors, British, 3, 28, 30, 42–3, 48, 50–1, 66–7, 77, 79, 87, 89–90, 92, 94–7, 105, 107–8, 131
Song in Praise of Liberty, 92
Sons of Liberty, 5, 88, 97–100, 103–4, 131, 136, 223
South Carolina, 12, 19, 35–8, 64, 85, 136, 176, 194, 202, 240; Regulators in, 75, 79–81, 121; and independence, 161–2, 164–5
Sovereign States, The, 177
Stagg, John, 225
Stamp Act, 4, 30, 33, 42, 47–52, 54–5, 57, 64, 67, 70, 81, 87–9, 91–2, 101, 103–4, 107, 118, 156, 175, 179; Congress of, 5, 64, 106

Stanton, Elizabeth Cady, 236
Steuben, Friedrich von, 142
suffrage, 17, 65–6, 127–8, 130, 132, 134, 150, 156, 159, 172
Sugar Act, 46–7, 49, 52, 54–5, 59, 65, 67, 87
Summary of the Rights of British America, A, 69–70
Sumter, Thomas, 162

Tarleton, Banastre, 161–2
taxation, after independence, 129, 139, 149–50, 152–3, 156–7, 172–3, 176, 179, 184, 208; *see also under* Parliament
Tea Act, 53–5, 70, 87, 105
Ten Broeck, Abraham, 26
Tennent, Gilbert, 23
theater, 30, 89, 91–3, 103
Thoreau, Henry David, 231
Thoughts on Government, 138
town meetings, 5, 21, 23, 32, 57, 84–5, 102, 114, 117, 158, 195
Townshend, Charles, 45, 52–4, 67
Townshend Acts, 4, 42, 53–5, 59, 67, 70, 87, 99, 105, 179
Treaty of Paris, 157, 180, 182, 184
Trenchard, John, 63
Tryon, William, 82, 116

United States, and world mastery, 43

Van Cortlandts, 13
Van Rensselaer, Johannes, 26
Van Rensselaers, 13, 24–6, 131
Van Schaicks, 26
Vermont, 25, 87, 135–6, 159, 239
violence, 74–6, 78, 97, 161–2; *see also* crowds *and* rebellion
Virginia, 12, 18–19, 30–7, 64, 180; Burgesses of, 31–3, 52, 64–5, 67, 71–2, 119; blacks in, 32, 34–5, 240; and Polity and Taxation, 52, 64, 67; and Revolution, 115–16, 119–22; and independence, 162–3, 166–7; and Constitution, 176, 195–6, 198; Plan, 186–8

Walpole, Robert, 63
Warner, Seth, 145
Warren, Mercy Otis, 234
Washington, George, 5, 44, 102, 108, 140–2, 175, 183, 192, 195–6, 216, 237
Wealth of Nations, The, 147, 212
Webster, Noah, 205
Wemyss, James, 161–2
Wentworth, Benning, 24
Whately, Thomas, pamphlet of, 65–6
Whiskey Rebellion, 75, 80
White, Hugh, 232–3
White Oaks, 220–1
White Pine Act, 45
Whitefield, George, 23
whites, diversity among, 16, 18–19; *see also* colonies *and* provinces
Whitestown, 232–3
Whitney, Eli, 165
Wilentz, Sean, 226–7
Wilkes, John, 107
Wills, Garry, 123
Wilson, James, 126, 153, 155, 205, 209, 216–17
Windsor, 22–4
women, subordination of, 18, 25, 39; and Philadelphia parade, 218, 235–6; and politics, 236, 241; and Revolution, 219, 233–8, 244
Women of the Republic, 237
Wood, Gordon S., 60, 109, 178, 199, 202, 212, 243
Worcester Magazine, 194
writers, *see* authors
Wythe, George, 196

Yates, Abraham, Jr., 20, 25–8, 38–40, 86, 205, 219
Yates, Robert, 186
Young, Alfred, 22, 102
Young, Dr. Thomas, 98, 127, 135–6